HINDI-ENGLISH

PHRASEBOOK

HINDI-ENGLISH
PHRASEBOOK

Kavita Kumar

Rupa & Co

First Published 2004
Eighth Impression 2011

Published by
Rupa Publications India Pvt. Ltd.
7/16, Ansari Road, Daryaganj,
New Delhi 110 002

Sales Centres:

Allahabad Bengaluru Chennai
Hyderabad Jaipur Kathmandu
Kolkata Mumbai

Printed in India by
Gopsons Papers Ltd.
A-14 Sector 60
Noida 201 301

CONTENTS

PREFACE

The Hindi Phrasebook is designed to enable non-Hindi speaking people from different countries to converse without difficulty with Hindi-speaking people on matters of daily life. It is a compilation of phrases ranging from one word to short sentences. A large number of situational sentences required in general conversation, useful for learning the language, making travel trouble-free and sightseeing enjoyable, are given in the text. The material provides tourists and business visitors with appropriate words and phrases to wade through diverse challenging encounters during their travel and stay in India.

The pronunciation guide explains the special sounds of the language. Phonetic spellings of each Hindi sentence are given to help you speak without any prior knowledge of script or grammar. At the same time, for those who may be interested, the text is given in Hindi script too.

It is equally profitable for students of Hindi in transition phase, where they have acquired the ability to read and comprehend written text in Hindi, but cannot speak due to lack of practice.

Sincere thanks are due to:

Shri R.K. Mehra and Ms. Sugeeta Roy Choudhry of Rupa & Co., for asking me to undertake this project and for their keen interest in its successful completion.

My husband Prof. Hardarshan Kumar for his sustained support in my work.

Mangla Prasad Dube for his assistance in composing the book.

My son-in-law Kant and daughter Anu for their

understanding and generosity in every way during my stay with them in the United States where the first draft of this book was written.

My grandsons Arman and Rahul, and my daughter Tara for propelling vital energy in me in some of my lone moments.

I shall welcome any feedback from the readers, especially any printing errors that might have escaped my notice.

December 28, 2003

Kavita Kumar

ABBREVIATIONS

adj.	adjective
adv.	adverb
f.	feminine
form.	formal
freq.	frequentative
G	gender
imper.	imperative
inf.	Informal
int.	intimate
m.	masculine
N	number
nom	nominative
obj.	object
obl.	oblique
pg.	page
pl.	plural
pp	postposition
pres.	present
sg.	singular
subj.	subject
v.i.	verb intransitive
v.t.	verb transitive

Transliteration

अ (a)	आ (ā)	इ (i)	ई (ī)	उ (u)
ऊ (ū)	ऋ (ṛ)	ए (e)	ऐ (ai)	ओ (o)
औ (au)		ँ (ṁ)		: (ḥ)
क (ka)	ख (kha)	ग (ga)	घ (gha)	ङ (ṅa)
च (ca)	छ (cha)	ज (ja)	झ (jha)	ञ (ña)
ट (ṭ)	ठ (ṭha)	ड (ḍa)	ढ (ḍha)	ण (ṇ)
		ड़ (ṛ)	ढ़ (ṛha)	
त (t)	थ (tha)	द (da)	ध (dha)	न (na)
प (pa)	फ (pha)	ब (ba)	भ (bha)	म (ma)
य (ya)	र (ra)	ल (la)	व (va)	
श (śa)	ष (ṣa)	स (sa)	ह (ha)	
क्ष (kṣa)	त्र (tra)	ज्ञ (gya)		

ṁ = vowel nasality
ṃ = nasality before ya, ra, ca, va, sa śa. ha.
ḥ = for voiced aspiration used chiefly in loan words from Sanskrit and pronounced as 'ah'

PRONUNCIATION GUIDE

Hindi uses the Devanāgarī script of Sanskrit. It is written from left to right. The alphabet is divided into five classifications (vargas) arranged in a systematic order, beginning with velars, moving forward through the prepalatals, palatals, dentals to the labials. Every classification has five letters consisting of two pairs of non-aspirate and aspirate characters each, followed by a nasal consonant.

The written script is uniform, with no distinction between capital or lower case letters. Hindi is a phonetic language. The letters of the alphabet have fixed sounds. There are no silent letters. The language is read almost the way it is written. Hence pronunciation ambiguities are minimal.

The pronunciation of aspirated characters sometimes appears problematic to foreigners at first but, with practice, this difficulty is readily overcome.

Given below is a quick guide to various sounds of the Hindi symbols. As far as possible, corresponding English equivalents or other suggestions have been given.

Vowels	Transliteration	Sound in English
a	अ	as in hut
ā	आ	as in car

i	इ	as in sit
ī	ई	as in meet
u	उ	as in put
ū	ऊ	ū as in fool
e	ए	as in hate
a	ऐ	i as in hat
o	ओ	as in hole
au	औ	au as in hot

CONSONANT

Hindi	English	Example
Velars:		
ka	क	as in **c**ool
kha	ख	The point of articulation is the same as K in English, but with aspiration. as in **kh**akī
ga	ग	as in game
gha	घ	as in aghast
ṅa	ङ	as in ri**ng**

Prepalatals: The point of articulation is the prepalatal region.

ca	च	as in church

cha	छ	same as ch in English, but with aspiration.
ja	ज	as in joy
jha	झ	same as j in English, but aspirated
ña	ञ	as in brinjal

Palatals: The point of articulation is the palatals region; the tongue touches the hard palate.

ṭa	ट	as in tea
ṭha	ठ	aspirated t
ḍa	ड	as in daddy
ḍha	ढ	aspirated d
ṇa	ण	nasal consonant

ṛa ड़ ṛha ढ़

These two sounds are not found in English. These are produced in the same region as d in dog. However the tongue is rolled and let slip for 'ṛ', and exactly the same effort is required for ṛha, but with aspiration.

Dentals: The tip of the tongue touches the hind part of the front teeth.

ta	त	This sound is alien for English language speakers. The tip of the tongue touches the hind part of the front teeth.

tha	थ	as in **th**ink
da	द	**th** as in **they**
dha	ध	same as **th** in English, but with aspiration.
na	न	n as in **none**

Labials. Sound is produced by joining both the lips.

pa	प	p as in **papa**
pha	फ	same as p in English, but with aspiration. This is different from 'f' of English. The lips close fully as in 'p' but with aspiration.
ba	ब	b as in boy
bha	भ	same as b in English, but with aspiration.
ma	म	m as in **mom**
ya	य	y as in **yes**
ra	र	r as in **r**ose
la	ल	l as in **l**ong
va	व	v as in vase
śa	श	sh as in **sh**ow
ṣa	ष	different from sh of English. The sound is produced in the prepalatal region. This is found only in words borrowed from Sanskrit. In practice, the Hindi speakers pronounce it the same as 'sh'.

sa	स	s as in **s**it
ha	ह	h as in **h**at

Arabic and persian sounds used in Hindi

qa	क़	as in queen
kha	ख़	as in german word bach (no English equivalent)
ga	ग़	as in persian gazal (no English equivalent)
za	ज़	as in zoo
fa	फ़	as in fool

WORD ORDER IN HINDI

In Hindi, unlike English, the verb comes at the end and the interrogatives usually come after the subject

Affirmative:

subject + noun object / adjective / adverb etc + verb.

I am sick.	maiṁ	bīmār	hūṁ.
	I	sick	am.
I eat rice.	maiṁ	cāval	khātā hūṁ.
	I	rice	eat.

Interrogative:

What is this? yah **kyā** hai?
This what is?

However when the answer to the question is yes or no, kyā comes at the beginning of the sentence.

Are you from India? **kyā** āp bhārat se haiṁ?
Are you India from ?

Negative sentences have the negative particles 'na', 'nahīṁ' before the verb.

Today is not Monday. āj somwār nahīṁ hai.
Today Monday not is.

Planning to visit Temples!

★ Most temples remain closed from 12 noon to 3 p.m.

★ Sikh temples require you to enter the sacred hall with your head covered.

★ Entry for non-Hindus is prohibited in some temples.

ASKING QUESTIONS

what (kyā) क्या

What is this?

yah kyā hai? यह क्या है?

What do you do?

āp kyā karte haiṁ? आप क्या करते हैं?

What did you say?

āp ne kyā kahā? आपने क्या कहा?

What is his occupation?

vah kyā kartā hai? वह क्या करता है?

What does she want?

usko kyā cāhie? उसको क्या चाहिए?

What day is it today?

āj kaun-sā vār hai? आज कौन–सा वार है?

What date is it today?

āj kyā tārīkh/ tithi hai? आज क्या तारीख़/तिथि है?

who (kaun) कौन

Who is she/he?

vah kaun hai? वह कौन है?

Who are those women?

ve aurteṁ kaun haiṁ? वे औरतें कौन हैं?

Who is shouting?

kaun chillā rahā hai? कौन चिल्ला रहा है?

8 • ASKING QUESTIONS

Who is at the door?
darvāze par kaun hai? दरवाज़े पर कौन है?

whom kis (किस)

to whom	**kisko**	किसको
with whom	**kisse**	किससे
in whom	**kismeṁ**	किसमें
on whom	**kispar**	किसपर
for whom	**kiske lie**	किसके लिए
with whom	**kiske sāth**	किसके साथ

With whom did you travel?
āpne kiske sāth yātrā kī?
आपने किसके साथ यात्रा की?

Whom do you want?
āp kisko milnā cāhte haiṁ?
आप किसको मिलना चाहते हैं?

With whom did you talk?
āpne kisse bāt kī? आपने किससे बात की?

From whom shall I take?
maiṁ kis se lūṁ? मैं किससे लूँ?

In whom do you have faith?
āpko kis meṁ viśvās hai? आपको किसमें विश्वास है?

why (kyoṁ) क्यों

Why is she/he crying?
vah kyoṁ ro rahī /rahā hai?
वह क्यों रो रही/रहा है?

Why are they (f./m.) running?
ve kyoṁ daur̤ rahī(f.)/rahe(m.) haiṁ?
वे क्यों दौड़ रही/रहे हैं?

Why are you (f./m.) going?
tum kyoṁ jā rahī (f.)/ rahe (m.) ho?
तुम क्यों जा रही/रहे हो?

where (kahāṁ) कहाँ

taxi stand	**taiksī aḍḍā**	टैक्सी अड्डा
airport	**hawāī aḍḍā**	हवाई अड्डा

Where is the bus stop?
bas aḍḍā kahāṁ hai?
बस अड्डा कहाँ हैं?

Where is the key to my room?
mere kamre kī cābhī kahāṁ hai?
मेरे कमरे की चाभी कहाँ हैं?

Where is the bathroom?
gusalkhānā kahāṁ hai?
गुसलख़ाना कहाँ हैं?

How	**kaise**	**कैसे**
how much	**kitnā** (m.sg.)	कितना
how many	**kitne** (m.pl.)	कितने
	kitnī (f.sg./pl.)	कितनी
how much sugar?	**kitnī cīnī?**	कितनी चीनी
How much milk?	**kitnā dūdh?**	कितना दूध
How many bananas?	**kitne kele?**	कितने केले

How many pears?
kitnī nāśpātiyāṁ? कितनी नाशपातियाँ

How many children does she have?
uske kitne bacce haiṁ?
उसके कितने बच्चे हैं?

How did she/he contact you?
vah āpse kaise milī/milā?
वह आपसे कैसे मिली/मिला?

How did you come?
āp kaise āe? आप कैसे आए?

How much is this?
yah kitne kā hai? यह कितने का है?

How could this be?
yah kaise ho saktā hai? यह कैसे हो सकता है?

when (kab) कब

When did she come?
vah kab āī? वह कब आई?

Since when have you been waiting for me?

āp kab se merī intzār kar rahe haiṁ?

आप कब से मेरा इन्तज़ार कर रहे हैं?

By when will my work be done?

merā kām kab tak ho jāegī?

मेरा काम कब तक हो जाएगा?

whose — kiskā (m.sg.) किसका/kiske(m.pl.) किसके/kiskī (f.sg/pl.) किसकी

kā, ke kī depends on the number and gender of the object possessed.

Whose bag(m.) is this?

yah kiskā thailā hai? यह किसका थैला है?

Whose watch(f.) is this?

yah kiskī gharī hai? यह किसकी घड़ी है?

Whose shoes are these?

ye kiske jūte (m.pl.) haiṁ? ये किसके जूते हैं?

which one — kaun-sā (m.sg) कौन-सा; kaun-sī (f.sg./pl.) कौन-सी

which ones — kaun-se(m.pl.) कौन-से

Which school do they go to?

ve kaun-se 'skūl' meṁ jāte haiṁ?

वे कौन से 'स्कूल' में जाते हैं?

sā, se, sī depends upon the number and gender of the object pointed to.

Which boy?	**kaun-sā laṛkā**	कौन–सा लड़का
Which girl?	**kaun-sī laṛkī**	कौन–सी लड़की
Which apples?	**kaun-se seb**	कौन–से सेब
Which saris?	**kaun-sī sāṛiyāṁ**	कौन–सी साड़ियाँ

Greetings

All time greetings among Hindus are:

namaste नमस्ते; namaskār नमस्कार; praṇām प्रणाम; pālāgi पालागी।

praṇām is more formal, used while greeting elders.

Good morning	śubh prabhāt	शुभ प्रभात
Good evening	śubh sandhyā	शुभ सन्ध्या
Good night	śubbh rātri	शुभ रात्रि

Muslims usually greet with :

salām सलाम; taslimāt तसलीमात; bandāgi बंदगी; assalāmālaikum अस्लामालेकम; ādāb आदाब

Sikhs usually greet each other with:

sat shri akal सत श्री अकाल

Young peole, particularly in the cities, use the international greeting, 'hi' or 'hello' at the time of meeting and 'bye' at the time of parting.

EVERYDAY PHRASES

A

Absolutely!

bilkul. बिल्कुल।

Absolutely not!

bilkul nahīṁ बिल्कुल नहीं।

Act your age!

apnī umra kā khyāl karo. अपनी उम्र का लिहाज़ करो।

Am I right?

hai na? है न?

And you?

aur āp? और आप?

Anything you say.

maiṁ āpke sāth hūṁ. मैं आपके साथ हूँ।

Anytime?

kabhī bhī. कभी भी।

(Are you)You doing okay?

sab ṭhīk cal rahā hai na? सब ठीक चल रहा है न?

(Are you)Ready to order?

āp aurḍar dījiegā. आप आर्डर दीजिएगा?

As far as I know.

jahāṁ tak maiṁ jāntā hūṁ. जहाँ तक मैं जानता हूँ।

As far as I am concerned

jahāṁ tak merā sawāl hai जहाँ तक मेरा सवाल है

As I was saying.
hāṁ, to maiṁ kah rahā thā हाँ, तो मैं कह रहा था

As such vaise bhī, ... वैसे भी, ... ।

Attention! dhyān se. ध्यान से।

Be quiet. chup ho jāo. चुप हो जाओ।

Be careful sāvdhan! सावधान!

Be seated! baiṭhie. बैठिए।

B

be talk of
carcā kā viṣay honā. चर्चा का विषय होना।

Boys will be boys.
bacce to bacce hī haiṁ बच्चे तो बच्चे ही हैं

Break a record.
kīrtimān sthāpit karnā कीर्तिमान स्थापित करना

Butt out!
jāo. jākar apnā kām karo.
जाओ। जाकर अपना काम करो

By chance saṁyog se, संयोग से

By the way. aur haṁ ... और हाँ ...

C

Catch me later.
mujh se bād meṁ bāt karnā.
मुझसे बाद में बात करना।

Clear the way!
rāste se hato! रास्ते से हटो।

D

Danger! <u>kh</u>atrā. ख़तरा।

Enough is enough.
bas bahut ho gayā. बस बहुत हो गया।

E

Everything will work for the best.
sab ṭhīk ho jāegā. सब ठीक हो जाएगा।

Excellent! bahut baṛhiā. बहुत बढ़िया।

Exuse me! kṣamā kījie. क्षमा कीजिए।

Farewell. alvidā. अल्विदा।

F

Forget it! jāne dījie. जाने दीजिए।

For sure. niścit hī. निश्चित ही।

Frankly. sac kahūṁ to. सच कहूँ तो।

From my point of view.
merī samajh se. मेरी समझ से।

Get lost! dūr ho jāo. दूर हो जाए।

Give it time. dhairyă rakho. धैर्य रखो।

G

Give it up!
ise bilkul choṛ do! इसे बिल्कुल छोड़ दो।

Give me a break. / Give me a chance.
mujhe ek maukā aur dījie. मुझे एक मौका और दीजिए।

Give me a rest.
merā khūn mat pio. मेरा खून मत पिओ।

God forbid!
bhagwān bacāy. भगवान बचाए!

God only knows.
īśvar hī jāntā hai. ईश्वर ही जानता है।

God willing.
yadi bhagvān ne cāhā to यदि भगवान ने चाहा तो

G

Good enough.
yah ṭhīk rahe gā. yah cale gā.
यह ठीक ही रहेगा। यह चलेगा।

Good luck!
śubh kāmnāyeṁ. शुभ कामनाएँ।

Good riddance!
jān chūṭī जान छूटी।

Good talking to you.
āp se bāt karke acchā lagā.
आपसे बात करके अच्छा लगा।

Go to hell. bhāṛh meṁ jāo. भाड़ में जाओ।

Greetings. namaste. नमस्ते।

H

Hail authority! kursī kī jai. कुर्सी की जय।

Have a nice trip.
āp kī yātrā maṅgalmay ho. आपकी यात्रा मंगलमय हो।

Have it your way.
maiṁ āp se sahmat hūṁ. मैं आपसे सहमत हूँ।
jaisā āp cāheṁge, vaisā hī hogā.
जैसा आप चाहेंगे, वैसा ही होगा।

Have to shove off.
ab mujhe jānā hai. अब मुझे जाना है

Haven't seen you in a long time.
bahut der se āp dikhāī nahīṁ die.
बहुत समय से आप दिखाई नहीं दिए।

Have you heard?

āp ne sunā hai? आपने सुना है?

Haven't we met before?

ham pahle kahīṁ mile lagte haiṁ.

हम पहले कहीं मिले लगते हैं।

Having a wonderful time; wish you were here.

bahut mazā ā rahā hai; kāś āp bhī sāth hote.

बहुत मज़ा आ रहा है, काश तुम यहाँ होते।

Having the time of my life.

bahut mazā ā rahā hai. बहुत मज़ा आ रहा है।

Heads up! sāvdhān सावधान!

Hold your horses! dhīre. itne uttejit na ho'o.

धीरे। इतने उत्तेजित न होओ।

Hold your tongue.

apnī zabān par lagām lagāo.

अपनी ज़बान पर लगाम लगाओ।

Hopefully. ummīd to hai. उम्मीद तो है।

Horsefeathers!

savāl hī nahīṁ uṭhatā. सवाल ही नहीं उठता ।

bakvās. बकवास!

How about you?

aur, āpkī kyā rāy hai? और, आपकी क्या राय है?

How can I help you?

maiṁ āp kī kyā sevā kar saktā hūṁ?

मैं आपकी क्या सेवा कर सकता हूँ ?

H

How do you know?
āpko kaise patā lagā?
आपको कैसे पता लगा?

How has the world been treating you?
sab kaise chal rahā hai? सब कैसे चल रहा है?

Hurry up! jaldī kījie. जल्दी कीजिए।

Hush your mouth!
kṛpayā śānt ho jāie. कृपया शान्त हो जाइए।

I

I am grateful to you.
maiṁ āpkā ābhārī hūṁ. मैं आपका आभारी हूँ।

I am tired.
maiṁ thakā (m.)/ thakī (f.) hūṁ.
मैं थका/थकी हूँ।

I am sorry. mujhe khed hai. मुझे खेद है।

I don't care!
mujhe koī parvāh nahīṁ. मुझे कोई परवाह नहीं।

I hope, mujh ko āśā hai, मुझको आशा है,

I know, maiṁ jāntā hūṁ, मैं जानता हूँ,
mujh ko mālūm hai, मुझको मालूम है,

I think, mere khyāl meṁ, मेरे ख़्याल में,
mere vicār meṁ, मेरे विचार में,

It is likely.. ho saktā hai... हो सकता है

It is none of your business!
is bat se apkā koī vāstā nahīṁ.
इस बात से आपका कोई वास्ता नहीं।

Its okay ṭhīk hai. ठीक है

It seems.. aisā lagtā hai.. ऐसा लगता है

Just a moment. ek kṣaṇ. एक क्षण

J

Keep in touch.
sampark banāe rakhnā/rakhiegā
सम्पर्क बनाए रखना/रखिएगा।

K

Keep it in mind that, ..
is bāt kā dhyān rahe ki, इस बात का ध्यान रहे कि....

Keep it up!
karte raho/rahie. करते रहो/ रहिए।

Keep on trying.
kośiś karte raho/rahie. कोशिश करते रहो/ रहिए।

Keep your opinion to yourself.
apnī rāy apne pās rakho/rakhie.
अपनी राय अपने पास रखो/रखिए।

Keep your chin up.
himmat banāe raho. हिम्मत बनाए रहो/ रहिए।

Keep your mouth shut.
apnā muṁh band rakhnā. / tum kuch na kahnā.
अपना मुँह बन्द रखना।/तुम कुछ न कहना।

L

Keep your shirt on!
dhairyă rakho/rakhie. धैर्य रखो/रखिए।

Later. bād meṁ. बाद में।

Leave me alone.
mujhe taṅg na karo. मुझे तंग न करो।

Leaving so soon?
.āp itnī jaldī jā rahe haiṁ?
आप इतनी जल्दी जा रहे हैं?

Let it go. jāne dījie. जाने दीजिए

Let me get back to you.
maiṁ āp se bād meṁ bāt kartā hūṁ.
मैं आपसे बाद में बात करता हूँ।

Let's call it a day.
bas, āj ke lie itnā hī.
बस, आज के लिए इतना ही।

Let's eat.
calie khānā khāeṁ. चलिए, खाना खाएँ।

Let's get down to business.
calie, ab kām kī bāt kī jāy.
चलिए, अब काम की बात की जाय।

Let's get together sometime.
kisī din milā jāy. किसी दिन मिला जाय।

Let's go somewhere it's quieter.
kisī śānt jagah par calā jāy.
चलिए किसी शान्त जगह पर चला जाय।

Like I was saying...

hāṁ, to jaisā maiṁ kah rahā thā....

हाँ, तो जैसा मैं कह रहा था.....

Like two peas in a pod.

ghaniṣṭh sambandh honā. घनिष्ठ सम्बन्ध होना।

Look! dekhie! देखिए।

Look me up when you are in town.

jab āp aglī bār āeṁ, to khabar kījiegā.

जब आप अगली बार आएँ, तो ख़बर कीजिएगा।

Look who is there!

dekhie, sāmne kaun hai? देखिए, सामने कौन है?

Lots of luck!

ḍher sārī śubh kāmnāyeṁ. ढ़ेर सारी शुभ कामनाएँ।

Make it snappy.

jaldī karo. जल्दी करो।

M

Make it two (while ordering in a restaurant)

mere lie bhī yahī lāie. मेरे लिए भी यही लाइए।

Make no mistake about it.

kisi galat fahmī meṁ na rahnā/rahiegā.

किसी ग़लत फ़हमी में न रहना/रहिएगा।

Makes me no difference.

mujhe koī farak nahīṁ paṛtā.

मुझे कोई फ़रक नहीं पड़ता।

Mind if...
āp ko burā to nahīṁ lage gā?
आपको बुरा तो नहीं लगेगा?

Mind your own business.
apne kām se kām rakho. अपने काम से काम रखो।

More power to you.
tum ne bahut acchā kiyā. तुमने बहुत अच्छा किया।

Mum's the word.
maiṁ kisī ko nahīṁ batāūṁ gā.
मैं किसी को नहीं बताऊँगा।

My house is your house.
ise apnā hī ghar samajhie.
इसे अपना ही घर समझिए।

My, how time flies.
vakt guzarte patā nahīṁ lagtā.
वक्त गुज़रते पता नहीं लगता।

My lips are sealed.
viśvās rakhie, maiṁ apnā muṁh nahīṁ kholūṁgā.
विश्वास रखिए, मैं अपना मुँह नहीं खोलूँगा।

My pleasure.
yah merā saubhāgyă hai. यह मेरा सौभाग्य है।

N

Need I remind you that?
kyā mujhe tumheṁ naye sire se batānā hogā?
क्या मुझे तुम्हें नए सिरे से बताना होगा?

Neither can I.
maiṁ bhī nahīṁ.. मैं भी नहीं।

Never hurts to ask.
pūchne meṁ harz hī kyā hai?
पूछने में हर्ज़ ही क्या है?

Never mind.
jāne do / dījie. जाने दो/दीजिए।

Never would have guessed.
koī soc bhī nahīṁ saktā thā.
कोई सोच भी नहीं सकता था।

No nahīṁ; jī nahīṁ नहीं; जी नहीं।

No comment.
is meṁ mujhe kuch nahīṁ kahnā.
इसमें मुझे कुछ नहीं कहना।

No doubt. niḥsandeh. निःसन्देह।

No lie? sac? सच?

No point in.
koi fāyadā nahīṁ. कोई फायदा नहीं।

Not bad. cale gā. चलेगा।

Not by a long shot.
kisī hāl meṁ nahīṁ. किसी हाल में नहीं।

Not right now. Thanks.
abhī nahīṁ. dhanyăvād. अभी नहीं। धन्यवाद।

Not to worry.
cintā na kareṁ. चिन्ता न करें।

Not worth mentioning.
Iskā zikra bhī bekār hai. इसका जिक्र भी बेकार है।

Nothing. kuch nahīṁ. कुछ नहीं।

Now then... hāṁ to phir,.... हाँ तो फिर,....

O

One moment, please.
ek kṣaṇ एक क्षण।

One more thing.
ek aur bāt. एक और बात।

or else
nahīṁ to,.. नहीं तो,...

P

Perhaps. śāyad शायद।

Perhaps a little later.
śāyad kuch bād meṁ. शायद कुछ बाद में।

Please. kṛpayā. कृपया।

Please show me.
kṛpayā mujhe dikhāie. कृपया मुझे दिखाइए।

Pleased to meet you.
āpse milkar bahut khuśī huī.
आपसे मिलकर बहुत खुशी हुई।

Pull up a chair.
kursī lekar baiṭh jāie. कुर्सी लेकर बैठ जाइए।

Put two and two together.
aṭkal lagānā. अटकल लगाना।

Really? sac? सच?

R

Remember me to ...
....ko merā pranām kahnā ....को मेरा प्रणाम कहना

Remember to write.
patra likhte rahnā. पत्र लिखते रहना।

Rest is history.
aur sab to āp jānte hī haiṁ.
और सब तो आप जानते ही हैं।

run rampant.
bekābū honā बेकाबू होना

S

Same to you.
āpko bhī. आपको भी।

Say cheese.
muskarāo मुस्कराओ। / muskarāie मुस्कराइए।

Say hello to ....
merī or se unko namaste kahnā/kahiegā.
मेरी ओर से उनको नमस्ते कहना/कहिएगा।

Says me!
maiṁ kahtā hūṁ. मैं कहता हूँ।

Says who?
kaun kahtā hai? कौन कहता है?

See you soon. jaldī mileṁge. जल्दी मिलेंगे।

Seen better.
maiṁne is se achhā samay dekhā hai.
मैंने इससे अच्छा समय देखा है।
Seen worse.
maiṁne is se burā samay bhī dekhā hai.
मैंने इससे बुरा समय भी देखा है।
Shame on you.
śarm karo. शर्म करो।
tumheṁ śarm ānī cāhie. तुम्हें शर्म आनी चाहिए।
Since time immemorial:

S

ek arse se. एक अर्से से।
Snap it up!
jaldī karo. जल्दी करो।
So do I.
maiṁ bhī. मैं भी।
So mad I could scream.
mujhe bahut gussā āyā. मुझे बहुत गुस्सा आया।
So much for that
bas bahut ho gayā बस बहुत हो गया।
So soon.
itnī jaldī? इतनी जल्दी?
So what?
to kyā? तो क्या?
Something's got to give.
gubbār to phūṭnā hī thā. गुब्बार तो फूटना ही था।
Somewhere in the neighbourhood of. lagbhag लगभग

sorry (that) I asked.
mujhe nahīṁ pūchnā cāhie thā. मुझे नहीं पूछना चाहिए था।

Soup's on! khānā taiyār hai. खाना तैयार है।

speak ill of. kisī kī burāī karnā किसी की बुराई करना

Speak up. zarā zor se bolie ज़रा ज़ोर से बोलिए।

Step aside. rāstā choṛie. रास्ता छोड़िए।

Stick with it. karte raho करते रहो।

stuck in traffic.
traifik meṁ faṁs jānā. ट्रैफ़िक में फंस जाना।

Suit yourself.
jaisā āp ṭhīk samjheṁ. जैसा आप ठीक समझें।

Suppose I do? yadi maiṁ karūṁ to? यदि मैं करूँ तो?

Sure. nischit hī. निश्चित ही।

Take it easy. sāvdhān rahiegā सावधान रहिएगा।

take it on the chin. muṁh kī khānā मुँह की खाना

T

Take it or leave it.
bas yahī hai, rakho yā phir choṛ do.
बस यही है, रखो या फिर छोड़ दो।

Take my word for it.
merā viśvās kijie. मेरा विश्वास कीजिए।

Take ... by surprise.
ko cauṁkā denā ...को चौंका देना

Take ... at face value.
jo jaisā dikhe, vaisā mān lenā.
जो जैसा दिखे, वैसा मान लेना।

talk through one's hat.
śekhī baghārnā. शेखी बघारना।
teething troubles.
śurū ki pareśāniyāṁ शुरू की परेशानियाँ
Thanks for you call.
taiifon karne ke lie dhanyăvād.
टेलीफ़ोन करने के लिए धन्यवाद।
Thank you for inviting me.
nimantraṇ ke lie dhanyăvād. निमन्त्रण के लिए धन्यवाद।
Thanks. dhanyăvād. धन्यवाद।
śukriyā. शुक्रिया।

T

Thanks awfully.
bahut-bahut dhanyăvād बहुत–बहुत धन्यवाद
That'll be the day!
us din sūryă paścim se nikalegā.
उस दिन सूर्य पश्चिम से निकलेगा।
That'll teach ...
tumheṁ achhā sabak milegā.
तुम्हें अच्छा सबक मिलेगा।
That's all. bas. बस
That's easy for you to say.
apke lie aisā kahnā āsān hai.
आपके लिए ऐसा कहना आसान है।
That's enough for now.
bas, abhī ke lie itnā hī kāfī hai.
बस, अभी के लिए इतना काफ़ी है।

That's fine with me. mujhe manzūr hai. मुझे मंजूर है।

That's just too much ! .
yah to zyādatī hai. यह तो ज़्यादती है।

That's more like it: yah kuch ṭhīk hai. यह कुछ ठीक है

There aren't enough hours in the day.
din pūrā nahīṁ paṛtā. दिन पूरा नहीं पड़ता।

There is no chance. asambhav. असम्भव।

There is no need to.
iskī koī zarūrat nahīṁ. इसकी कोई ज़रूरत नहीं

There will be hell to pay.
bahut muśkil meṁ paṛ jāoge बहुत मुश्किल में पड़ जाओगे।

Things will work out .
sab ṭhīk ho jāegā सब ठीक हो जाएगा।

Under no circumstances.
kisī hāl meṁ nahīṁ, किसी हाल में नहीं,

Under normal circumstances.
ām hālāt meṁ आम हालात में

Use your head!
dimāg se kām lo. दिमाग से काम लो।

U

Wait a minute. ek kṣaṇ. एक क्षण।

wake the dead. gaṛhe murde jagānā गढ़े मुर्दे जगाना

Watch out! sāvdhān! सावधान।

Watch your tongue.
zabān saṁbhāl kar bāt karo. जबान सम्भाल कर बात करो।

We must do this again.
hameṁ ek bār phir yah karnā cāhie.
हमें एक बार फिर यह करना चाहिए।

We were just talking about you.
ham tumhārī / āpkī hī bāt kar rahe the.
हम तुम्हारी/आपकी ही बात कर रहे थे।

Welcome. swāgtam. स्वागतम्।

Well said. khūb kahā. खूब कहा।

What brings you here?
kaise ānā huā.? कैसे आना हुआ?

W

What happened? kya huā? क्या हुआ

What is the matter?
kyā bāt hai? क्या बात है?

What makes you think so?
tum aisā kyoṁ socte ho? तुम ऐसा क्यों सोचते हो?

What else can I do?
maiṁ aur kar hī kyā saktā hūṁ?
मैं और कर ही क्या सकता हूँ?

What else is new?
yah to koī naī bāt nahīṁ. यह तो कोई नई बात नहीं।

What number did you dial?
āpne kaun sā nambar milāyā ?
आपने कौन–सा नम्बर मिलाया?

Whatever turns you on.
agar tumheṁ is se khuśī mile.
अगर तुम्हें इससे खुशी मिले।

W

What is coming off?
yahāṁ kyā cal rahā hai? यहाँ क्या चल रहा है?

What's in it for me?
is meṁ mera kyā fāyadā hai? इसमें मेरा क्या फ़ायदा है?

What's it to you?
is se tumhārā kyā vāstā hai?
इससे तुम्हारा क्या वास्ता है?

What'a new with you?
koi naī bāt? कोई नई बात?

Who do you want to speak to?
āp kis se bāt karnā cāhte haiṁ?
आप किससे बात करना चाहते हैं?

Yes hāṁ; jī hāṁ हाँ; जी हाँ

You are welcome.
koi bāt nahīṁ. कोई बात नहीं।

You'd better get moving.
ab tumheṁ / āpko jānā chāie?
अब तुम्हें/आपको जाना चाहिए?

Y

You're just wasting my time.
tum sirf merā samay barbād kar rahe ho.
तुम सिर्फ़ मेरा समय बरबाद कर रहे हो।

Y

You're out of your mind!
tumhārā dimāg kharāb ho gayā hai.
तुम्हारा दिमाग़ ख़राब हो गया है।

You said a mouthful.
tumne bilkul ṭhīk kahā. तुमने बिल्कुल ठीक कहा।

You think you are so smart.
tum apne ko zyādā hī hośyār samajhte ho.
तुम अपने को ज़्यादा ही होशियार समझते हो।

you took words out of my mouth.
āpne mere muṁh kī bāt chīn lī.
आपने मेरी मुँह की बात छीन ली।

LANGUAGE PROBLEMS

I know very little Hindi.
maiṁ bahut thoṛī hindī jāntā hūṁ.
मैं बहुत थोड़ी हिन्दी जानता हूँ।

Do you speak English?
kyā āp aṅgrezī bolte haiṁ? क्या आप अंग्रेज़ी बोलते हैं?

What does it mean?
iskā kyā matlab hai? इसका क्या मतलब है?

How does one say it in Hindi?
ise hindī meṁ kaise kahte haiṁ?
इसे हिन्दी में कैसे कहते हैं?

What is it called in Hindi?
ise hindī meṁ kyā kahte haiṁ?
इसे हिन्दी में क्या कहते हैं?

You are speaking very fast.
āp bahut jaldī bol rahe (m.)/rahī (f.)haiṁ.
आप बहुत जल्दी बोल रहे/रही हैं।

I didn't understand.
maiṁ samjhā (m.)/samjhī (f.) nahīṁ.
मैं समझा/समझी नहीं।

I beg your pardon!
kṛpayā phir se kahie. कृपया फिर से कहिए।

Please repeat.
kṛpayā ek bār aur kahie. कृपया एक बार और कहिए।
Please speak slowly.
kṛpayā dhīre bolie. कृपया धीरे बोलिए।

INTRODUCTORY MEETING

What is your name?
āpkā nām kyā hai? आपका नाम क्या है?

How do you do?
āp kaise(m.)/kaisī(f.) haiṁ? आप कैसे/कैसी हैं?

Do you like it here?
āpko yahāṁ kaisā lag rahā hai?
आपको यहाँ कैसा लग रहा है?

Where are you from?
āp kis deś se haiṁ? आप किस देश से हैं?

I am from France.
maiṁ 'frāns' se hūṁ. मैं फ्रान्स से हूँ।

I am very pleased to meet you.
āpse milkar bahut prasannatā huī.
आपसे मिलकर बहुत प्रसन्नता हुई।

PARTING SENTENCES

Phone me as soon as you reach home.
ghar pahuṁcte hī 'ṭailifon' kījiegā.
घर पहुँचते ही टेलीफ़ोन कीजिएगा।

Come soon again!
jaldī phir āiegā. जल्दी फिर आइएगा।

Keep writing mail.
patra likhte rahiegā. पत्र लिखते रहिएगा।

Wish you a happy journey.
āpkī yātrā maṅgalmay ho. आपकी यात्रा मंगलमय हो।

USEFUL TIPS **Your host in traditional families might say:**

kṛpayā jute utarkār andar āeṁ.
Please remove your shoes and come in!
कृपया जूते उतारकर अन्दर आएँ।

BASIC NEEDS

I am feeling very hungry.
mujhe bahut bhūkh lagī hai. मुझे बहुत भूख लगी है।

I am very thirsty.
mujhe bahut pyās lagī hai. मुझे बहुत प्यास लगी है।

I want cold water.
mujhe ṭhaṇḍā pānī cāhie. मुझे ठण्डा पानी चाहिए।

I am feeling very tired.
mujhe bahut thakān lag rahī hai.
मुझे बहुत थकान लग रही है।

I am feeling sleepy.
mujhe nīṁd ā rahī hai. मुझे नींद आ रही है।

I would like to sleep now.
ab maiṁ sonā cāhūṁgā. अब मैं सोना चाहूँगा।

BASIC EMOTIONS

I am happy.
maiṁ khuś hūṁ मैं खुश हूँ।

I am unhappy.
maiṁ dukhī hūṁ. मैं दुःखी हूँ।

I am worried.
maiṁ cintit hūṁ मैं चिन्तित हूँ।

I am surprised.
maiṁ cakit hūṁ. मैं चकित हूँ।

I am upset.
maiṁ pareśān hūṁ. मैं परेशान हूँ।

I am curious.
maiṁ utsuk hūṁ. मैं उत्सुक हूँ।

I am frustrated.
maiṁ kuṇṭhit hūṁ. मैं कुण्ठित हूँ।

I am afraid.
mujhe ḍar hai... मुझे डर है...

I am repenting.
maiṁ pachtā rahā hūṁ. मैं पछता रहा हूँ।

I am sorry...
mujhe khẹd hai... मुझे खेद है...

MEETING THE NEIGHBOURS

Namaste I am Kamal. I am your next door neighbor.
Namaste, maiṁ kamal hūṁ. maiṁ āpkā paṛosī hūṁ.
नमस्ते। मैं कमल हूँ। मैं आपका पड़ोसी हूँ।

What is your name?
āpkā nām kyā hai? आपका नाम क्या है?

Where are you from?
āp kahāṁ se haiṁ? आप कहाँ से हैं?

My name is Robert.
merā nām 'raubarṭ' hai. मेरा नाम रॉबर्ट है।

I am from America.

maiṁ amrīkā se hūṁ. मैं अमरीका से हूँ।

This is my wife.

yah merī patnī hai. यह मेरी पत्नी है।

This is my son.

yah merā beṭā hai. यह मेरा बेटा है।

Our sons are the same age.

hamāre beṭe ek umra ke haiṁ.

हमारे बेटे एक उम्र के हैं।

Please come in.

kṛpayā andar āie. कृपया अन्दर आइए।

Have a seat please!

sthān grahaṇ kījie. स्थान ग्रहण कीजिए।

What would you like to have? Something cold or hot?

āp kyā leṁge? kuch ṭhaṇḍā yā garam?

आप क्या लेंगे? कुछ ठण्डा या गरम?

What do you do here?

āp yahāṁ kyā karte haiṁ? आप यहाँ क्या करते हैं?

I work for a bank.

maiṁ baiṅk meṁ kām kartā hūṁ.

मैं बैंक में काम करता हूँ।

I study at the university here.

maiṁ viśvavidyālayă meṁ paṛhtā hūṁ.

मैं विश्वविद्यालय में पढ़ता हूँ।

I am learning Hindi and Sanskrit.
maiṁ hindī aur saṁskṛt sīkh rahā hūṁ.
मैं हिन्दी और संस्कृत सीख रहा हूँ।

I am learning to play the sitar / the tabla.
maiṁ sitār / tablā bajānā sīkh rahā hūṁ.
मैं सितार/तबला बजाना सीख रहा हूँ।

I have come to India for traveling.
maiṁ bhārat yātrā karne āyā hūṁ.
मैं भारत यात्रा करने आया हूँ।

This is my first visit to India.
maiṁ pahlī bār bhārat āyā hūṁ.
मैं पहली बार भारत आया हूँ।

I have come to India several times before.
maiṁ pahle kaī bār bhārat āyā hūṁ.
मैं पहले कई बार भारत आया हूँ।

I have truly liked India.
mujhe bhārat sacmuc pasand āyā hai.
मुझे भारत सचमुच पसन्द आया है।

People here are very generous.
yahāṁ ke log bahut udār haiṁ.
यहाँ के लोग बहुत उदार हैं।

This city is very interesting.
yah śahar bahut rocak hai. यह शहर बहुत रोचक है।

Shopping is very difficult here.
yahāṁ kharīdārī bahut muśkil hai.

यहाँ ख़रीदारी बहुत मुश्किल है।

There is no fixed price. One has to bargain all the time.
ek dām nahīṁ hai. hameśā mol-bhāv karnā paṛtā hai.
एक दाम नहीं है। हमेशा मोल–भाव करना पड़ता है।

This is difficult. It is not like this in our country.
yah muśkil hai. hamāre deś meṁ aisā nahīṁ hotā.
यह मुश्किल है। हमारे देश में ऐसा नहीं होता।

I will be here ... a couple of days.
maiṁ yahāṁ do-cār din hūṁ.
मैं यहाँ दो–चार दिन हूँ।

... about two weeks
... lagbhag do hafte ... . . . लगभग दो हफ़्ते. . .

... perhaps a month
... śāyad ek mahīnā ... . . . शायद एक महीना...

I will certainly come here again.
maiṁ zarūr yahāṁ phir āūṁgā.
मैं जरूर यहाँ फिर आऊँगा।

Are you alone or with family?
āp akele haiṁ, yā parivār ke sāth?
आप अकेले हैं, या परिवार के साथ?

Inviting Friends to Tea or Movie

Would you like to join me for a cup of tea or coffee?
āp mere sāth ek pyālā cāy, yā 'kāufī' leṁge?

आप मेरे साथ एक प्याला चाय, या कॉफी लेंगे?

Are you free Saturday evening?

ap śanivār śām ko khālī haiṁ?

आप शनिवार शाम को खाली हैं?

Would you come with me to see a Hindi film?

kyā āp mere sāth hindī film dekhne caleṁge?

क्या आप मेरे साथ हिन्दी फ़िल्म देखने चलेंगे?

I love Hindi films.

mujhe hindī filmeṁ bahut pasand haiṁ.

मुझे हिन्दी फिल्में बहुत पसन्द हैं।

What is your phone number?

āpkā dūrbhāṣ -nambar kyā hai?

आपका दूरभाष नम्बर क्या है?

What kinds of films do you like?

āpko kaisī filmeṁ pasand haiṁ?

आपको कैसी फ़िल्में पसन्द हैं?

I like action films/movies.

mujhe mār-pīt wālī filmeṁ acchī lagtī haiṁ.

मुझे मार–पीट वाली फ़िल्में अच्छी लगती हैं।

... musical film ...

. . .gane-bajane walī film. . . . . .गाने–बजाने वाली फ़िल्म.

...social film...

...sāmājik film... . . .सामाजिक फ़िल्म. . .

...horror films...

...ḍarāvnī film... . . .डरावनी फ़िल्म. . .

...hackneyed film...

...ghisī-piṭī film... . . .घिसी–पिटी फ़िल्म. . .

...powerful film...

...zordār/damdār film... . . .जोरदार/दमदार फ़िल्म.

☞ **Both the words 'pikcar' and 'film' are interchangeably used. The use of the word 'movie' is getting more popular.**

I will pick you up at the hotel.

maiṁ āpko 'hoṭal' se le lūṁgā.

मैं आपको होटल से ले लूँगा।

Thanks. I will meet you in front of the cinema hall.

dhanyavād. maiṁ āpko sinemāghar ke sāmne milūṁgā.

धन्यवाद। मैं आपको सिनेमाघर के सामने मिलूँगा।

It was fantastic.

bahut mazā āyā. बहुत मज़ा आया।

I will always remember this evening.

mujhe yah śām hameśā yād rahegī.

मुझे यह शाम हमेशा याद रहेगी।

AT THE CUSTOMS

Don't get irritated or upset by the time-consuming controls and tight checks at the airport. With growing terrorism, for security reasons, this has become a necessity internationally. India is no exception. Cooperate patiently with the airport staff on duty. Tourists are truly very welcome in India.

IMMIGRATION

Here is my passport.

yah merā pāsporṭ hai. यह मेरा पासपोर्ट है।

I am a tourist. I will be here for three weeks.

maiṁ paryaṭak hūṁ. maim yahāṁ tīn hafte rahūṁgā.

मैं पर्यटक हूँ। मैं यहाँ तीन हफ़्ते रहूँगा।

I am on business trip.

maiṁ vyāpār ke silsile meṁ āyā hūṁ.

मैं व्यापार के सिलसिले में आया हूँ।

I am travelling alone.

maiṁ ... akelā ... safar kar rahā hūṁ

मैं ... अकेला ... सफ़र कर रहा हूँ।

... with family...

... parivār ke sāth ... . . . परिवार के साथ. .

.... with my business partner...

.... apne vyāpārī sahyogī ke sāth ...

. . . अपने व्यापारी सहयोगी के साथ . . .

Please stamp the date of departure on my passport.
kṛpayā mere pāsporṭ meṁ deś choṛne kī tārīkh ḍāl dījie.
कृपया मेरे पासपोर्ट में देश छोड़ने की तारीख़ डाल दीजिए।

I am on a transit visa.
mere pās 'ṭrānsiṭ vīsā' hai. मेरे पास ट्रांजिट वीसा है।

Please grant me transit visa.
kṛpayā mujhe 'ṭrānsiṭ vīsā' de dījie.
कृपया मुझे ट्रांजिट वीसा दे दीजिए।

CUSTOMS

Do you have something to declare?
kyā āpke pās śulk dene lāyak kuch sāmān hai?
क्या आपके पास शुल्क देने लायक कुछ सामान है?

These are all my used personal belongings.
ye sab merā pahle istemāl kiyā huā nijī sāmān hai.
ये सब मेरा पहले इस्तेमाल किया हुआ निजी सामान है।

I don't have any alcohol or cigarettes.
mere pās na śarāb hai, na sigreṭ.
मेरे पास न शराब है, न सिगरेट।

I don't have any electronics except my lap top and this small portable CD player.
mere pās apne laip-ṭaup aur is choṭe, 'porṭebal' sī. dī. ke alāvā koī aur bijlī kā sāmān nahīṁ hai.
मेरे पास अपने लैप–टॉप और इस छोटे, पोरटेबल सी.डी. के अलावा कोई और बिजली का सामान नहीं है।

These are for my personal use.

ye mere nijī istemāl ke lie haiṁ.

ये मेरे निजी इस्तेमाल के लिए हैं।

Open your box please.

apnā sandūk kholie. अपना सन्दूक खोलिए।

May I shut the box now?

kyā maiṁ ab apnā sandūk band kar saktā hūṁ?

क्या मैं अब अपना सन्दूक बन्द कर सकता हूँ?

Do I need to pay any duty?

kyā mujhe kuch śulk denā hogā?

क्या मुझे कुछ शुल्क देना होगा?

No. You may go through the green channel.

nahīṁ. āp 'grīn-cainel' se jā sakte haiṁ.

नहीं। आप ग्रीन चैनल से जा सकते हैं।

Have a good time in my country, sir!

mere deś meṁ āpkā samay maṅgalmay ho.

मेरे देश में आपका समय मंगलमय हो।

Thanks.

dhanyăvād. धन्यवाद।

I need a cart to carry luggage to the taxi stand.

mujhe sāmān ṭaiksī aḍḍe tak le jāne ke lie 'kārṭ' cāhie.

मुझे सामान टैक्सी अड्डे तक ले जाने के लिए 'कार्ट' चाहिए।

Can I get a porter here?

yahāṁ koī kulī milegā? यहाँ कोई कुली मिलेगा?

Those two boxes over there are mine.

vahāṁ par, ve do bakse mere haiṁ.

वहाँ पर, वे दो बक्से मेरे हैं।

This small bag I will carry myself.

yah choṭā 'baig' maiṁ apne āp uṭhā lūṁgā.

यह छोटा बैग मैं अपने आप उठा लूँगा।

Be careful! That one has fragile things.

dhyān se! usmeṁ ṭūṭne kā sāmān hai.

ध्यान से! उसमें टूटने का सामान है।

One of my bags is missing.

merā ek 'baig' nahīṁ mil rahā.

मेरा एक बैग नहीं गिल रहा।

I have a booking in a hotel. How can I get there?

ek hoṭal meṁ merī 'buking' hai. maiṁ vahāṁ kaise jā saktā hūṁ?

एक होटल में मेरी बुकिंग है। मैं वहाँ कैसे जा सकता हूँ।

Can I go there by bus?

kyā maiṁ 'bas' se jā saktā hūṁ?

क्या मैं बस से जा सकता हूँ।

It is walking distance from here. You may go on foot if you like.

yahāṁ se paidal kā rāstā hai. āp cāheṁ to paidal jā sakte haiṁ.

यहाँ से पैदल का रास्ता है। आप चाहें तो पैदल जा सकते हैं।

USEFUL TIPS

Beware of Pickpockets!

★ Prepaid taxi is the safest and most reasonably priced mode of transport at airports and railway stations.

★ Some licensed travel agencies run their buses to bring passengers downtown from where they can take a private or shared taxi to their destination.

★ Use of credit cards is relatively new in India. Only big stores and hotels accept them.

★ ATM machines are available in big cities.

★ Change money at the airport. You need to carry cash all the time.

HIRE A TAXI

Is this taxi free?

ṭaiksī khālī hai? टैक्सी खाली है?

How much will it cost to go from here to Hotel Taj?
yahāṁ se 'hoṭal' tāj tak ke kitne paise lageṁge?
यहाँ से होटल ताज तक के कितने पैसे लगेंगे?

The meter of my taxi is out of order. You may give me a hundred rupees.
merī ṭaiksī kā mīṭar kharāb hai; sau rupae de dījiegā.

मेरी टैक्सी का मीटर ख़राब है, सौ रुपए दे दीजिएगा।

This sounds too much.

yah to bahut zyādā lag rahā hai.

यह तो बहुत ज़्यादा लग रहा है।

Please, charge reasonable price.

ṭhīk-ṭhīk batāie. ठीक–ठीक बताइए।

Final price, ninety rupees.

ākhirī dām nabbe rupae. आखिरी दाम नब्बे रुपए।

Alright. Take me to the main station/ hotel Taj please.
ṭhīk hai. mujhe mukhyă sṭeśan/ hoṭal taj tak le calie.
ठीक है। मुझे मुख्य स्टेशन/होटल ताज तक ले चलिए।

Let us go.

calie! चलिए!

IN THE TAXI

Why is there so much traffic on the road?
is saṛak par itnā 'traifik' (yātāyāt) kyoṁ hai?
इस सड़क पर इतना ट्रैफ़िक (यातायात) क्यों है?

I am a bit in a hurry.

maiṁ kuch jaldī meṁ hūṁ. मैं कुछ जल्दी में हूँ।

If possible, I would like to get there faster.
yadi sambhav ho, to maiṁ vahāṁ kuch jaldī pahuṁcnā cāhtā hūṁ.
यदी सम्भव हो, तो मैं वहाँ कुछ जल्दी पहुँचना चाहता हूँ।

Please don't drive so fast!
kṛpayā itnī tez na calāie.
कृपया इतनी तेज़ न चलाइए।

Please drive a bit slow.
kṛpayā thoṛa dhīre calāie.. कृपया थोड़ा धीरे चलाइए।
Is there another route to get there.
kyā vahāṁ pahuṁcne kā koī aur rāsta hai?
क्या वहाँ पहुँचने का कोई और रास्ता है?

TOURIST INFORMATION

Is there a travel bureau nearby?
yahāṁ pās meṁ koī 'traival byoro' (yātrī sevak maṇḍal) hai?
यहाँ पास में कोई ट्रेवेल ब्यूरो (यात्री सेवक मंडल) है?

Are good tourist buses available?
kyā yahāṁ acchī paryaṭak 'baseṁ' miltī haiṁ?
क्या यहाँ अच्छी पर्यटक बसें मिलती हैं?

Air-conditioned tourist buses are frequently available here.
yahāṁ vātānukūlit paryaṭak 'baseṁ' bahut miltī haiṁ.
यहाँ वातानुकूलित पर्यटक बसें बहुत मिलती हैं।

They are comfortable, and also not very expensive.
ye ārāmdeh hotī haiṁ, aur bahut mahaṁgī bhī nahīṁ hotīṁ.
यह आरामदेह होती हैं, और बहुत महँगी भी नहीं होतीं।

They have a qualified guide who narrates the significance as well as the history of the place.
inke sāth yogyă mārgdarśak hotā hai, jo yatriyoṁ ko har sthān kā itihās aur zarūrī jānkārī detā rahtā hai.
इनके साथ योग्य मार्गदर्शक होता है, जो यात्रियों को हर स्थान का इतिहास और जरूरी जानकारी देता रहता है।

What time does the next bus leave for Red Fort?
lāl kile ke lie aglī 'bas' kitne baje chūṭegī?
लाल किले के लिए अगली बस कितने बजे छूटेगी?

I don't like crowded places.
mujhe bahut bhīṛwāle sthān pasand nahīṁ āte.
मुझे बहुत भीड़वाले स्थान पसन्द नहीं आते।

I wish to visit some place where not many tourists go.
maiṁ kisī aisī jagah jānā cāhtā hūṁ jahāṁ bahut yātrī na jāte hoṁ.
मैं किसी ऐसी जगह जाना चाहता हूँ जहाँ बहुत यात्री न जाते हों।

During summer very few tourists visit this city.
garmī ke mausam meṁ is śahar meṁ bahut kam yātrī āte haiṁ.
गर्मी के मौसम में इस शहर में बहुत कम यात्री आते हैं।

It has several good and inexpensive hotels.
yahāṁ kaī acche aur saste 'hoṭal' haiṁ.
यहाँ कई अच्छे और सस्ते होटल हैं।

BOOKING A ROOM IN A HOTEL

ENQUIRY AND BOOKING

I want a single room with an attached bathroom.
mujhe ek ādmī ke lie gusalkhanewālā kamrā cāhie.
मुझे एक आदमी के लिए गुसलखानेवाला कमरा चाहिए।

I need an air-conditioned room.
mujhe vātānukūlit kamrā cāhie.
मुझे वातानुकूलित कमरा चाहिए।

I want a room with T.V. and telephone.
mujhe kamre meṁ ṭī. vī. aur 'ṭailifon' cāhie.
मुझे कमरे में टी.वी. और टेलिफ़ोन चाहिए।

I want a room with a view of the river.
mujhe nadī kī or khulnewālā kamrā cahie.
मुझे नदी की ओर खुलनेवाला कमरा चाहिए।

I need a tranquil place. Here there is too much noise of temple bells.
mujhe śānt jagah cāhie. yahāṁ mandir kī ghaṇṭiyoṁ kā śor bahut zyādā hai.
मुझे शान्त जगह चाहिए। यहाँ मन्दिर की घण्टियों का शोर बहुत ज़्यादा है।

How much is the room rent in this hotel?.
is 'hoṭal' meṁ ek kamre kā kirāyā kitnā hai?
इस होटल में एक कमरे का किराया कितना है?

This is too high for me.
mere lie yah bahut zyādā hai.

मेरे लिए यह बहुत ज्यादा है।

Please suggest some cheaper place.
koī is se sastī jagah batāie.
कोई इससे सस्ती जगह बताइए।

There is a small hotel on the other side of the road. You will get a room there for less money.
saṛak ke us pār ek choṭā 'hoṭal' hai. āpko vahāṁ sastā kamrā milegā.
सड़क के उस पार एक छोटा होटल है। आपको वहाँ सस्ता कमरा मिलेगा।

Across from here, there is a monastery.
vahāṁ sāmne ek maṭh hai.
वहाँ सामने एक मठ है।

Next door from here is an aśram.
yahāṁ bagal meṁ ek āśram hai.
यहाँ बगल में एक आश्रम है।

They don't ask for any money.
ve kuch paisā nahīṁ māṁgte.
वे कुछ पैसा नहीं माँगते।

You may donate a small amount if you like.
āp cāheṁ to kuch rāśī dān de sakte haiṁ.
आप चाहें तो कुछ राशि दान दे सकते है।

ASKING FOR ADDITIONAL SERVICE

I need one more blanket.
mujhe ek aur kambal cāhie. मुझे एक और कम्बल चाहिए।

...two more pillows...
...do aur sirhāne/takiye... . . .दो और सिरहाने/तकिये.

...a clean towel...
...ek sāf tauliyā.... . . .एक साफ़ तौलिया. . .

...two or three hangers...
...do-tīn 'haiṅgar'... . . .दो–तीन हैंगर. . .

ashtray	**rākhdānī**	राखदानी
stationery	**lekhan-sāmagrī**	लेखन–सामग्री
envelopes	**lifāfe**	लिफ़ाफ़े
glue	**goṁd**	गोंद
postal stamps	**ḍāk-ṭikaṭ**	डाक–टिकट

ROOM SERVICE

Are meals served in the room?
kyā āp log khānā kamre meṁ pahuṁcāte haiṁ?
क्या आप लोग खाना कमरे में पहुँचाते हैं?

Morning breakfast is served in the room.
subah kā nāśtā kamre meṁ pahuṁcāyā jātā hai.
सुबह का नाश्ता कमरे में पहुँचाया जाता है।

Lunch and dinner are served in the dining room of the hotel.
din kā khānā aur rāt kā khānā 'hoṭal' ke bhojan kakṣ meṁ miltā hai.

दिन का खाना और रात का खाना होटल के भोजन कक्ष में मिलता है।

COMPLAINTS

Where is the manager?
'manejar' sāhab kahāṁ haiṁ?
मनेजर साहब कहाँ है?

There is no running water in the bathroom.
gusalkhāne ke nal meṁ pānī nahīṁ ā rahā.
गुसलख़ाने के नल में पानी नहीं आ रहा।

Both the fan as well as the cooler are not working.
paṅkhā aur 'kūlar' donoṁ hī kharāb haiṁ.
पंखा और कूलर, दोनों ही ख़राब हैं।

The bathroom drain is clogged.
gusalkhāne kī nālī band ho gaī hai.
गुसलख़ाने की नाली बन्द हो गई है।

The T.V. is not working.
ṭī. vī. nahīṁ cal rahā.
टी.वी. नहीं चल रहा।

Also the A.C. is not working.
'e. sī.' bhī kåm nahīṁ kar rahā.
ए.सी. भी काम नहीं कर रहा।

ORDERING BREAKFAST

What would you like to have for breakfast?
āp nāśte meṁ kyā leṁge?

आप नाश्ते में क्या लेंगे?

What do you serve for breakfast?
āpke yahāṁ nāśte meṁ kyā-kyā miltā hai?
आपके यहाँ नाश्ते में क्या–क्या मिलता है?

Our Indian breakfast has poori, paratha, kacauri, jalebi, halwa etc.
hamāre hindustānī nāśte meṁ pūrī,parāṭhā,kacaurī, jalebī, halwā ādi haiṁ.
हमारे हिन्दुस्तानी नाश्ते में पूरी, पराठा, कचौड़ी, जलेबी, हलवा आदि हैं।

We have lassi and tea for drink.
pīne ke lie lassī aur cāy.
पीने के लिए लस्सी और चाय।

Also we serve bread, butter, jam,omelette, cutlet etc.
ḍabal roṭī, makkhan, jaim, aumleṭ, kaṭleṭ ādi bhī haiṁ.
डबल रोटी, मक्खन, जैम, ऑमलेट, कटलेट आदि भी हैं।

I will have bread with butter and omelette,please.
maiṁ makkhan ke sāth ḍabal roṭī aur 'aumleṭ' lūṁgā.
मैं मक्खन के साथ डबल रोटी और आमलेट लूँगा।

I will have tea without sugar and milk.
pīne ke lie binā dūdh aur binā cīnī kī cāy .
पीने के लिए बिना दूध और बिना चीनी की चाय।

AT THE FRONT DESK OF A HOTEL

My name is Robert. I have a reservation here.
merā nām 'raubarṭ' hai. yahāṁ mere nām se kamrā ārakṣit hai.
मेरा नाम रॉबर्ट है। यहाँ मेरे नाम से कमरा आरक्षित है।

Room number 15. Would you register, please.
kamrā namber pandrah. āp 'rajisṭar' meṁ apnā nām likhie.
कमरा नम्बर पन्द्रह। आप रजिस्टर में अपना नाम लिखिए।

Could you lend me your pen please?
kṛpayā apnā kalam dījie.
कृपया अपना कलम दीजिए।

I will be here until the evening tomorrow.
maiṁ kal śām tak yahāṁ rahūṁgā.
मैं कल शाम तक यहाँ रहूँगा।

Do you accept traveler's checks?
āp 'ṭraivlar caik' lete haiṁ? आप ट्रैवलर चैक लेते हैं?

Would you like the payment now?
āp paise abhī leṁge? आप पैसे अभी लेंगे?

You may pay when you leave. Here is your key.
āp jāte samay de dījiegā. yah āpkī cābhī hai.
आप जाते समय दे दीजिएगा। यह आपकी चाभी है।

Is there a lift here?
kyā yahāṁ 'lifṭ' hai? क्या यहाँ लिफ़्ट है?

Please wake me up at four in the morning.
mujhe subah cār baje jagā dījiegā.
मुझे सुबह चार बजे जगा दीजिएगा।

I want to have the morning view of the Ganges.
maiṁ prabhāt meṁ gaṅgā dekhnā cāhtā hūṁ.
मैं प्रभात में गंगा देखना चाहता हूँ।

I would like to take a boat ride and enjoy the sunrise.
maiṁ nāv lekar sūryoday dekhnā cāhtā hūṁ.
मैं नाव लेकर सूर्योदय देखना चाहता हूँ।

RENT A ROOM / APARTMENT

I am looking for some accommodation for myself.
maiṁ apne rahne ke lie koī jagah ḍhūṁḍh rahā hūṁ.
मैं अपने रहने के लिए कोई जगह ढूँढ रहा हूँ।

My basic requirement is a room with a small kitchen and a private bathroom.
merī mūl zarūrat hai, ek kamrā, ek choṭī-sī rasoī aur nijī gusalkhānā.
मेरी मूल ज़रूरत है, एक कमरा, एक छोटी–सी रसोई और निजी गुसलख़ाना।

I have problem climbing the stairs. I prefer to live on the ground floor.
mujhe sīṛhiyāṁ caṛhne meṁ muśkil hotī hai. maiṁ nīce kī mañzil par rahnā zyādā pasand kartā hūṁ.
मुझे सीढ़ियाँ चढ़ने में मुश्किल होती है। मैं नीचे की मंज़िल पर रहना ज्यादा पसन्द करता हूँ।

This is a fairly large room.

yah kamra kāfī baṛā hai. यह कमरा काफ़ी बड़ा है।

This room is too small for my needs.

yah kamrā merī zarūrtoṁ ke lie bahut choṭā hai.

यह कमरा मेरी जरूरतों के लिए बहुत छोटा है।

The rent is rupees 1500/= per month, water and electricity extra.

kirāyā pandrah sau rupae prati mahīnā hai; bijlī-pānī alag.

किराया पन्द्रह सौ रुपए प्रति महीना है; बिजली–पानी अलग,

There is a fixed water charge of rupees 20/= per month.

pānī ke bīs rupae mahīnā. पानी के बीस रुपए महीना।

Electricity as per meter reading.

bijlī mītar ke anusār. बिजली मीटर के अनुसार।

There is a separate meter to record your electricity use.

āpke lie bijlī ka mītar alag hai.

आपके लिए बिजली का मीटर अलग है।

You pay as much as you use.

āp jitnī bijlī istemal kareṁge, utnā paisā deṁge.

आप जितनी बिजली इस्तेमाल करेंगे, उतना पैसा देंगे।

This is a small apartment.

yah ek choṭa 'apārṭmainṭ' hai.

यह एक छोटा अपार्टमेण्ट है।

It has a bed room, a living room and a small study room.

ismeṁ ek sone kā kamrā, ek baiṭhak aur ek choṭā-sā paṛhne kā kamrā hai.

इसमें एक सोने का कमरा, एक बैठक, एक छोटा–सा पढ़ने का कमरा है।

Besides , it has a small balcony.
iske atirikt, ismeṁ ek choṭī 'bālkanī' bhī hai.
इसके अतिरिक्त, इसमें एक छोटी 'बालकनी' भी है।

In winter you can sit in the sun.
sardī meṁ āp dhūp meṁ baiṭh sakte haiṁ.
सर्दी में आप धूप में बैठ सकते हैं।

You can dry your washed clothes there.
āp apne dhule kapṛe vahāṁ sukhā sakte haiṁ.
आप अपने धुले कपड़े वहाँ सुखा सकते हैं।

The monthly rent is rupees 3000/-, water and electricity charge excluded.
kirāyā tīn hazār rupae mahīnā, bijlī-pānī alag.
किराया तीन हजार रुपए महीना, बिजली–पानी अलग।

The rooms are airy.
kamre havādār haiṁ. कमरे हवादार हैं।

During the day there is sufficient sun light.
din meṁ paryāpt sūryă kā prākaś hotā hai.
दिन में पर्याप्त सूर्य का प्रकाश होता है।
The rent is very reasonable.
kirāyā vājib hai.
किराया वाजिब है।

I think I will take this apartment.
maiṁ soctā hūṁ, maiṁ yah apārṭmainṭ lūṁgā.
मैं सोचता हूँ, मैं यह अपार्टमेन्ट लूँगा।

PAYING GUEST ACCOMMODATION

I would like to live as a paying guest with some Hindi speaking Indian family.
maiṁ kisī hindī bolnewāle hindustānī parivār ke sāth 'peiṅg gaisṭ' ho kar rahnā cāhtā hūṁ.
मैं किसी हिन्दी बोलनेवाले हिन्दुस्तानी परिवार के साथ पेइंग गेस्ट होकर रहना चाहता हूँ।

This way I could very easily learn both the Indian culture and Hindi language.
is tarah maiṁ āsānī se bhārtīyă saṃskṛti aur hindī bhāṣā donoṁ sīkh sakūṁgā.
इस तरह मैं आसानी से भारतीय संस्कृति और हिन्दी भाषा दोनों सीख सकूँगा।

It is not difficult to find paying guest accommodation in India.
bhārat meṁ 'peiṅg gaisṭ' jagah milnā muśkil nahīṁ.
भारत में पेइंग गेस्ट जगह मिलना मुश्किल नहीं।

Indians are by nature very hospitable and foreigner-friendly.
hindustānī log swabhāv se baṛe satkārśīl aur videśiyoṁ ke śubhcintak hote haiṁ.
हिन्दुस्तानी लोग स्वभाव से बड़े सत्कारशील और विदेशियों के शुभचिन्तक होते हैं।

HOLIDAY BOOKING

I have read your advertisement about 'Banaras Tour In Winter' in the Statesman.
maiṁne sṭeṭsmain meṁ āpkā 'Sardiyoṁ Meṁ Banāras Yātrā' vijñāpan paṛhā hai.
मैंने स्टेट्स्मैन में आपका 'सर्दियों में बनारस यात्रा विज्ञापन' पढ़ा है।

I would like more information about this travel plan
maiṁ is yātrā yojnā ke bāre meṁ aur jānkārī cāhta hūṁ.
मैं इस यात्रा योजना के बारे में और जानकारी चाहता हूँ।

How far is your hotel from the river Ganges?
āpkā 'hoṭal' gaṅgā se kitnī dūr hai?
आपका होटल गंगा से कितनी दूर है?

The hotel is across from the Ganges.
'hoṭal' gaṅgā ke ṭhīk sāmne hai.
होटल गंगा के ठीक सामने है।

Single room with attached bathroom is for Rs 400/= per day.
ek ādmī ke lie gusalkhāne sahit kamrā cār sau rupae roz.
एक आदमी के लिए गुसलख़ाने सहित कमरा चार सौ रुपए रोज़।

It is 15 minutes away from the city center.
śahar se pandrah 'minaṭ' ke fāsle par hai.
शहर से पन्द्रह मिनट के फ़ासले पर है।

Our travel guides will be with you.
hamāre 'gāīḍ' āp ke sāth raheṁge.
हमारे गाईड आपके साथ रहेंगे।

Do you charge extra for that?
kyā āp uske lie aur paisā leṁge?
क्या आप उसके लिए और पैसा लेंगे?

No, this is included in our services.
jī nahīṁ, ye hamārī sevāoṁ kā hissā hai.
जी नहीं, ये हमारी सेवाओं का हिस्सा है।

Very good. Please book me four places in November.
bahut baṛhiā. kṛpayā mere lie navambar meṁ cār sthān ārakṣit kar dījie.
बहुत बढ़िया। कृपया मेरे लिए नवम्बर में चार स्थान आरक्षित कर दीजिए।

USEFUL TIPS

Some Leading Newpapers in India

English : Hindustan Times, The Times of India, The Statesman, The Hindu.

Hindi : Dainik Jagran, Navbharat Times.

Some leading magazines are:

English : India Today, Frontline, Femina, Eves Weekly.

Hindi : India Today, Outlook, Saheli, Manorama..

ASKING DIRECTIONS

THE FOREIGNER'S REGISTRATION OFFICE

Which way is the foreigners' registration office here?
videśī pañjīkaraṇ daftar kis or hai?
विदेशी पंजीकरण दफ़्तर किस ओर है?

I arrived in India on the 3rd of this month and in this city yesterday.
maiṁ bhārat meṁ tīn tārīkh ko pahuṁcā, aur is śahar meṁ kal.
मैं भारत में तीन तारीख को पहुँचा, और इस शहर में कल।

I have already been to the CID office.
maiṁ sī-āī-ḍī daftar ho āyā hūṁ.
मैं सी–आई–डी दफ़्तर हो आया हूँ।

I have found a place to stay, but I have not moved in yet.
mujhe rahne kī jagah mil gaī hai, parantu maiṁ abhī us meṁ gayā nahīṁ hūṁ.
मुझे रहने की जगह मिल गई है, परन्तु मैं अभी उसमें गया नहीं हूँ।

Your ID please?
āpkā paricayă patra? आपका परिचय पत्र?

Will my passport do?
mer 'pāsporṭ' se kām calegā?
मेरे पासपोर्ट से काम चलेगा?

Do you have a driver's license?
āpke pās 'ḍrāivars lāisens' hai?

आपके पास ड्राइवर्स लाइसेन्स है?

Yes, I have an international driver's license.
jī, mere pas antarrāṣṭrīyă 'ḍrāivars lāisens' (vāhan cālak patra) hai.
जी, मेरे पास अन्तर्राष्ट्रीय ड्राइवर्स लाइसेन्स (वाहन चालक पत्र) है।

Here is the address and phone number of my landlord.
mere makān mālik kā patā aur dūrbhāś nambar yah hai.
मेरे मकान मालिक का पता और दूरभाष नम्बर यह है।

TELEPHONE BOOTH

I am looking for a telephone booth around here.
maiṁkoi 'ṭailifon būth' khoj rahā hūṁ.
मैं कोई टेलीफ़ोन बूथ खोज रहा हूँ।

There is one round the corner.
vahāṁ kone par ek hai.
वहाँ कोने पर एक है।

Can one make international calls there?
kyā vahāṁ antarrāṣṭrīyă 'fon' ho saktā hai?
क्या वहाँ अन्तर्राष्ट्रीय फ़ोन हो सकता है?

You can phone from there anywhere in the world.
āp vahāṁ se viśva meṁ kahīṁ bhī 'fon' kar sakte haiṁ.
आप वहाँ से विश्व में कहीं भी फ़ोन कर सकते हैं।

Can I make collect calls there?
kyā yahāṁ se 'kalaikṭ kaul' kar sakte haiṁ?
क्या यहाँ से 'कलेक्ट कॉल' कर सकते हैं?

Can I use credit card?
kyā maiṁ 'kraiḍit kārḍ' istemāl kar saktā hūṁ?
क्या मैं क्रेडिट कार्ड इस्तेमाल कर सकता हूँ?

You must have one rupee coins with you to use the phone.
'ṭailifon' karne ke lie apne pās ek rupae ke sikke rakhiegā.
टेलिफ़ोन करने के लिए अपने पास एक रुपए के सिक्के रखिएगा।

LOST MY WAY

I think I am lost.
maiṁ rāstā bhūl gayā lagtā hūṁ.
मैं रास्ता भूल गया लगता हूँ।

I want to go to the railway station.
maiṁ 'relwe sṭeśan' jānā cāhtā hūṁ.
मैं रेलवे स्टेशन जाना चाहता हूँ।

I feel I am going the wrong way.
mujhe lagtā hai maiṁ galat diśā meṁ jā rahā hūṁ.
मुझे लगता है मैं ग़लत दिशा में जा रहा हूँ।

I might miss my train.
kahīṁ merī gāṛī nā chūṭ jāy.
कहीं मेरी गाड़ी ना छूट जाय।

Could you put me right for the station, please.
kṛpayā mujhe ṭhīk rāstā batāie.
कृपया मुझे ठीक रास्ता बताइए।

Walk straight. **sīdhe jāie.** सीधे जाइए।

Turn right at the first crossing.
pahle moṛ par dāyeṁ muṛie.
पहले मोड़ पर दायें मुड़िए।

Then take the next turning to the left.
phir bāyeṁ muṛie. फिर बायें मुड़िए।

Walk down two more blocks.
do 'blauk' aur calie. दो ब्लॉक और चलिए।

The station is right there.
ṭhīk vahīṁ par 'sṭeśan' hai. ठीक वहीं पर स्टेशन है।

AT THE CROSSING

Does this road go to Sarnath?
kyā yah saṛak sārnāth jātī hai?
क्या वह सड़क सारनाथ जाती है?

Where does this road go?
yah saṛak kahāṁ jātī hai? यह सड़क कहाँ जाती है?

Which road goes to Sarnath?
kaun-sī saṛak sārnāth jātī hai?
कौन–सी सड़क सारनाथ जाती है?

How far is Sarnath from here?
yahāṁ se sārnāth kitnī dūr hai?

यहाँ से सारनाथ कितनी दूर है?

Please show it to me on this map.
kṛpayā mujhe is nakśe meṁ dikhāie.
कृपया मुझे इस नक्शे में दिखाइए।

Turn right at the third crossing from here.
yahāṁ se tīsre caurāhe par dāyīṁ or muṛie.
यहाँ से तीसरे चौराहे पर दायीं ओर मुड़िए।

Go straight about two kilometers.
lagbhag do kilomīṭar sīdhe jāie.
लगभग दो किलोमीटर सीधे जाइए।

You will come to the highway.
āp 'hāiwe' par ā jāeṁge. आप हाइवे पर आ जाएँगे।

You will find signboards on the highway.
'hāiwe' par āpko saṅketstambh mileṁge.
हाइवे पर आपको संकेतस्तम्भ मिलेंगे।

In any case we are going to Sarnath too.
vaise ham bhī sārnāth jā rahe haiṁ.
वैसे हम भी सारनाथ जा रहे हैं।

You can follow us if you like.
āp cāheṁ to hamāre pīche-pīche āie.
आप चाहें तो हमारे पीछे–पीछे आइए।

This will be the best. Thanks.
yah sab se thīk rahegā. dhanyăvād.
यह सबसे ठीक रहेगा। धन्यवाद।

SARNATH

Located 8 km. from Varanasi, the holy city of light, in Uttar Prades, Sarnath is a pilgrim place for Buddhists from all over the world. After attaining enlightenment in Bodh Gaya, Lord Buddha gave his first sermon to his five disciples in the Deer Park. Countries such as Korea, Thailand, China, Vietnam, and Myanmar have built magnificent temples with their distinctive architecture. Devotees in large numbers are seen cleaning temples, meditating, reading scriptures and helping the needy.

BOOKING FOR MUSIC CONCERT

I would like to book two seats for the music concert on Sunday evening.

mujhe ravivār śām kī saṅgīt goṣṭhī ke lie do ṭikaṭeṁ cāhie.

मुझे रविवार शाम की संगीत गोष्ठी के लिए दो टिकटें चाहिए।

May I see the seating plan of the hall please.

kṛpayā 'haul' meṁ baiṭhne kī vyavasthā batāie.

कृपया हॉल में बैठने की व्यवस्था बताइए।

How much will the middle place in the first five rows cost?

pahlī pāṁc paṅktiyoṁ meṁ bīc kī jagah ke kitne paise hoṁge?

पहली पाँच पंक्तियों में बीच की जगह के कितने पैसे होंगे?

The middle seats in the first two rows cost Rs 200 each.
pahlī do paṅktiyoṁ meṁ bīc kī 'sīṭeṁ' do-do sau rupae kī haiṁ.
पहली दो पंक्तियों में बीच की सीटें दो–दो सौ रुपए की हैं।

Please give me two seats in the third row.
kṛpayā tīsrī paṅkti meṁ do 'ṭikaṭeṁ' de dījie.
कृपया तीसरी पंक्ति में दो टिकटें दे दीजिए।

What time will the concert start?
goṣṭhī kitne baje śurū hogī?
गोष्ठी कितने बजे शुरू होगी?

SIGHT SEEING

I have two days to spend in Varanasi.
mere pās vārāṇasī ke lie do din haiṁ.
मेरे पास वाराणसी के लिए दो दिन हैं।

I would like to see all the temples in this city.
maiṁ is śahar meṁ sab mandir dekhnā cāhtā hūṁ.
मैं इस शहर में सब मन्दिर देखना चाहता हूँ।

If possible, I would like to bathe in the River Ganges.
yadi sambhav ho, to maiṁ gaṅgā nadī meṁ nahānā cāhūṁgā.

यदि सम्भव हो, तो मैं गंगा नदी में नहाना चाहूँगा।

Are there any historical monuments here? I would love to visit them.
kyā yahāṁ koī aitihāsik imārteṁ haiṁ? maiṁ unheṁ zarūr dekhnā cāhūṁgā.
क्या यहाँ कोई ऐतिहासिक इमारतें हैं? मैं उन्हें ज़रूर देखना चाहूँगा।

What souvenirs can I buy here?
yahāṁ maiṁ yādgār kī taur par kyā kharīd saktā hūṁ?
यहाँ मैं यादगार की तौर पर क्या ख़रीद सकता हूँ?

Is there a market near my hotel?
kyā mere 'hoṭal' ke pās koī bāzār hai?
क्या मेरे होटल के पास कोई बाज़ार है?

If we pass by a market, we can stop there.
agar ham kisī 'mārkiṭ' ke pās se guzre, to vahāṁ ruk sakte haiṁ.
अगर हम किसी मार्केट के पास से गुज़रे, तो वहाँ रूक सकते हैं।

I wish I had more time to spend here.
kāś mere pās yahāṁ ke lie zyādā samay hotā!
काश मेरे पास यहाँ के लिए ज़्यादा समय होता।

I think this is enough for the day.
mere vicār meṁ āj ke lie bahut ho gayā.
मेरे विचार में आज के लिए बहुत हो गया।

Let us go back to the hotel.
calie, 'hoṭal' vāpas caleṁ! चलिए, होटल वापस चलें।

BOAT RIDE

I want to take an early morning boat ride.
maiṁ subah-subah naukā vihār karnā cāhtā hūṁ.
मैं सुबह–सुबह नौका विहार करना चाहता हूँ।
I want to see the sunrise on a boat.
maiṁ nāv par se sūryoday dekhnā cāhtā hūṁ.
मैं नाव पर से सूर्योदय देखना चाहता हूँ।
It will be very expensive to go alone by boat.
akele nāv se jānā bahut mahaṁgā paṛegā.
अकेले नाव से जाना बहुत महँगा पड़ेगा।

It will be cheaper to go in a group.
dūsre yāṭriyoṁ ke sāṭh jānā sastā paṛegā.
दूसरे यात्रियों के साथ जाना सस्ता पड़ेगा।

EATING OUT

Tell me the names of some good restaurants here.
yahāṁ kinhīṁ acche 'raisṭorainṭoṁ' ke nām batāie.
यहाँ किन्हीं अच्छे रेस्टोरेन्टों के नाम बताइए।

It is not safe to eat meat here.
yahāṁ māṁs khānā surakṣit nahīṁ.
यहाँ मांस खाना सुरक्षित नहीं।

For vegetarian food, Kesri is a good place to eat. Food is good; also not too expensive.

śākāhārī khāne ke lie 'kesrī' acchī jagah hai. khānā acchā hai; aur bahut mahaṁgā bhī nahīṁ.
शाकाहारी खाने के लिए 'केशरी' अच्छी जगह है। खाना अच्छा है, और बहुत महँगा भी नहीं।

Can you recommend some good vegetarian dishes?
kuch acche śākāhārī khānoṁ ke nām batāie.
कुछ अच्छे शाकाहारी खानों के नाम बताइए।

You may have sag-panir with nan, or bhaṭhūre chole. Iḍlī, ḍosa, sambhar-vaṛa etc. are some south Indian dishes.
āp nān ke sāth sāg-panīr, yā chole-bhathūre le sakte haiṁ. iḍlī, ḍosā, sāmbhar-vaṛā ādi kuch dakṣiṇ bhārat ke khāne haiṁ.
आप नान के साथ साग–पनीर, या छोले–भठूरे ले सकते हैं। इडली, डोसा, साम्भर–वड़ा आदि कुछ दक्षिण भारत के खाने हैं।

Bring me a menu please.
kṛpayā 'menyū' (vyañjan sūcī) lāie.
कृपया मेन्यू (व्यन्जन सूची) लाइए।

What is bhaṭhūra?
bhaṭhūrā kyā hai? भठूरा क्या है?

Bhathūra is fried bread made from fermented white flour.
bhaṭhūrā maide se banī, talī huī roṭī hai.
भठूरा मैदे से बनी, तली हुई रोटी है।

It is made from leavened dough. We eat it with chickpeas
yah khamīre āte se bantā hai. ham ise choloṁ ke sāth khāte haiṁ.

यह खमीरे आटे से बनता है। हम इसे छोलों के साथ खाते हैं।

What would you like to drink sir?
āp kyā pīnā cāheṁge? आप क्या पीना चाहेंगे?

Mineral water for me please.
kṛpayā mere lie 'minral wautar' lāie.
कृपया मेरे लिए 'मिनरल वॉटर' लाइए।

My friend will have lassi, please
mere dost ke lie lassī lāie.
मेरे दोस्त के लिए लस्सी लाइए।

I would like to reserve a table for ten for 6 p.m. today.
maiṁ āj śām ko chah baje das ādmiyoṁ ke lie mez ārakṣit karnā cāhtā hūṁ.
मैं आज शाम को छः बजे दस आदमियों के लिए मेज़ आरक्षित करना चाहता हूँ।

Do you serve beer here?
yahāṁ 'biyar' milegī? यहाँ बियर मिलेगी?

'rohu' fish of this place is considered to be very good.
yahāṁ kī rohū machlī bahut acchī mānī jātī hai.
यहाँ की रोहू मछली बहुत अच्छी मानी जाती है।

Taste some.
thoṛā cakh kar dekhie. थोड़ा चख कर देखिए।

Give me a small piece from that one.
mujhe uswāle meṁ se choṭā-sā ṭukṛā dījie.
मुझे उसवाले में से छोटा–सा टुकड़ा दीजिए।

I particularly like lightly spiced fish baked in oven.
mujhe tandūr meṁ sikī huī, halke masālewālī machlī bahut pasand hai.
मुझे तन्दूर में सिकी हुई, हल्के मसालेवाली मछली बहुत पसन्द है।

Please remove the bone from the fish.
machlī meṁ se haḍḍī nikāl dījie.
मछली में से हड्डी निकाल दीजिए।

Some more lentil soup please!
thoṛī aur dāl lāie!
थोड़ी और दाल लाइए।

The food was excellent. We enjoyed much.
khānā bahut baṛhiyā thā. hameṁ bahut mazā āyā.
खाना बहुत बढ़िया था। हमें बहुत मज़ा आया।

The service was excellent.
sevā bahut acchī thī. सेवा बहुत अच्छी थी।

Bring me the bill please.
kṛpayā bil lāie. कृपया बिल लाइए।

INDIAN FOODS

BREADS

ordinary breads :
roṭī रोटी **rūmālī roṭī** रूमाली रोटी

deep fried breads :
pūrī पूरी bhaṭhūrā भटूरा,

shallow fried breads :

parāṭhā पराठा   **bharvāṁ parāṭhā** भरवां पराठा

nān नान,   **kulcā** कुल्चा,
baked   baked

RICE PREPARATIONS

ublā cāval (boiled rice)   **pulāo** (fried rice)   **biryānī**
उबला चावल   पुलाव   बिरयानी

SNACKS

samosā	**ṭikkī**	**pakoṛā**	**vaṛā**
समोसा	टिक्की	पकोड़ा	वड़ा
ḍhoklā	**kacaurī**	**maṭhrī**	**gol gappā**
ढोकला	कचौरी	मठरी	गोल गप्पा
cāṭ			
चाट			

DRINKS

lassī	**śikañjvī**	**ṭhaṇḍāī**	**śarbat**
लस्सी	शिकञ्जवी	ठण्डाई	शरबत

COMMON APPETIZERS

jaljīrā	**panā**	**kāñjī**
जलजीरा	पना	काञ्जी

DESSERTS

khīr खीर	**kulfī** कुल्फ़ी	**rasmalāī** रसमलाई
rasgullā रसगुल्ला	**gulābjāmun** गुलाबजामुन	**halwā** हलवा

YOGURT PREPARATIONS

sādā dahī (plain yogurt) सादा दही	**rāyatā** रायता	**dahī -baṛā** दही–बड़ा

VEGETARIAN CURIES

dam ālū दम आलू	**maṭar-panīr** मटर–पनीर	**sāg-panīr** साग–पनीर	**malāī-koftā** मलाई–कोफ्ता

NON-VEGETARIAN CURRIES

tandūrī chicken तन्दूरी चिकन	**murg musallam** मुर्ग मुसल्लम	**makkhānī murg,** मक्खनी मुर्ग
nargasī kofta curry नरगसी कोफ्ता करी		**śāhī kormā** शाही कोरमा

PICKLES AND CHUTNEYS

lemon/mixed pickle	**nīmbū/navratan kā acār** नींबू/नवरतन का अचार
mint-coriander chutney	**podīnā-dhaniyā caṭnī** पुदीना–धनिया चटनी

RELATED VOCABULARY

roasted	**bhunā huā**	भुना हुआ
fried	**talā huā**	तला हुआ
boiled	**ublā huā**	उबला हुआ
baked	**bhaṭṭhī meṁ sikā huā**	भट्ठी में सिका हुआ
steamed	**bhāp meṁ pakā huā**	भाप में पका हुआ
stuffed	**bharvāṁ**	भरवाँ
grilled	**tez āṁc par bhūnanā**	तेज आंच पर भूना हुआ
garnished	**sajāyā huā**	सजाया हुआ

USEFUL TIPS

Food Habits

The majority of Indian people are vegetarians. They obtain their proteins from a variety of pulses (dal) and beans as well as dairy products such as milk and yogurt.

★ Rice, wheat and corn serve as the staple cereals.

★ Coarse grains like millets, sorghum and barley are also used, especially in rural families.

★ **Commonly used flours are :**
black gram flour (besan), semolina (sūjī), white flour (maidā), whole wheat flour (gehūṁ kā āṭā).

★ **Commonly used pulses are:**
mūṅg, masūr, urad, arhar, canā etc.

FINDING LOST BELONGINGS

I left my money bag in the bus. What shall I do?
merā baṭuā 'bas' meṁ chūṭ gayā hai. mujhe kyā karnā cāhie.
मेरा बटुआ बस में छूट गया है। मुझे क्या करना चाहिए।

You can go and find out at the head office of the Transport Corporation.
āp basoṁ ke baṛe daftar meṁ jākar patā lagā sakte haiṁ.
आप बसों के बड़े दफ्तर में जाकर पता लगा सकते हैं।

You may lodge a report at the police station.
āp thāne meṁ rapaṭ likhwā sakte haiṁ.
आप थाने में रपट लिखवा सकते हैं।

It is not common to find lost goods here.
yahāṁ khoyā huā sāmān ām taur par nahīṁ miltā.
यहाँ खोया हुआ सामान आम तौर पर नहीं मिलता।

In my opinion it would be better to forget it. You won't get anything by all this.
merī rāy meṁ use bhūl jānā hī ṭhīk rahegā. is sab se kuch milegā nahīṁ.
मेरी राय में उसे भूल जाना ही ठीक रहेगा। इस सबसे कुछ मिलेगा नहीं।

Only your time will be wasted.
sirf āpkā samay kharāb hogā.
सिर्फ आपका समय ख़राब होगा।

ACCIDENT

You have damaged my car!
āpne merī gāṛī* toṛ dī hai. आपने मेरी गाड़ी तोड़ दी है।

I will call the police. I need a lawyer too!
maiṁ pulis ko bulāūṁgā. mujhe vakīl bhī cāhie!
मैं पुलिस को बुलाऊँगा। मुझे वकील भी चाहिए!

Let us not involve the police and lawyers!
hameṁ vakīloṁ aur pulis ke cakkar meṁ nahīṁ paṛnā cāhie.
हमें वकीलों और पुलिस के चक्कर में नहीं पड़ना चाहिए।

Let us settle the matter between us.
hameṁ āpas meṁ māmlā suljhā lenā cāhie.
हमें आपस में मामला सुलझा लेना चाहिए।

☞ **The word gāṛī is used as common noun for most vehicles such as car, bicycle, scooter, train etc. The meaning is derived contextually.**

ACCIDENT AVERTED

Suddenly a cow came in front of my car. An accident almost happened.
merī kār ke sāmne acānak gāy ā gaī; durghaṭna hote-hote bacī.
मेरी कार के सामने अचानक गाय आ गई; दुर्घटना होते–होते बची।

Our riksa collided with a bullock-cart
hamārā rikśā bailgāṛī se bhiṛ gayā.
हमारा रिक्शा बैलगाड़ी से भिड़ गया।

USEFUL TIPS

Be Mentally Prepared. Not Afraid!

The roads in most cities, other than the metropolitan, contain countless craters, pits, curves and potholes of weird shapes and dimensions, some even unknown to science.

Drivers of heterogeneous variety of vehicles ply on the roads with scant respect to any traffic rules.

To top the misery, you find cows, bulls and stray dogs running rampant anywhere, anytime.

Beggars make their own contribution to this chaotic road scenario!

SHOPPING

ASKING PRICE

How much is this sari?

yaha sāṛī kitane kī hai? यह साड़ी कितने की है?

How much is this umbrella?

yaha chātā kitane kā hai? यह छाता कितने का है?

How much are these gloves?

ye dastāne kitne ke haiṁ? ये दस्ताने कितने के हैं?

ASKING OPINION

How do you like this book?

āpko yaha kitāb kaisī lag rahī hai?
आपको यह किताब कैसी लग रही है?

How do you like my umbrella?
āpko merā chātā kaisā lag rahā hai?
आपको मेरा छाता कैसा लग रहा है?

How do you like my gloves?
āpko mere dastāne kaise lag rahe haiṁ?
आपको मेरे दस्ताने कैसे लग रहे हैं?

EXPRESSING OPINION

I like this book.
mujhe yah kitāb acchī lag rahī hai.
मुझे यह किताब अच्छी लग रही है।

I find this umbrella too expensive.
mujhe yah chātā bahut mahaṁgā lag rahā hai.
मुझे यह छाता बहुत महँगा लग रहा है।

I find these gloves a bit too small.
mujhe ye dastāne kuch chote lag rahe haiṁ.
मुझे ये दस्ताने कुछ छोटे लग रहे हैं।

...tastes stale.
...bāsī lag rahā hai. बासी लग रहा है।

...feels rough.
...khurdarā lag rahā hai. खुरदरा लग रहा है।

ENQUIRING ABOUT AVAILABILITY

Where can one get English Newspaper
yahāṁ angrezī kā akhbār kahāṁ milegā?
यहाँ अंग्रेज़ी का अख़बार कहाँ मिलेगा?

Where can one get milk and yogurt here?
yahāṁ dūdh aur dahi kahāṁ milegā?
यहाँ दूध, दही कहाँ मिलेगा?

Where can one get shoes and clothes here?
yahāṁ jute aur kapṛe kahāṁ mileṁge?
यहाँ जूते और कपड़े कहाँ मिलेगें?

Can one get English newspaper here?

kyā yahāṁ angrazī kā akhbār miltā hai?
क्या यहाँ अंग्रेज़ी का अख़बार मिलता है?

...milk and yogurt here?
...dūdh, dahī miltā hal?
...दूध, दही मिलता है?

...sweets here?
...miṭhaī milti hai?
...मिठाई मिलती है?

EXPRESSING DESIRE TO SEE MORE

Do you have something bigger than this?
āpke pās kuch aur is se baṛā hogā?
आपके पास कुछ और इससे बड़ा होगा?

better than this
is se baṛhiyā
इससे बढ़िया

cheaper than this
is se sastā
इससे सस्ता

BUYING CLOTHES

Are there any good department stores here?
kyā yahāṁ koī acche 'ḍipārṭmaiṇṭ sṭor' (bahuvibhāgīyă bhaṇḍăr) haiṁ?
क्या यहाँ कोई अच्छे डिपार्टमेण्ट स्टोर (बहुविभागीय भण्डार) हैं?

We don't have department stores in this city.
is śahar meṁ bahuvibhāgīyă bhaṇḍār nahīṁ haiṁ.
इस शहर में बहुविभागीय भण्डार नहीं हैं।

What exactly would you like to buy?
āp kyā kharīdnā cāhte haiṁ?
आप क्या खरीदना चाहते हैं?

This place is famous for silk and wooden toys.
yah sthān reśam aur lakṛī ke khilaunoṁ ke lie maśhūr hai.
यह स्थान रेशम और लकड़ी के खिलौनों के लिए मशहूर है।

In Delhi you can visit the government emporiums.
dillī meṁ āp sarkārī bhaṇḍāroṁ meṁ jā sakte haiṁ.
दिल्ली में आप सरकारी भण्डारों में जा सकते हैं।

They have all kinds of things from different regions.
ve vibhinn kṣetroṁ se sab tarah kā sāmān rakhte haiṁ.
वे विभिन्न क्षेत्रों से सब तरह का सामान रखते हैं।

Their quality is very good. The have fixed prices.
unke māl kī guṇvattā ūṁcī aur dām ek hotā hai.
उनके माल की गुणवत्ता ऊँची और दाम एक होता है।

Thank you for your advice.
āpkī salāh ke lie dhanyăvād.
आपकी सलाह के लिए धन्यवाद।

I would like to buy myself a silk suit.
maiṁ yahāṁ se apne lie ek reśam ka 'sūṭ' kharīdnā cāhtā hūṁ.
मैं यहाँ से अपने लिए एक रेशम का सूट ख़रीदना चाहता हूँ।

You can buy a ready-made one.
āp banā-banāyā bhī kharīd sakte haiṁ.
आप बना–बनाया भी ख़रीद सकते हैं।

But it may be a bit tight or loose, short or long.
lekin yah kuch taṅg yā ḍhīlā, choṭā yā baṛā ho saktā hai.
लेकिन यह कुछ तंग या ढीला, छोटा या बड़ा हो सकता है।

Usually some alteration is required.
ām taur par kuch ṭhīk karvānā paṛtā hai.
आम तौर पर कुछ ठीक करवाना पड़ता है।

You can buy material of your choice and have it made to measure.
āp apnī pasand ka kapṛā kharīdkar apne nāp se banvā sakte haiṁ.
आप अपनी पसन्द का कपड़ा खरीदकर अपने नाप से बनवा सकते हैं।

It is less expensive and more satisfactory.
yah kam dām meṁ aur zyādā santoṣprad hotā hai.
यह कम दाम में और ज़्यादा सन्तोषप्रद होता है।

That sounds like a good plan.
yah ṭhīk rahegā. यह ठीक रहेगा।

Where is a good place to buy the material?
kapṛā kharīdne ke lie koī acchā sthān batāie.
कपड़ा खरीदने के लिए कोई अच्छा स्थान बताइए।

And some good tailor too.
aur koī acchā darzī bhī. और कोई अच्छा दर्जी भी।

Show me some material for men's suit.
mujhe puruṣoṁ ke 'sūṭ' ke lie koī kapṛā dikhāie.
मुझे पुरुषों के सूट के लिए कोई कपड़ा दिखाइए।

Any specific color?
koī viśeṣ raṅg? कोई विशेष रंग?

I like brown.
mujhe bhūrā raṅg pasand hai.
मुझे भूरा रंग पसन्द है।

Please show me something in a lighter color.
kṛpayā is se halke raṅg meṁ kuch dikhāie.
कृपया इससे हल्के रंग में कुछ दिखाइए।

What kind of silk is this?
yah kaisī 'silk' hai? यह कैसी सिल्क है?

Do you have anything better?
āpke pās is se baṛhiā kuch aur hai?
आपके पास इससे बढ़िया कुछ और है?

Can I pay by credit card?
kyā maiṁ 'kraiḍiṭ kārḍ' se bhugtān kar saktā hūṁ?
क्या मैं क्रेडिट कार्ड से भुगतान कर सकता हूँ?

I would like to get a dress made for my wife too.
maiṁ apnī patnī ke lie bhī ek pośāk banvānā cāhtā hūṁ.
मैं अपनी पत्नी के लिए भी एक पोशाक बनवाना चाहता हूँ।

I have her measurements.
mere pās unkā nāp hai.
मेरे पास उनका नाप है।

How long will it take you to do it?
āpko banāne meṁ kitnā samay lagegā?
आपको बनाने में कितना समय लगेगा?

I am here for three days only.
maiṁ yahāṁ sirf tīn din hūṁ.
मैं यहाँ सिर्फ़ तीन दिन हूँ।

Please send it to my hotel.
kṛpayā mere 'hoṭal' meṁ bhej dījiegā.
कृपया मेरे होटल में भेज दीजिएगा।

USEFUL TIPS

No Panic! No Stress Syndrome!

An oft heard phrase in India is:
jo honā hai, so hogā.
जो होना है, सो होगा।
whatever has to happen, will happen.

What marvellous self-abandonment by the people, in the midst of entire hectic mundane activity to the all pervasive Will of the Lord.

BUYING BOOKS

I am looking for a book store.
maiṁ koī kitāb kī dukān khoj rahā hūṁ.
मैं कोई किताब की दुकान खोज रहा हूँ।

What kind of books are you planning to buy?
āp kaisī kitābeṁ kharīdne kī soc rahe haiṁ?
आप कैसी किताबें खरीदने की सोच रहे हैं?

I am interested in bilingual books on indology.
mujhe iṇḍaulaugī kī dubhāṣīyă kitāboṁ meṁ ruci hai.
मुझे इण्डोलॉजी की दुभाषीय किताबों में रुचि है।

The largest book store in this town is Vishvavidyalaya Prakashan.
is śahar meṁ sab se baṛī kitāboṁ kī dukān viśvavidyālayă Prākaśan hai.
इस शहर में सबसे बड़ी किताबों की दुकान विश्वविद्यालय प्रकाशन है।

The best place to buy indology books is Harmony at Assi Ghat.
iṇḍaulaugī kī kitāboṁ ke lie sab se acchī jagah assī ghāt par hārmanī pustak bhaṇḍār hai.
इन्डोलॉजी की किताबों के लिए सबसे अच्छी जगह अस्सी घाट पर हारमनी पुस्तक भण्डार है।

I am particularly interested in books on the Goddess Durga.
mujhe viśeṣkar Devī Durgā par kitāboṁ meṁ ruci hai.

मुझे विशेषकर देवी दुर्गा पर किताबों में रुचि है।

I don't have in mind any specific titles or authors.
mere dimāg meṁ koī viśeṣ kitāboṁ ya lekhkoṁ ke nām nahīṁ haiṁ.
मेरे दिमाग में कोई विशेष किताबों या लेखकों के नाम नहीं हैं।

Please show me where to look for these books.
kṛpayā mujhe batāeṁ maiṁ in kitāboṁ ko kahāṁ dekhūṁ.
कृपया मुझे बताएँ मैं इन किताबों को कहाँ देखूँ।

Also where could I buy a map of the city?
aur, śahar ka nakśā kahāṁ milegā?
और, शहर का नक्शा कहाँ मिलेगा?

Please show some good translation and commentary of Kaṭhopnisad.
kṛpayā kaṭhopniṣad kā koī acchā tīkā sahit anuvād dikhāie.
कृपया कठोपनिषद का कोई अच्छा टीका सहित अनुवाद दिखाइए।

PHOTOGRAPHY

With your permission, may I take a picture of you, as a remembrance?
yadi āp ijāzat deṁ, to maiṁ yādgār ke lie āpkī tasvīr le luṁ?
यदि आप इजाज़त दें, तो मैं यादगार के लिए आपकी तस्वीर ले लूँ?

Look in the camera, over here please.
kṛpayā idhar 'kaimre' meṁ dekhie.
कृपया इधर कैमरे में देखिए।

Smile a little please.
thoṛā muskarāie. थोड़ा मुस्कराइए।

Don't move.
hilie nahīṁ. हिलिए नहीं।

I would like to buy a couple of color film rolls.
maiṁ kuch 'kaimere' kī raṅgīn filmeṁ khárīdnā cāhtā hūṁ.
मैं कुछ कैमरे की रंगीन फिल्में खरीदना चाहता हूँ।

Please load this camera for me.
kṛpayā mere 'kaimre' meṁ film ḍāl dījie.
कृपया मेरे कैमरे में फ़िल्म डाल दीजिए।

VISA OFFICE

I wish to apply for a visa. What am I supposed to do?
maiṁ vīsā ke lie āvedan patra denā cāhtā hūṁ. mujhe kyā karnā hogā?
मैं वीसा के लिए आवेदन पत्र देना चाहता हूँ। मुझे क्या करना होगा?

Please give in your application at the front desk.
kṛpayā āp sāmnewālī mez par āvedan patra de deṁ.
कृपया आप सामनेवाली मेज़ पर आवेदन पत्र दे दें।

Enclose character certificate from the police station of your area and two photographs.

sāth meṁ apne ilāke ke thāne se caritra pramāṇ patra aur do foto bhī lagā deṁ.

साथ में अपने इलाके के थाने से चरित्र प्रमाण पत्र और दो फोटो भी लगा दें।

Deposit the Visa fee.

vīsā śulk jamā karā deṁ. वीसा शुल्क जमा करा दें।

How much is the Visa fee?

vīsā śulk kitnā hai? वीसा शुल्क कितना है?

When will the visa be ready?

vīsā kab tak taiyār hogā? वीसा कब तक तैयार होगा?

You may come back any time after 2 p:m to collect your passport. Our office closes at 4 p:m.

āp dopahar do baje ke bād kabhī bhī ākar apnā 'pāsporṭ' le sakte haiṁ. hamārā daftar śām cār baje band ho jātā hai.

आप दोपहर दो बजे के बाद कभी भी आकर अपना पासपोर्ट ले सकते हैं। हमारा दफ़्तर शाम चार बजे बन्द हो जाता है।

Please come with your personal identification card.

kṛpayā apnā paricay patra sāth lekar āeṁ.

कृपया अपना परिचय पत्र साथ लेकर आएँ।

Here is my identity card.

yah merā paricay patra hai.

यह मेरा परिचय पत्र है।

How long is my visa valid?

merā vīsā kab tak vaidh rahegā?

मेरा वीसा कब तक वैध रहेगा?

EXPLORING BUSINESS

I would like to contact a firm that makes men's wear.
maiṁ kisī puruṣoṁ ke kapṛe banānewālī 'farm' se sampark karnā cāhtā hūṁ
मैं किसी पुरुषों के कपड़े बनानेवाली फ़र्म से सम्पर्क करना चाहता हूँ।

I am here to survey the market.
maiṁ yahāṁ bāzār kā sarvekṣaṇ karne āyā hūṁ.
मैं यहाँ बाजार का सर्वेक्षण करने आया हूँ।

I need a local distributor/ manufacturer for my product.
mujhe apne māl ke lie sthānīyă vitrak / utpādak kī zarūrat hai.
मुझे अपने माल के लिए स्थानीय वितरक/उत्पादक की ज़रूरत है।

Labor in my country is very expensive.
mere deś meṁ mazdūrī bahut mahaṁgī hai.
मेरे देश में मज़दूरी बहुत महंगी है।

What is your capital?
āpkī pūñjī rāśī kitnī hai?
आपकी पूँजी राशी कितनी है?

How can I check on the firm's credit rating?
maiṁ 'farm' kī sākh ke bare meṁ kaise patā lagā saktā hūṁ?
मैं फ़र्म की साख के बारे में कैसे पता लगा सकता हूँ?

I would like to show you some of my samples.
maiṁ āpko apne kuch namūne dikhānā cāhūṁgā.
मैं आपको अपने कुछ नमूने दिखाना चाहूँगा।

Can these be made here?
kyā ye yahāṁ banāe jā sakte haiṁ?
क्या ये यहाँ बनाए जा सकते हैं?

How large is your factory?
āpkā kārkhānā kitnā baṛā hai?
आपका कारखाना कितना बड़ा है?

How many people do you employ on permanent basis?
āpke yahāṁ sthāī karmcārī kitne haiṁ?
आपके यहाँ स्थाई कर्मचारी कितने हैं?

I would like bank references.
mujhe 'baiṅk' kā havālā cāhie hogā.
मुझे बैंक का हवाला चाहिए होगा।

I am authorized to make payment in pounds.
maiṁ pāuṇḍ mcṁ rakam cuktā karne ko prādhikṛt hūṁ.
मैं पौंड में रकम चुकता करने को प्राधिकृत हूँ।

Where can you ship the merchandise to?
āp māl kahāṁ bhej sakte haiṁ?
आप माल कहाँ भेज सकते हैं?

BANKING

I wish to open a bank account here.
maiṁ yahāṁ baiṅk meṁ khātā kholnā cāhtā hūṁ.
मैं यहाँ बैंक में खाता खोलना चाहता हूँ।

A savings account or a current account?
bacat khātā yā cālū khātā?
बचत खाता या चालू खाता?

What is the interest rate on savings?
bacat par byāj dar kyā hai?
बचत पर ब्याज दर क्या है?

Please fill in this form?
kṛpayā yah 'fāram' bharie.
कृपया यह फ़ारम भरिए।

I have just come to this country.
maiṁ abhī-abhī is deś meṁ āyā hūṁ.
मैं अभी–अभी इस देश में आया हूँ।

I have nobody to introduce me.
maiṁ apne paricay ke lie kisī ko nahīṁ jāntā.
मैं अपने परिचय के लिए किसीको नहीं जानता।

Please show me your passport.
kṛpayā apnā 'pāsporṭ' dikhāie.
कृपया अपना पासपोर्ट दिखाइए।

Is a small bank locker available?
kyā āpke 'baiṅk' meṁ choṭā 'lāukar' uplabdh hai?
क्या आपके बैंक में छोटा लॉकर उपलब्ध है?

You will need to wait quite some time for that.
uske lie āpko kāfī intzār karnā hogā.
उसके लिए आपको काफ़ी इन्तज़ार करना होगा।

It is okay. Please put me on the waiting list.
kṛpayā merā nām pratīkṣā sūcī meṁ dāl dījie.
कृपया मेरा नाम प्रतीक्षा सूची में डाल दीजिए।

I want to send some money to America.
maiṁ kuch paisā amrīkā bhejnā cāhtā hūṁ.
मैं कुछ पैसा अमरीका भेजना चाहता हूँ।

Please go to window three.
kṛpayā khiṛkī nambar tīn par jāeṁ.
कृपया खिड़की नम्बर तीन पर जाएँ।

You can buy a bank draft there.
vahāṁ āp 'baiṅk ḍrāfṭ' kharīd sakte haiṁ.
वहाँ आप बैंक ड्राफ्ट ख़रीद सकते हैं।

USEFUL TIPS

It Takes Longer in India!

Don't be disappointed to find the counters in a bank or a government office sometimes unattended during working hours especially in the morning. Many clerks or employees habitually arrive and start their day late.

Be prepared to spend a long time for doing any business in a government office or a government bank!

CHANGING MONEY

I will have tc change some money today.
āj mujhe kuch paisā badalnā hogā.
आज मुझे कुछ पैसा बदलना होगा।

What is the legal exchange rate on a dollar today?
āj 'ḍaular' kī sarkārī vinimaydar kyā hai?
आज डॉलर की सरकारी विनिमयदर क्या है?

Is free market rate here very different from the legal rate?
kyā yahāṁ bāzār meṁ vinimaydar sarkārī dar se bahut bhinn hotī hai?
क्या यहाँ बाजार में विनिमयदर सरकारी दर से बहुत भिन्न होती है?

Do you have cash or traveler's checks?
āpke pās 'kaiś (nakdī) hai yā 'ṭraivlar caik'?
आपके पास कैश (नकदी) है या ट्रेवलर चैक?

I have travelers' checks.
mere pās 'ṭraivlar caik' haiṁ. मेरे पास ट्रेवलर चैक हैं।

Can I encash traveler's checks here?
kyā maiṁ yahāṁ 'ṭraivlar caik' bhunvā saktā hūṁ?
क्या मैं यहाँ ट्रेवलर चैक भुनवा सकता हूँ?

Please sign here.
yahāṁ dastkhat kījie. यहाँ दस्तख़त कीजिए।

Please give me some ten rupee notes.
kṛpayā mujhe kuch das rupae ke 'noṭ' dījiye.
कृपया मुझे कुछ दस रुपए के नोट दीजिए।

MISCELLANEOUS SERVICES

CAR REPAIR

My car developed some fault half way through the journey.
safar meṁ ādhe rāste par merī 'kār' kharāb ho gaī.
सफ़र में आधे रास्ते पर मेरी कार ख़राब हो गई।

My car suddenly stopped moving.
merī kār acānak calte-calte ruk gaī.
मेरी कार अचानक चलते–चलते रुक गई।

Battery seems to have gone low.
baiṭarī kamzor paṛ gaī lagtī hai.
बैटरी कमज़ोर पड़ गई लगती है।

Battery is not functioning.
baiṭarī kām nahīṁ kar rahī.
बैटरी काम नहीं कर रही।

The tube is punctured.
ṭyūb paṅkcar ho gaī hai. ट्यूब पंकचर हो गई है।

The tire burst.
ṭāyar phaṭ gayā hai. टायर फट गया है।

The handle of the back door has come out.
pichle darvāze kā haiṇḍal nikāl āyā hai.
पिछले दरवाजे का हैण्डल निकल आया है।

The trunk wouldn't open.
ḍikkī nahīṁ khul rahī. डिक्की नहीं खुल रही।

The car radio is not working.
kār kā reḍiyo kām nahīṁ kar rahā.
कार का रेडियो काम नहीं कर रहा।

Brake-pedal is stuck.
brek-paiḍal jām ho gayā hai.
ब्रेक–पैडल जाम हो गया है।

Steering moves with great difficulty.
'sṭīyariṅg' bahut muśkil se ghūmtā hai.
स्टीयरिंग बहुत मुश्किल से घूमता है।

Please check the entire car thoroughly.
kṛpayā sārī gāṛī acchī tarah dekh dījie.
कृपया सारी गाड़ी अच्छी तरह देख दीजिए।

Will you be able to repair it by evening?
āp śām tak marammat kar pāeṁge?
आप शाम तक मरम्मत कर पाएँगे?

Is everything in order now?
sab ṭhīk ho gayā?
सब ठीक हो गया?

Please fill 20 liters of petrol in.
kṛpayā bīs liṭar paiṭrol bhar dījie.
कृपया बीस लीटर पैट्रोल भर दीजिए।

How much does it come to?
kitne paise hue? कितने पैसे हुए?

☞ **In India, the american words 'gas' or 'gas station', though not unheard of, are unusual. Instead 'petrol' and 'petrol-pump' are used.**

WATCH REPAIR

My watch has stopped.
merī gharī ruk gaī hai. मेरी घड़ी रुक गई है।

My watch is running 10-15 minutes slow.
merī gharī das-pandrah minaṭ pīche cal rahī hai.
मेरी घड़ी दस–पन्द्रह मिनट पीछे चल रही है।

This watch is running very fast.
yah gharī bahut tez cal rahī hai.
यह घड़ी बहुत तेज़ चल रही है।

This watch often stops.
yah gharī aksar calte-calte ruk jātī hai.
यह घड़ी अक्सर चलते–चलते रुक जाती है।

I feel its battery needs replacement.
mujhe lagtā hai, is kī baiṭrī badalne kī zarūrat hai.
मुझे लगता है, इसकी बैटरी बदलने की जरूरत है।

Perhaps the battery is fully discharged.
śāyad baiṭrī khatm ho gaī hai.
शायद बैटरी ख़त्म हो गई है।

The long hand of this watch has come out.
is gharī kī barī suī nikal āī hai.
इस घड़ी की बड़ी सुई निकल आई है।

The glass of this watch has fallen off somewhere
is gharī kā śīśā kahīṁ gir gayā hai.
इस घड़ी का शीशा कहीं गिर गया है।

Across from here, on the other side of the road, there is a watch repairer's shop. You may talk with him.
sāmne, saṛak ke us pār, ek ghaṛīsāz kī dukān hai. āp us se bāt kar leṁ.
सामने सड़क के उस पार, एक घड़ीसाज़ की दुकान है। आप उससे बात कर लें।

How much will the repair of this watch cost?
is ghaṛī kī marammat karne meṁ kitnā paisā lagegā?
इस घड़ी की मरम्मत करने में कितना पैसा लगेगा?

It will cost you more to have this clock/watch repaired, and cheaper to buy a new one.
āpko yah ghaṛī ṭhīk karānā mahaṁgā paṛegā, aur naī ghaṛī kharīdnā sastā.
आपको यह घड़ी ठीक कराना महँगा पड़ेगा, और नई घड़ी खरीदना सस्ता।

In my opinion, it would better to buy a new one.
merī rāy meṁ, naī ghaṛī kharīdnā ṭhīk rahegā.
मेरी राय में, नई घड़ी खरीदना ठीक रहेगा।

SHOE REPAIR

My shoe broke.
merā jūtā ṭūṭ gayā hai. मेरा जूता टूट गया है।

Can it be repaired?
kyā yah ṭhīk ho sakegā? क्या यह ठीक हो सकेगा?

Any cobbler will repair it.
koī bhī mocī ise ṭhīk kar degā.

कोई भी मोची इसे ठीक कर देगा।

Where can I find a cobbler here?

mujhe yahāṁ mocī kahāṁ milegā? मुझे यहाँ मोची कहाँ मिलेगा?

There is a cobbler sitting every couple of meters by the roadside.

saṛak ke kināre, cappe-cappe par, mocī baiṭhā rahtā hai.

सड़क के किनारे, चप्पे–चप्पे पर, मोची बैठा रहता है।

The sole of your shoe has become bad.

āpke jūte kā talā kharāb ho gayā hai.

आपके जूते का तला ख़राब हो गया है।

As it is, even the heel seems weak.

vaise to eṛhī bhī kamzor lag rahī hai.

वैसे तो ऐड़ी भी कमज़ोर लग रही है।

How much will all this repair cost?

is sab ko ṭhīk karne kā kitnā paisā hogā?

इस सबको ठीक करने का कितना पैसा होगा?

And how much time?

aur kitnā samay lagegā? और कितना समय लगेगा?

It is all right. Please do it.

ṭhīk hai. banā dījie. ठीक है। बना दीजिए।

Please also polish the shoes.

kṛpayā jūte pālīś bhī kar dījie.

कृपया जूते पालिश भी कर दीजिए।

I will come and collect at 4 o'clock in the evening.
maiṁ śām ko cār baje ākar le lūṁgā.
मैं शाम को चार बजे आकर ले लूँगा।

WASHERMAN

All my clothes have become dirty.
mere sab kapṛe gande ho gae haiṁ.
मेरे सब कपड़े गन्दे हो गए हैं।

Is there a laundromat or a dry cleaner's shop nearby?
kyā yahāṁ pās meṁ koī lāuṇḍrī yā ḍrāi-klīnar kī dukān hai?
क्या यहाँ पास में कोई लाण्ड्री या ड्राइ–क्लीनर की दुकान है?

There is a washerman next door. He also drycleans.
bagal meṁ ek dhobī hai. vah ḍrāiklīn bhī kartā hai.
बगल में एक धोबी है। वह ड्राईक्लीन भी करता है।

Please clean my clothes.
kṛpayā mere kapṛe sāf kar deṁ.
कृपया मेरे कपड़े साफ़ कर दें।

I want to have my shirts and pants ironed.
maiṁ apnī kamīzeṁ aur paiṇṭeṁ prais karvānā cāhtā hūṁ.
मैं अपनी कमीजें और पैन्टें प्रेस करवाना चाहता हूँ।

How much will it cost?
kitne paise lageṁge? कितने पैसे लगेंगे?

Please clean these handkerchieves and socks too.
ye rūmāl aur jurābeṁ bhī sāf kar dījiegā.
ये रूमाल और जुराबें भी साफ़ कर दीजिएगा।

Please don't starch my clothes.
mere kapṛoṁ meṁ māṁḍī nā lagāeṁ.
मेरे कपड़ों में मांडी ना लगाएँ।

Iron the synthetics carefully and lightly.
sinthaiṭik kapṛoṁ ko dhyān se halkī prais kareṁ.
सिन्थेटिक कपड़ों को ध्यान से हल्की प्रेस करें।

There is this spot on the collar of my shirt. Please remove it.
merī kamīz ke 'kāular' par yah dāg lag gayā hai. Ise nikāl deṁ.
मेरी कमीज़ के कॉलर पर यह दाग लग गया है। इसे निकाल दें।

When will the washing be ready?
dhulāī kab tak taiyār ho jāegī?
धुलाई कब तक तैयार हो जाएगी?

When will you bring the clothes back?
āp kab tak kapṛe vāpas lāeṁge?
आप कब तक कपड़े वापस लाएँगे?

Please make them all ready by evening today.
āj śām tak sab taiyār kar deṁ.
आज शाम तक सब तैयार कर दें।

- by tomorrow morning
  kal subah tak कल सुबह तक

- as soon as possible
  jitnī jaldī ho sake जितनी जल्दी हो सके

I certainly must have them by evening tomorrow.
mujhe har hāl meṁ kal śām tak ye mil jāne cāhie.
मुझे हर हाल में कल शाम तक ये मिल जाने चाहिए।

One button of my shirt broke. Please change it.
merī kamīz kā ek baṭan ṭuṭ gayā hai. isko badal deṁ.
मेरी कमीज़ का एक बटन टूट गया है। इसको बदल दें।

There is a hole in my sweater. Please darn it.
mere swaiṭar meṁ ched ho gayā hai. ise rafū kar deṁ.
मेरे स्वेटर में छेद हो गया है। इसे रफू कर दें।

My skirt got torn. If possible, please fix a patch in here.
merā skarṭ phaṭ gayā hai. yadi ho sake to ismeṁ paiband lagā dījie.
मेरा स्कर्ट फट गया है। यदि हो सके तो इसमें पैबन्द लगा दीजिए।

Sir, I am a washerman.
jī, maiṁ dhobī hūṁ. जी, मैं धोबी हूँ।

I just wash and iron clothes.
maiṁ sirf kapṛe dhotā aur prais kartā hūṁ.
मैं सिर्फ़ कपड़े धोता और प्रेस करता हूँ।

Fixing buttons and darning is the task of a tailor.
baṭan lagānā aur rafū karnā darzī kā kām hai.
बटन लगाना और रफू करना दर्ज़ी का काम है।

Forgive me, please. I did not know this.

mujhe kṣamā kījie. maiṁ yah nahīṁ jāntā thā.
मुझे क्षमा कीजिए। मैं यह नहीं जानता था।

ASTROLOGY

I am looking for an astrologer
maiṁ kisī jyotiṣī kī talāś meṁ hūṁ.
मैं किसी ज्योतिषी की तलाश में हूँ।

Do you know some good astrologer?
āp kisī acche jyotiṣī ko jānte haiṁ?
आप किसी अच्छे ज्योतिषी को जानते हैं?

Please tell me the name and address of some good astrologer.
mujhe kisī acche jyotiṣī kā nām aur patā batāie.
मुझे किसी अच्छे ज्योतिषी का नाम और पता बताए।

I want to get my horoscope made.
maiṁ apnī janam kuṇḍlī banvānā cāhta hūṁ.
मैं अपनी जनमकुण्डली बनवाना चाहता हूँ।

How much will it cost to get a horoscope made?
janamkuṇḍlī banvāne meṁ kitne paise lageṁge?
जनमकुण्डली बनवाने में कितने पैसे लगेंगे?

And how much time will it take?
aur kitnā samay lagegā?
और कितना समय लगेगा?

What all information is required for getting a horoscope made?
janampatrī banvāne ke lie kyā-kyā sūcnā zarūrī hai?

जनमपत्री बनवाने के लिए क्या–क्या सूचना ज़रूरी है?

Well, the required information for getting a horoscope made is:
janampatrī banvāne ke lie zarūrī sūcnā hai:
जनमपत्री बनवाने के लिए जरूरी सूचना है :

time of birth	**janma kā samay**	जन्म का समय
date of birth	**janma kī tārīkh**	जन्म की तारीख़
place of birth	**janma kā sthān**	जन्म का स्थान

I don't believe in astrology.
maiṁ jyotiṣ ko nahīṁ māntā.
मैं ज्योतिष को नहीं मानता।

I have much faith in astrology.
maiṁ jyotiṣ meṁ bahut viśvās rakhtā hūṁ.
मैं ज्योतिष में बहुत विश्वास रखता हूँ।

COMMUNICATIONS

TELEGRAM

I would like to send a telegram to Mumbai.
maiṁ mumbaī tār bhejnā cāhtā hūṁ.
मैं मुम्बई तार भेजना चाहता हूँ।

How much will thirty words cost?
tīs śabdoṁ ke kitne paise hoṁge?
तीस शब्दों के कितने पैसे होंगे?

Do you wish to send it during the day time or at night ?
āp din ke samay bhejnā cāhte haiṁ yā rāt ko?
आप दिन के समय भेजना चाहते हैं, या रात को?

Are day rates different from night rates?
kyā din kī dareṁ rāt se alag hotī haiṁ?
क्या दिन की दरें रात से अलग होती हैं?

Send it immediately, please.
kṛpayā turant bhej dījie.
कृपया तुरन्त भेज दीजिए।

INTERNET CAFE

Is there an Internet Café nearby?
kyā pās meṁ koī 'iṇṭarnaiṭ kaifé' hai?
क्या पास में कोई इण्टरनेट कैफ़े है?

I do all my work by e-mail.
maiṁ apnā sab kām 'ī-mel' se kartā hūṁ.
मैं अपना सब काम ई–मेल से करता हूँ।

I need to read as well as write e-mail every day.
mere lie roz 'ī -mel' paṛhnā aur likhnā zarūrī hotā hai.
मेरे लिए रोज़ ई–मेल देखना और लिखना ज़रूरी होता है।

TELEPHONE

It is my father's 60th birthday today.
āj mere pitā jī ka sāṭhvāṁ janamdin hai.
आज मेरे पिता जी का साठवाँ जनमदिन है।

I would like to call him in New York tonight.
āj maiṁ New York meṁ unko 'ṭailīfon' karnā cāhūṁgā.
आज मैं न्यूयॉर्क में उनको टेलिफोन करना चाहूँगा।

How much does it cost to phone New York from here?

yahāṁ se nyū yaurk 'ṭailīfon' karne ke kitne paise lagte haiṁ?
यहाँ से न्यूयॉर्क टेलिफ़ोन करने के कितने पैसे लगते हैं?

I would like to call when it is 7 a.m. in New York.
maiṁ aise vakt 'fon' karnā cāhtā hūṁ jab nyū yaurk meṁ subah ke sāt baje hoṁ.
मैं ऐसे वक्त फ़ोन करना चाहता हूँ जब न्यूयॉर्क में सुबह के सात बजे हों।

The time difference between New York and New Delhi is ten hours.
naī dillī aur nyū yāurk ke sthānīyă samay meṁ das ghaṇṭoṁ kā antar hai.
नई दिल्ली और न्यूयॉर्क के स्थानीय समय में दस घण्टों का अन्तर है।

If you phone at 5 p.m. from New Delhi, it should be 7 a.m. in New York.
yadi āp naī dillī meṁ śām ke pāṁc baje fon kareṁ, to nyū yāurk meṁ subah ke sāt baje hoṁge.
यदि आप नई दिल्ली में शाम के पाँच बजे फोन करें, तो न्यूयॉर्क में सुबह के सात बजे होंगे।

Oh, I am sorry. Operator, I seem to have dialled the wrong number.
mujhe khed hai. 'āupreṭar', maiṁne galat namber milā diyā lagtā hai.
मुझे खेद है। ऑपरेटर, मैंने गलत नम्बर मिला दिया लगता है।

I am sorry. All the lines on this route are busy at the moment.
mujhe khed hai, is vakt is 'rūṭ' kī sabhī lāineṁ vyast haiṁ.
मुझे खेद है, इस वक्त इस रुट की सभी लाइनें व्यस्त हैं।

Happy birthday, dad, this is Robert here.
janamdin mubārak, pitā jī, maiṁ 'raubarṭ' bol rahā hūṁ.
जनमदिन मुबारक पिता जी, मैं रॉबर्ट बोल रहा हूँ।

Please do not interrupt me
kṛpayā mujhe bīc meṁ nā ṭokiegā.
कृपया मुझे बीच में ना टोकिएगा।

Just let me know when ten minutes are over.
jab das 'minaṭ' ho jāeṁ to mujhe batā dījiegā.
जब दस मिनट हो जाएँ तो मुझे बता दीजिएगा।

I have another appointment.
mujhe kisī aur se milnā hai.
मुझे किसी और से मिलना है।

May I speak with Mr. Kant Pathak please?
maiṁ śrī kānt pāṭhak se milnā cāhtā hūṁ.
मैं श्री कान्त पाठक से बात करना चाहता हूँ।

He is out at the moment.
ve abhī bāhar gae haiṁ.
वे अभी बाहर गए हैं।

He is not at his desk at the moment.
ve is vakt apnī mez par nahīṁ haiṁ.

वे इस वक्त अपनी मेज़ पर नहीं हैं।

When is he expected back?
ve kab tak lauṭeṁge? वे कब तक लौटेंगे?

Tell him Ram called.
unheṁ batā deṁ ki Rām kā fon āyā thā.
उन्हें बता दें कि राम का फ़ोन आया था।

POSTAL SERVICES

What time is the mail delivered here?
yahāṁ ḍāk kitne baje ātī hai?
यहाँ डाक कितने बजे आती है?

And how many times during the day?
aur din meṁ kitnī bār? और दिन में कितनी बार?

How far is the nearest post office?
ḍāk ghar kitnī dūr hai? डाक घर कितनी दूर है?

What time does the post office open?
ḍāk ghar kitne baje khultā hai?
डाक घर कितने बजे खुलता है?

And until when is it open?
aur kab tak khulā rahtā hai?
और कब तक खुला रहता है?

I need to buy some envelopes and postage stamps.
maiṁ kuch lifāfe aur ḍāk-ṭikaṭ <u>kh</u>arīḍnā cāhtā hūṁ.
मैं कुछ लिफ़ाफ़े और डाक–टिकट ख़रीदना चाहता हूँ।

Which window do I go to for sending this packet?
yah paikeṭ bhejne ke lie mujhe kis khiṛkī par jānā hogā?
यह पैकेट भेजने के लिए मुझे किस खिड़की पर जाना होगा?

How long will this packet take to reach London?
yah paikit lonḍon kab tak pahūṁcegā?
यह पैकेट लन्दन कब तक पहुँचेगा?

I want to send it express mail.
maiṁ ise 'aiksprais' ḍāk se bhejnā cāhtā hūṁ.
मैं इसे एक्सप्रेस डाक से भेजना चाहता हूँ।

Also I want to register this letter.
maiṁ is patra kā pañjīkaraṇ karvānā cāhtā hūṁ.
मैं इस पत्र का पंजीकरण करवाना चाहता हूँ।

Is a registered letter also automatically insured?
kyā pañjīkṛt patra svataḥ bīmākṛt bhī hotā hai?
क्या पंजीकृत पत्र स्वतः बीमाकृत भी होता है?

No, every registered letter is not automatically insured.
ji nahīṁ, har pañjīkṛt patra svataḥ bīmākṛt nahīṁ hotā.
जी नहीं, हर पंजीकृत पत्र स्वतः बीमाकृत नहीं होता।

But every insured letter is automatically registered.
lekin har bīmākṛt patra svataḥ pañjīkṛt hotā hai.
लेकिन हर बीमाकृत पत्र स्वतः पंजीकृत होता है।

An insured letter or parcel must be sealed properly.
bīmākṛt patra, yā 'pārsal' ṭhīk se band kiyā jānā cāhie.
बीमाकृत पत्र, या पार्सल ठीक से बन्द किया जाना चाहिए।

Registration and insurance of the letter or parcel will be at this window.
patra yā 'pārsal' kā pañjīkaraṇ aur bīmā isī khiṛkī par hogā.
पत्र या पार्सल का पंजीकरण और बीमा इसी खिड़की पर होगा।

Please get a form for the parcel at window number 5.
kṛpayā pārsal' ke lie khiṛkī number pāñc se 'faurm' le lījie.
कृपया पार्सल के लिए खिड़की नम्बर पाँच से फॉर्म ले लीजिए।

The form is quite self-explanatory.
is 'faurm' meṁ sab spaṣṭ likhā hotā hai.
इस फॉर्म में सब स्पष्ट लिखा होता है।

Please write the postal addresses of both the sender and the receiver.
āp bhejnewāle aur pānewāle, donoṁ ka ḍāk-patā likhie.
आप भेजनेवाले और पानेवाले, दोनों का डाक–पता लिखिए।

You declare the value of the contents of the parcel.
āp 'pārsal' meṁ vastuoṁ ke mūlyă kā vivraṇ dījie.
आप पार्सल में वस्तुओं के मूल्य का विवरण दीजिए।

How much postage is required for this?
is meṁ ḍāk kharc kyā lagegā?
इसमें डाक खर्च क्या लगेगा?

At window five they will tell you every thing, sir!
khiṛkī number pāṁc par āpko sab sūcnā deṁge.

खिड़की नम्बर पाँच पर आपको सब सूचना देंगे।

I am going out of town for one month.
maiṁ ek mahīne ke lie śahar se bāhar jā rahā hūṁ.
मैं एक महीने के लिए शहर से बाहर जा रहा हूँ।

Please hold my mail till I return.
kṛpayā merī ḍāk mere vāpas āne tak yahīṁ rakheṁ.
कृपया मेरी डाक मेरे वापस आने तक यहीं रखें।

Please keep redirecting all my mail at my new address.
kṛpayā merī ḍāk mere nae pate par bhejte raheṁ.
कृपया मेरी डाक मेरे नए पते पर भेजते रहें।

Please give me 10 aerograms and twenty postcards.
kṛpayā mujhe das hawāī patra aur bīs 'posṭkārḍ' de dījie.
कृपया मुझे दस हवाई पत्र और बीस पोस्टकार्ड दे दीजिए।

PERSONAL GROOMING

HAIRCUT

I want to get my hair cut.
maiṁ apne bāl kaṭvānā cāhtā hūṁ.
मैं अपने बाल कटवाना चाहता हूँ।

Where is a haircutting saloon?
nāī kī dukān kahāṁ par hai?
नाई की दुकान कहाँ पर है?

Please give me a hair cut.
mere bāl kāṭ dījie. मेरे बाल काट दीजिए।

Please don't cut too short.

bahut zyādā nā kāṭeṁ. बहुत ज़्यादा न काटें।

Trim a little bit more on the temples please.
kanpaṭiyoṁ par se thoṛe aur kāṭeṁ.
कनपटियों पर से थोड़े और काटें।

I am somewhat in a hurry.
maiṁ kuch jaldī meṁ hūṁ. मैं कुछ जल्दी में हूँ।

How long does it take to get the beard shaved?
dāṛhī banāne meṁ kitnā samay lagegā.
दाढ़ी बनाने में कितना समय लगेगा।

Sir, about ten minutes.
jī, lagbhag das minaṭ. जी, लगभग दस मिनट।

In that case, I still have time. Please give me a shave too.
tab to abhī mere pās samay hai. kṛpayā merī dāṛhī bhī banā deṁ.
तब तो अभी मेरे पास समय है। कृपया मेरी दाढ़ी भी बना दें।

Would you like it clean shaven, sir?
āp bilkul sāf kaṭvānā cāhte haiṁ?
आप बिल्कुल साफ़ कटवाना चाहते हैं?

No, no. Just trim it short with scissors please.
nahīṁ, nahīṁ, sirf kaiṁcī se choṭā kar deṁ.
नहीं, नहीं, सिर्फ़ कैंची से छोटा कर दें।

Please lightly trim my moustache and sideburns too.
mūcheṁ aur galmucche bhī thoṛe-thoṛe kāṭ deṁ.
मूछें और गलमुच्छे भी थोड़े–थोड़े काट दें।

How much do I owe you?

kitne paise hue? कितने पैसे हुए?

You did a really god job. Thank you.

āpkā kām bahut baṛhiyā thā. dhanyăvād.

आपका काम बहुत बढ़िया था। धन्यवाद।

Here you are! Keep the balance please.

yah lījie. bākī paise āp rakh lījie.

यह लीजिए। बाकी पैसे आप रख लीजिए।

- These days in India there are many haircutting saloons. Also there are individual barbers giving personalized service to their clientele.

BODY MASSAGE

I want to get body massage done.

maiṁ badan par māliś karvānā cāhtā hūṁ.

मैं बदन पर मालिश करवाना चाहता हूँ।

It is very expensive to get massage done in our country.

hamāre deś meṁ māliś karvānā bahut mahaṁgā hotā hai.

हमारे देश में मालिश करवाना बहुत महँगा होता है।

MANICURE AND PEDICURE

My finger and toe nails have groin.

mere hāṭhoṁ aur pairoṁ ke nākhūn baṛh gae haiṁ.

मेरे हाथों और पैरों के नाखून बढ़ गए हैं।

My heels have cracked.

merī eṛīyāṁ phat gaī haiṁ. मेरी एड़ियाँ फट गई हैं।

My hands here became rough.
mere hāth khurdure ho gae haiṁ.
मेरे हाथ खुरदुरे हो गए हैं।

How much do you charge for manicure and pedicure?
āp hast aur pād nakh prasādhan kā kyā lete haiṁ?
आप हस्त और पाद नख प्रसाधन का क्या लेते हैं?

EMERGENCY SERVICES

POLICE STATION

police station	**thānā**	थाना
officer incharge of a police station	**thānedār**	थानेदार
constable	**sipāhī**	सिपाही
crime	**aprādh**	अपराध
criminal	**aprādhī**	अपराधी
ciminal law	**daṇḍvidhān**	दण्डविधान

I want to register a complaint.
maiṁ śikāyat darz karānā cāhtā hūṁ.
मैं शिकायत दर्ज़ कराना चाहता हूँ।

At the corner over there somebody pickpocketed me.
vahāṁ nukkaṛ par kisī ne merī jeb kāṭ lī hai.
वहाँ नुक्कड़ पर किसी ने मेरी जेब काट ली है।

And also snatched away my bicycle.
aur merā 'sāikil' bhī chīn liyā hai.
और मेरा साइकिल भी छीन लिया है।

You are charged with eve teasing.
āp par laṛkiyoṁ se cheṛ-chaṛ karne kā ārop hai.
आप पर लड़कियों से छेड़–छाड़ करने का आरोप है।

You are charged with entering the country without a visa.
āp par binā 'vīsā' deś meṁ ghusne kā ārop hai.
आप पर बिना वीसा देश में घुसने का आरोप है।

You have been charged with manufacturing and selling fake medicines.
āp par naklī dwāiyāṁ banākar becne kā ārop hai.
आप पर नकली दवाइयाँ बनाकर बेचने का आरोप है।

You will be kept in police custody for three days.
āpko tīn din ke lie hirāsat meṁ rakhā jāegā.
आपको तीन दिन के लिए हिरासत में रखा जाएगा।

You wil have to pay Rs. five hundred fine
āpko pāṁc sau rupae jurmānā bharnā hogā.
आपको पाँच सौ रुपए जुर्माना भरना होगा।

FIRE

My house has caught fire.
mere ghar meṁ āg lag gaī hai.
मेरे घर में आग लग गई है।

Somebody please immediately inform the fire station
koī jaldī se agniśaman kendra ko sūcnā karo.
कोई जल्दी से अग्निशमन केन्द्र को सूचना करो।

Does someone know the phone number of fire station?
kisīko agniśaman kendra kā fon namber patā hai?

किसीको अग्निशमन केन्द्र का फ़ोन नम्बर पता है?

Fire engine is coming.
damkal gāṛī ā rahī hai. दमकल गाड़ी आ रही है।

AMBULANCE

My father fell in the bathroom. I need an ambulance.
mere pitā ji gusalkhāne meṁ gir gae haiṁ. mujhe rogī vāhan cāhie.
मेरे पिता जी गुसलखाने में गिर गए हैं। मुझे रोगी वाहन चाहिए।

What is the ambulance phone number?
rogī vāhan kā dūrbhāṣ nambar kyā hai.
रोगी वाहन का दूरभाष नम्बर क्या है?

The ambulance phone number is 102 but please don't waste time.
rogī vāhan dūrbhāṣ nambar ek sau do, hai lekin āp samay barbād na kareṁ.
रोगी वाहन दूरभाष नम्बर एक सौ दो है, लेकिन आप समय बरबाद न करें।

Here ambulance is not easily available.
yahāṁ rogī vāhan āsānī se nahīṁ miltā.
यहाँ रोगी वाहन आसानी से नहीं मिलता।

Quickly call a taxi and take the patient to hospital.
jaldī se taiksī bulāie aur marīz ko aspatāl le jāie.
जल्दी से टैक्सी बुलाइए और मरीज़ को अस्पताल ले जाइए।

TRANSPORTATION

TRAVEL PREFERENCES

I like to travel by train.
maiṁ rel gāṛī se safar karnā pasand kartā hūṁ.
मैं रेल गाड़ी से सफ़र करना पसन्द करता हूँ।

I don't like to travel by air.
mujhe hawāī jahāz se safar karnā pasand nahīṁ.
मुझे हवाई जहाज़ से सफ़र करना पसन्द नहीं।

You can also go there by bus.
vahāṁ āp 'bas' se bhī jā sakte haiṁ.
वहाँ आप बस से भी जा सकते हैं।

by air	**hawāī jahāz se**	हवाई जहाज़ से
by bus	**bas se**	बस से
by train	**gāṛī se**	गाड़ी से
by bicycle	**sāikil se**	साइकिल से
on foot	**paidal**	पैदल

AT THE RAILWAY ENQUIRY

Could you give me some information about trains from Delhi to Kanyakumari.
mujhe dillī se kanyākumārī kī gāṛiyoṁ ke bāre meṁ jānkārī dījie.
मुझे दिल्ली से कन्याकुमारी की गाड़ियों के बारे में जानकारी दीजिए।

There is one direct train from Delhi to Kanyakumari.
dillī se kanyākumārī ke lie ek sīdhī gāṛī hai.
दिल्ली से कन्याकुमारी के लिए एक सीधी गाड़ी है।

How much is one-way fare?
ek taraf kā kirāyā kitnā hai?
एक तरफ़ का किराया कितना है?

One way fare by A.C. 2-tier is Rs. 2400.
e.sī. ṭū ṭiyar se ek taraf kā kirāyā do hazār cār sau rupae hai.
ए.सी. टू टियर से एक तरफ़ का किराया दो हज़ार चार सौ रुपए है।

Where can I buy the ticket?
ṭikaṭ kahāṁ milegā? टिकट कहाँ मिलेगा?

How long is the travel time?
yātrā meṁ kitnā samay lagtā hai?
यात्रा में कितना समय लगता है?

I am sorry to tell you, sir, trains in India usually run behind schedule.
mujhe āpko batāne meṁ khed hai ki bhārat meṁ gāṛiyāṁ aksar der se caltī haiṁ.
मुझे आपको बताने में खेद है कि भारत में गाड़ियाँ अक्सर देर से चलती हैं।

Normally, it takes fifty-four hours from Delhi to Kanyakumari
sāmānyatā, dillī se kanyākumārī tak cauvan ghaṇṭe lagne cāhie.

सामान्यता, दिल्ली से कन्याकुमारी तक चौवन घण्टे लगने चाहिए।

Thanks for the information.
sūcnā ke lie dhanyăvād. सूचना के लिए धन्यवाद।

By the way, today the train is running four hours late.
vaise, āj gāṛī cār ghaṇṭe der se cal rahī hai.
वैसे, आज गाड़ी चार घण्टे देर से चल रही है।

KANYAKUMARI

Kanyakumari, located at the southernmost tip of India at the confluence of Arabian Sea and Indian Ocean, is famous for its spectacular sunrise and sunset.

RESERVATIONS

Please give me a ticket from Delhi to Kolkata.
mujhe dillī se kolkātā tak kā ek ṭikaṭ dījie.
मुझे दिल्ली से कोलकाता तक का एक टिकट दीजिए।

By which class would you like to travel?
āp kaun-sī śreṇī se safar karnā pasand kareṁge?
आप कौन–सी श्रेणी से सफ़र करना पसन्द करेंगे?

What classes do you have?
kaun-kaun sī śreṇī hai? कौन–कौन सी श्रेणी है?

A.C. first class is the highest class.
e-sī farsṭ klās sab se ūṁcī śreṇī hai.
ए.सी. फर्स्ट क्लास सबसे ऊँची श्रेणी है।

This is very comfortable, but also the most expensive.
yah bahut ārāmdeh hai, lekin sab se mahṁgī bhī hai.
यह बहुत आरामदेह है, लेकिन सबसे महँगी भी है।

Its fare is almost the same as air fare.
iskā kirāyā lagbhag hawāī yātrā ke barābar hotā hai.
इसका किराया लगभग हवाई यात्रा के बराबर होता है।

Bedding and meals are included in the fare.
bistar aur khānā kirāye meṁ juṛā rahtā hai.
बिस्तर और खाना किराये में जुड़ा रहता है।

A.C. two tier and A.C. three tier. Both of these are air conditioned sleeper coaches. You get a bedding in these coaches.
e.sī. ṭū ṭiyar aur e.sī. thrī ṭiyar: ye donoṁ vātānukūlit śayanyān śreṇiyāṁ haiṁ. in meṁ bistar miltā hai.
ए.सी. टू टियर और ए.सी. थ्री टियर : ये दोनों वातानुकूलित शयनयान श्रेणियाँ हैं। इनमें बिस्तर मिलता है।

A.C. two tier has some more space. It costs twice as much.
e.sī. ṭū ṭiyar meṁ kuch zyādā jagah hotī hai. paisā lagbhag dugunā lagtā hai.
ए.सी. टू टियर में कुछ ज़्यादा जगह होती है। पैसा लगभग दुगना लगता है।

Sleeper class: In this class, berth is reserved but the coach is not airconditioned.
slīpar klās: is śreṇī meṁ sthān to ārakṣit hotā hai, parantu yah yān vātānukūlit nahīṁ hotā.
स्लीपर क्लास : इस श्रेणी में स्थान तो आरक्षित होता है,

परन्तु यह यान वातानुकूलित नहीं होता।

Of course it costs much less. But you don't get any bedding.
beśak is meṁ paisā kāfī kam lagtā hai. lekin bistar nahīṁ miltā.
बेशक इसमें पैसा काफ़ी कम लगता है। लेकिन बिस्तर नहीं मिलता।

Ordinary class: One can sit in here without reservation.
sāmānyă śreṇī: is meṁ binā ārakṣaṇ ke baiṭh sakte haiṁ.
सामान्य श्रेणी : इसमें बिना आरक्षण के बैठ सकते हैं।

But it is not easy to find a seat in it. It is very crowded.
lekin is meṁ jagah milnā āsān nahīṁ hotā. bahut bhīṛ hotī hai.
लेकिन इसमें जगह मिलना आसान नहीं होता। बहुत भीड़ होती है।

Often there are thefts on trains here.
yahām gāṛiyoṁ meṁ aksar corī ho jātī hai.
यहाँ गाड़ियों में अक्सर चोरी हो जाती है।

You are a foreigner. You should take special care of your belongings.
āp videśī haiṁ. āp apne sāmān kā viśeṣ dhyān rakhiegā.
आप विदेशी हैं। आप अपने सामान का विशेष ध्यान रखिएगा।

Here is your ticket and this is your balance.
yah rahā āpkā ṭikaṭ aur ye haiṁ āpke bākī paise.
यह रहा आपका टिकट और ये हैं आपके बाकी पैसे।

One more thing. You don't get toilet paper on trains.
ek aur bāt. hamāre yahāṁ gāṛī meṁ 'ṭauleṭ pepar' nahīṁ miltā.
एक और बात। हमारे यहाँ गाड़ी में टॉएलेट पेपर नहीं मिलता।

Please carry your own toilet paper with you.
āp apnā 'ṭauleṭ pepar' sāth rakhiegā.
आप अपना टॉएलेट पेपर साथ रखिएगा।

Good wishes to you during your journey through my country.
mere deś meṁ āpkī yātrā ke lie śubh kāmnāeṁ.
मेरे देश में आपकी यात्रा के लिए शुभ कामनाएँ।

ON THE PLATFORM

Coolie, take my luggage on this train in AC two-tier!
kulī, merā sāmān is gāṛī meṁ ' e-sī-ṭū-ṭiyar' meṁ le calo.
कुली, मेरा सामान इस गाड़ी में ए.सी. टू. टियर में ले चलो।

How much will you charge for it?
kitnā paisā loge?
कितना पैसा लोगे?

Sir, give me whatever you consider appropriate.
sāhib, jo ṭhīk samjheṁ, de dījiegā.
साहिब, जो ठीक समझें, दे दीजिएगा।

No, no, tell me beforehand. There shouldn't be any dispute later.

nahīṁ, nahīṁ, pahale hī batā do. bād meṁ jhagṛā nahīṁ honā cāhie.
नहीं, नहीं, पहले ही बता दो। बाद में झगड़ा नहीं होना चाहिए।

Give me 25 rupees.
paccīs rupae de dījiegā. पच्चीस रुपए दे दीजिएगा।

This is too much.
yah to bahut zyādā hai. यह तो बहुत ज़्यादा है।

No sir, I wil have to carry very far. Your compartment is at the rear end of the train.
nahīṁ sāhib, mukhko bahut dūr ḍhonā paṛegā. āpkā ḍabbā bahut pīche lagtā hai.
नहीं साहिब, मुझको बहुत दूर ढोना पड़ेगा। आपका डब्बा बहुत पीछे लगता है।

ON THE TRAIN

What station is this?
yah kaun-sā 'sṭeśan' hai? यह कौन–सा स्टेशन है?

How long will the train stop here?
yahāṁ gāṛī kitnī der ruktī hai?
यहाँ गाड़ी कितनी देर रुकती है?

Is this seat vacant?
kyā yah sthān khālī hai? क्या यह स्थान खाली है?

May I sit here, please?
kyā maiṁ yahāṁ baiṭh saktā hūṁ?

क्या मैं यहाँ बैठ सकता हूँ?

I have to get off at the next station.
mujhe agle sṭeśan par utarnā hai.
मुझे अगले स्टेशन पर उतरना है।

We have both vegetarian and non-vegetarian food.
hamāre pās śākāhārī or māṁsāhārī donoṁ bhojan haiṁ.
हमारे पास शाकाहारी और मांसाहारी, दोनों भोजन है।

Vegetarian thālī is for rupees twenty-five, and the non-vegetarian thālī is for rupees 45.
śākāhārī thālī paccīs rupae kī, aur māṁsāhārī thālī paiṁtālīs rupae kī.
शाकाहारी थाली पच्चीस रुपए की, और मांसाहारी थाली पैंतालीस रुपए की।

Please bring me one vegetarian meal. Also bring mineral water.
mere lie ek śākāhārī thālī lāie. minral wāuṭar bhī lāie.
मेरे लिए एक शाकाहारी थाली और मिनरल वॉटर लाइए।

Conductor, please bring me a bedding.
kondakar, kṛpayā mere lie bistar le āie.
कंडक्टर, कृपया मेरे लिए बिस्तर ले आइए।

I would like to go down to buy a magazine. Could you please look after my things.
maiṁ zarā nīce utarkar maigzīn kharīdnā cāhtā hūṁ. kṛpayā mere sāmān kā dhyān rakheṁ.
मैं ज़रा नीचे उतरकर मैगज़ीन ख़रीदना चाहता हूँ। कृपया मेरे सामान का ध्यान रखें।

USEFUL TIPS

Check At The Enquiry For Reliable Information

Don't depend totally on the railway or the airlines time tables. The train and flight timings usually change after the time table has been printed. New trains and flights are often introduced that are not included in the time table. Some trains and flights are cancelled or their schedules changed every now and then, so the time table can be misleading, Always check at the rail or airlines ènquiry for the latest and reliable information.

A special quota is reserved for foreign tourists and sometimes for women on many trains.

BUS TRAVEL

I must catch the 5 o'clock bus tomorrow morning.
mujhe kal subah pāṁc bajewālī 'bas' pakaṛnī hai.
मुझे कल सुबह पाँच बजेवाली बस पकड़नी है।

Where exactly is the bus stop.
'bas' aḍḍā ṭhīk kahāṁ par hai.
बस अड्डा ठीक कहाँ पर है?

How far is the bus stop from here?
'bas' aḍḍā yahāṁ se kitnī dūr hai?

बस अड्डा यहाँ से कितनी दूर है?

The bus stops in front of the main gate of the hotel.
bas hoṭal ke mukhyă dwār ke ṭhīk sāmne ruktī hai.
बस होटल के मुख्य द्वार के ठीक सामने रुकती है।

Can I buy the ticket at the bus stop ?
kyā maiṁ 'bas' aḍḍe par ṭikaṭ kharīd sakūṁgā?
क्या मैं बस अड्डे पर टिकट ख़रीद सकूँगा?

Yes, of course!
ji, beśak! जी, बेशक!

A single one-way ticket to Bodh Gaya please.
bodh gayā ke lie ek iktarfā ṭikaṭ dījie.
बोध गया के लिए एक इकतरफ़ा टिकट दीजिए।

How long will the journey take?
safar meṁ kitnā samay lagegā?
सफ़र में कितना समय लगेगा?

How often do the buses run?
baseṁ kitne-kitne samay par caltī haiṁ?
बसें कितने–कितने समय पर चलती हैं?

Please tell me when Bodh Gaya comes.
jab bodh gayā ā jāe, to mujhe batā deṁ.
जब बोध गया आ जाए, तो मुझे बता दें।

RICKSHAW RIDE

The most common mode of transportation in small towns is a cycle rickshaw. It is very convenient in

narrow crowded lanes, relatively inexpensive and ideal for short distances.

Rickshaw driver, will you take me to ..?
rikshāwāle, ... caloge/caliegā?
रिक्शावाले, ... चलोगे/चलिएगा?

How much money will you charge?
kitnā paisā loge / lījiegā? कितना पैसा लोगे/लीजिएगा?

Please drive slowly.
dhīre calāo / calāie. धीरे चलाओ/चलाइए।

Turn to the right / left.
dāeṁ / bāeṁ muṛie. दाएँ/बाएँ मुड़िए।

Enough. Stop at the corner over there.
bas. vahāṁ nukkaṛ par rukie.
बस। वहाँ नुक्कड़ पर रुकिए।

Please wait for me right here.
yahīṁ merī pratīkṣā kījie. यहीं मेरी प्रतीक्षा कीजिए।

It might take me half an hour.
mujhe ādhā ghaṇṭā lag saktā hai.
मुझे आधा घण्टा लग सकता है।

Please don't worry. I will pay you extra money.
āp cintā nā kareṁ. maiṁ āpko intzār karne kā atirikt paisā dūṁgā.
आप चिन्ता ना करें। मैं आपको इन्तजार करने का अतिरिक्त पैसा दूँगा।

AT THE AIRLINES

I want to fly from Denver to Delhi.
maiṁ ḍainvar se dillī jānā cāhtā hūṁ.
मैं डेनवर से दिल्ली जाना चाहता हूँ।

Is there a direct flight or do I need to change flights?
koī sīdhī uṛān hai, yā mujhe jahāz badalnā hogā?
कोई सीधी उड़ान है, या मुझे जहाज़ बदलना होगा?

Your preferences, sir?
āpkī khās pasand ? आपकी ख़ास पसन्द?

Shortest route and cheapest fare.
choṭe-se-choṭā rāstā, aur saste-se-sastā ṭikaṭ.
छोटे–से–छोटा रास्ता, और सस्ते–से–सस्ता टिकट।

How much is a four month round trip ticket?
cār mahīne kā āne-jāne kā ṭikaṭ kitne kā hai?
चार महीने का आने–जाने का टिकट कितने का है?

How much is one way ticket?
aur ek tarfā ṭikaṭ kitne kā hai?
और एक तरफ़ा टिकट कितने का है?

By economy class or business class?
ikaunomī klās se yā biznes klās se?
इकॉनमी क्लास से या बिज़नेस क्लास से?

Please give me fares of both.
kṛpayā donoṁ kā kirāyā batāie.
कृपया दोनों का किराया बताइए।

I want one-day stopover in Frankfurt.
maiṁ ek din fraiṅkfarṭ meṁ ruknā cāhtā hūṁ.
मैं एक दिन फ्रैंकफ़र्ट में रुकना चाहता हूँ।

Can I get hotel at the expense of the airline?
kyā mujhe eyarlāins ke kharce par hoṭal mil saktā hai?
क्या मुझे एयरलाइन्स के ख़र्चे पर होटल मिल सकता है?

I want a window seat seat.
mujhe khiṛkī ke pāswālā sthān cāhie.
मुझे खिड़की के पासवाला स्थान चाहिए।

I need an aisle seat.
mujhe galiyārewālā sthān cāhie.
मुझे गलियारेवाला स्थान चाहिए।

I want vegetarian meals, no eggs, no fish either.
mujhe śākāhārī bhojan cāhie, aṇḍe nahīṁ, machlī bhī nahīṁ.
मुझे शाकाहारी भोजन चाहिए, अण्डे नहीं, मछली भी नहीं।

Can I keep this bag with me on the plane?
kyā maiṁ yah 'baig' jahāz meṁ sāth rakh saktā hūṁ?
क्या मैं यह बैग जहाज़ में साथ रख सकता हूँ?

What are the exact departure and arrival times of this flight?
is uṛān ke chūṭne aur pahuṁcne ke ṭhīk samay kyā haiṁ?
इस उड़ान के छूटने और पहुँचने के ठीक समय क्या हैं?

What is the time difference between Denver and Delhi.
ḍainvar aur dillī ke sthānīyă samay meṁ kitnā farak hai?
डेनवर और दिल्ली के स्थानीय समय में कितना फ़रक है?

What time will the flight take off?
jahāz kitne baje chūṭegā? जहाज कितने बजे छूटेगा?

And what time will it land in Delhi?
aur yah dillī kitne baje utăregā?
और यह दिल्ली कितने बजे उतरेगा?

Please give me some earplugs.
kṛpayā mujhe kān band karne ke lie ruī dījie.
कृपया मुझे कान बन्द करने के लिए रुई दीजिए।

I suffer from air sickness.
hawāī jahāz meṁ merā jī miclāne lagtā hai.
हवाई जहाज में मेरा जी मिचलाने लगता है।

Related Vocabulary:

to land	hawāī jahāz kā zamīn par utarnā हवाई जहाज का ज़मीन पर उतरना	
to take off	uṛān bharnā	उड़ान भरना
flight	uṛān (f.)	उड़ान
security	surakṣā (f.)	सुरक्षा
arrival	āgman	आगमन
departure	ravāngī (f.)	रवानगी,
	chūṭnā	छूटना

USEFUL TIPS

Allow Sufficient Time

For domestic flights passengers are required to be at the airport 90 minutes before departure and for international flights three hours before departure.

For security reasons, avoid carrying cameras, alarm clocks or other gadgets containing batteries. They may cause unnecessary interrogation, search and delays.

In India you never know when and where, because of strikes, religious processions or political rallies, you might get caught in serious traffic jams! Always allow sufficient time to arrive at the railway station, the airport or for that matter any place where arrival on time is required.

VISITING THE CHURCH

Is there a church in this city?
is śahar meṁ girjāghar hai?
इस शहर में गिरजाघर है?

There are three churches here.
yahāṁ tīn girjāghar haiṁ. यहाँ तीन गिरजाघर हैं।

One catholic and two protestant churches.
ek 'kaitholik' aur do proṭaisṭainṭ.
एक कैथोलिक और दो प्रोटेस्टेन्ट।

Do they hold service in English?
kyā ve prārthnā aṅgrezī meṁ karte haiṁ?
क्या वे प्रार्थना अंग्रेजी में करते हैं?

In this city the Christian community is largely Hindi speaking.
is śahar meṁ zyādātar īsāī log hindī bolnewāle haiṁ.
इस शहर में ज़्यादातर ईसाई लोग हिन्दी बोलनेवाले हैं।

Therefore the church service is held in Hindi only.
is lie girjāghar meṁ prārthnā aur updeś hindī meṁ hī hote haiṁ.
इसलिए गिरजाघर में प्रार्थना और उपदेश हिन्दी में ही होते हैं।

Good for me. This way I will pick up some Hindi.
mere lie acchā rahegā. is tarah maiṁ kuch hindī sīkh jāūṁgā.
मेरे लिए अच्छा रहेगा। इस तरह मैं कुछ हिन्दी सीख जाऊँगा।

Are there many Christians here?
kyā yahāṁ bahut īsāī log haiṁ?
क्या यहाँ बहुत ईसाई लोग हैं?

Where is the nearest church?
yahāṁ sab se nikaṭ kaun-sā girjāghar hai?
यहाँ सबसे निकट कौन–सा गिरजाघर है?

I would like to meet the priest.
maiṁ pādrī se milnā cāhtā hūṁ.
मैं पादरी से मिलना चाहता हूँ।

HEALTH AND MEDICINE

AT THE GENERAL PHYSICIAN'S

I am not feeling well today.
āj merī tabīyat ṭhīk nahīṁ.
आज मेरी तबीयत ठीक नहीं।

I need a doctor who speaks English.
mujhe aṅgrezī bolnewālā 'dāukṭar' cāhie.
मुझे अंग्रेजी बोलनेवाला डॉक्टर चाहिए।

I have an upset stomach.
merā peṭ kharāb hai. मेरा पेट ख़राब है।

I have a bad cold.
mujhe bahut jukām hai. मुझे बहुत जुकाम है।

I have some fever.
mujhe kuch bukhār hai. मुझे कुछ बुख़ार है।

My whole body aches.
merā sārā śarīr dukh rahā hai.
मेरा सारा शरीर दुख रहा है।

I have not been able to sleep well for several nights .
mujhko kaī dinoṁ se rāt ko ṭhīk se nīṁd nahīṁ ā rahī.
मुझको कई दिनों से रात को ठीक से नींद नहीं आ रही।

Please give me some sleeping pill.
kṛpayā mujhe koī nīṁd kī golī dījie.
कृपया मुझे कोई नींद की गोली दीजिए।

I feel breathless while climbing stairs.
sīṛhiyāṁ caṛhne se merā sāṁs phūltā hai.
सीढ़ियाँ चढ़ने से मेरा सांस फूलता है।

I have had this problem for a couple of days.
mujhe do-tīn din se yah taklīf hai.
मुझे दो–तीन दिन से यह तकलीफ़ है।

I am diabetic and take insulin.
maiṁ madhumeh kā marīz hūṁ aur 'insulin' kā sevan kartā hūṁ.
मैं मधुमेह का मरीज़ हूँ और इन्सुलिन का सेवन करता हूँ।

I am allergic to pollen.
mujhe parāg se alarjī hai.
मुझे पराग से एलर्जी है।

...groundnuts...
... mūṅgphalī se ... ... मूंगफली से ...
...insect bites...
... kīṭāṇuoṁ ke kāṭne se ... ... कीटाणुओं के काटने से
...tetracycline...
... ṭaiṭrāsaiklin se ... ... टैट्रासेकलिन से ...

Is there a drugstore nearby?
kyā pās meṁ koī dawāī kī dukān hai?
क्या पास में कोई दवाई की दुकान है?

AT THE ORTHOPAEDICS CLINIC

I hurt my leg.
merī ṭāṁg meṁ coṭ lag gaī hai.
मेरी टांग में चोट लग गई है।

I sprained my ankle.
mere ṭakhne meṁ moc ā gaī hai.
मेरे टखने में मोच आ गई है।

Where does it hurt?
dard kahāṁ hai? दर्द कहाँ है?

The bone seems to have broken. It will have to be x-rayed.
haḍḍī ṭūṭ gaī lagtī hai. 'aiksre' karnā hogā.
हड्डी टूट गई लगती है। एक्सरे करना होगा।

Will I have to stay in the hospital? / in bed?
kyā mujhe aspatāl meṁ / bistar meṁ rahnā hogā?
क्या मुझे अस्पताल में/बिस्तर में रहना होगा।

What is your fee, doctor?
dāukṭar, āpkī 'fīs' kitnī hai?
डॉक्टर, आपकी फ़ीस कितनी है?

AT THE OPHTHALMOLOGIST'S/OPTICIAN'S

I have a stye in the left eye.
merī bāyīṁ āṁkh meṁ bilnī nikal āī hai.
मेरी बायीं आँख में बिलनी निकल आई है।

There is much burning / irritation in both my eyes.
merī donoṁ āṁkhoṁ meṁ bahut jalan/ khujlāhat hai.
मेरी दोनों आँखों में बहुत जलन/खुजलाहट है।

Both my eyes are very red.
merī donoṁ āṁkheṁ bahut lāl haiṁ.

मेरी दोनों आँखें बहुत लाल हैं।

I have difficulty in keeping my eyes open.
mujhe āṁkheṁ khulī rakhne meṁ dikkat hotī hai.
मुझे आँखें खुली रखने में दिक्कत होती है।

Wash your eyes with cold water several times.
āp apnī āṁkheṁ kaī bār ṭhaṇḍe pānī se dhoie.
आप अपनी आँखें कई बार ठण्डे पानी से धोइए।

Put this ointment twice a day in your eye.
yah marham subah-śām apnī āṁkh meṁ lagāeṁ.
यह मरहम सुबह–शाम अपनी आँख में लगाएँ।

I need to see an oculist/optician.

- **mujhe kisī prākaś dṛṣṭī prīkṣak se milnā hai.**
  मुझे किसी प्रकाश दृष्टि परीक्षक से मिलना है।
- **mujhe kisī ainak banāne kī dukān par jānā hai.**
  मुझे किसी ऐनक बनाने की दुकान पर जाना है।

I want my eye-sight checked.
mujhe apnī āṁkheṁ 'ṭaisṭ' karvānī haiṁ.
मुझे अपनी आँखें टेस्ट करवानी हैं।

I broke my glasses.
merī ainak ṭūṭ gaī hai. मेरी ऐनक टूट गई है।

Could you put a new lens in this frame.
kṛpayā is frem meṁ nayā śīśā (lains) lagā dījie.
कृपया इस 'फ्रेम' में नया शीशा (लेन्स) लगा दीजिए।

The stem of my glasses came off. Could you fix it for me, please?
merī ainak kī ḍaṇḍī nikal gaī hai. kṛpayā ise ṭhīk kar deṁ.

मेरी ऐनक की डण्डी निकल गई है। कृपया इसे ठीक कर दें।

When will it be ready?
yah kab tak taiyār ho jāegā?
यह कब तक तैयार हो जाएगा?

I will come back to pick it up.
maiṁ ise śām ko lene āūṁgā.
मैं इसे शाम को लेने आऊँगा।

AT THE DENTIST'S

I have severe toothache today.
āj mere dāṁt meṁ bahut dard hai.
आज मेरे दाँत में बहुत दर्द है।
This toothache is driving me crazy.
is dāṁt ke dard ne mujhe pāgal kar rakhā hai.
इस दाँत के दर्द ने मुझे पागल कर रखा है।

Is there a dentist nearby?
koī dāṁt kā 'dauktar' pās meṁ hai?
कोई दाँत का डॉक्टर पास में है?

Is filling absolutely necessary?
kyā dāṁt bharnā nihāyat zarūrī hai?
क्या दाँत भरना निहायत ज़रूरी है?

Will it have to be extracted?
kyā ise nikālnā paṛegā? क्या इसे निकालना पड़ेगा?

I don't want my tooth pulled. Can it not be saved?
maiṁ apnā dāṁt nikalvānā nahīṁ cāhtā. kyā ise bacāyā nahīṁ jā saktā.
मैं अपना दाँत निकलवाना नहीं चाहता। क्या इसे बचाया नहीं जा सकता।

I have difficulty chewing on the right side.
mujhe dāyīṁ or cabāne meṁ taklīf hotī hai.
मुझे दायीं ओर चबाने में तकलीफ़ होती है।

I think I have lost a filling.
mujhe lagtā hai merī 'filling' gir gaī hai.
मुझे लगता है मेरी फिलिंग गिर गई है।

My lower gums bleed when I brush my teeth.
mere nīce ke masūṛoṁ meṁ se buruś karte samay khūn nikaltā hai.
मेरे नीचे के मसूड़ों में से बुरुश करते समय खून निकलता है।

AT THE PHYSIOTHERAPIST'S

I have a frozen shoulder.
merā kandhā jām ho gayā hai.
मेरा कन्धा जाम हो गया है।

I cannot move my hand backwards.
maiṁ apnā hāth pīche nahīṁ le jā saktā/saktī.
मैं अपना हाथ पीछे नहीं ले जा सकता/सकती।

Right hand is very bad.
dāyāṁ hāth bahut kharāb hai.

दायाँ हाथ बहुत ख़राब है।

It becomes numb in sleep.
yah nīṁd meṁ sunn ho jātā hai.
यह नींद में सुन्न हो जाता है।

My right knee joint also pains.
mere dāyeṁ ghutne ke joṛ meṁ bhī dard hai.
मेरे दायें घुटने के जोड़ में भी दर्द है।

You need regular exercise under the supervision of the physiotherapist.
āpko 'fiziothairepist' ke nirīkṣaṇ meṁ niyamit vyāyām kī āvaśyaktā hai.
आपको फिज़ियोथेरेपिस्ट के निरीक्षण में नियमित व्यायाम की आवश्यकता है।

Then excercise by yourself at home at least thirty minutes daily.
phir ghar par roz tīs minaṭ apne se vyāyām kījie.
फिर घर पर रोज़ तीस मिनट अपने से व्यायाम कीजिए।

Take long walks regularly.
niyamit taur par lambī sair kījie.
नियमित तौर पर लम्बी सैर कीजिए।

This will strengthen your muscles and make the joints limber.
is se āpkī māṁspeśiyāṁ mazbūt hoṁgī aur āpke joṛ dhīle ho jāeṁge.
इससे आपकी मांसपेशियाँ मज़बूत होंगी और आपके जोड़ ढीले हो जाएँगे।

ALTERNATIVE MEDICINE

Besides modern medicine, several alternative medical facilities are available in India.

ayurvedic	**āyurvaidik**	आयुर्वैदिक
homeopathy	**homiyopaithī**	होमियोपैथी
nursing	**paricaryā**	परिचर्या
naturopathy	**prākṛtik cikitsā**	प्राकृतिक चिकित्सा
sorcerer	**ojhā**	ओझा
unani	**yūnānī**	यूनानी
meditation	**dhyān**	ध्यान
yoga	**yog**	योग

USEFUL TIPS

Beware of Quacks!

There are many unqualified or unethical people practising medicine and manufacturing and selling spurious medicines in India.

India does not provide many special services for the disabled and handicapped on trains and buses.

Special toilets for such people are almost unheard of.

Use of wheelchair is not very common, leave alone ramps or an elevator for the people in wheel chair!

PROPOSING FRIENDSHIP

Could we be friends?
kyā ham dost ban sakte haiṁ?
क्या हम दोस्त बन सकते हैं?

Would you (m.) be friends with me?
āp (m.) mujhse dostī kareṁge / kareṁgī?
आप मुझसे दोस्ती करेंगे/करेंगी?

I want to be friends with you.
maiṁ (m.) āpse dostī karnā cāhtā/cāhtī hūṁ.
मैं आपसे दोस्ती करना चाहता/चाहती हूँ।

EXPRESSING LOVE

I love you.
maiṁ (m.) tumse pyār kartā/kartī hūṁ.
मैं तुमसे प्यार करता/करती हूँ।

I have fallen in love with you.
mujhe tumse pyār ho gayā hai.
मुझे तुमसे प्यार हो गया है।

PROPOSING MARRIAGE

Will you marry me?
tum (m./f.) mujhse śādī karoge/karogī?
तुम मुझसे शादी करोगे/करोगी?

I want to marry you.
maiṁ (m./f.) tumse śādī karnā cāhtā/cāhtī hūṁ.
मैं तुमसे शादी करना चाहता/चाहती हूँ।

USEFUL TIPS

International Marriages

A foreigner getting involved with an Indian girl should understand the cultural differences between India and the West. Friendships between boys and girls are becoming more common, sometimes culminating into marriage. Hence the use of the English terms *boyfriend* and *girlfriend* are not alien to young people. (There are no appropriate translations for these terms in Hindi). Physical relationship is not an accepted part of premarital courtship. Inter-caste marriages are no longer rare.

WEATHER

The weather is excellent.
mausam bahut baṛhiyā hai. मौसम बहुत बढ़िया है।

It seems it will rain today.
lagtā hai āj bāriś hogī. लगता है आज बारिश होगी।

It is raining outside.
bāhar pānī paṛ rahā hai. बाहर पानी पड़ रहा है।

It is raining cats and dogs.
mūslādhār bāriś ho rahī hai.
मूसलाधार बारिश हो रही है।

It is drizzling.
būṁdā-bāṁdī ho rahī hai. बूंदा–बांदी हो रही है।

Dew is falling.

os paṛ rahī hai. ओस पड़ रही है।

It is hailing.

ole paṛ rahe haiṁ. ओले पड़ रहे हैं।

It is sunny today.

āj dhūp hai. आज धूप है।

It is very foggy today.

āj bahut kuhrā hai. आज बहुत कुहरा है।

It is cloudy today.

āj bādal haiṁ. आज बादल हैं।

It is very hot these days.

ājkal bahut garmī paṛ rahī hai.

आजकल बहुत गर्मी पड़ रही है।

Today's highest temperature is fifty one degrees Celsius.

āj kā adhiktam tāpmān ikyāvan digrī selsias hai.

आज का अधिकतम तापमान इक्यावन डिग्री सेल्सियस है।

Today's lowest temperature is fifteen degrees Celsius.

āj kā nayūntam tāpmān pandrah digrī selsias hai.

आज का न्यूनतम तापमान पन्द्रह डिग्री सेल्सियम है।

There is much humidity these days.

ājkal bahut umas ho rahī hai.

आजकल बहुत उमस हो रही है।

It is very cold.

bahut ṭhaṇḍ paṛ rahī hai. बहुत ठण्ड पड़ रही है।

It seems there will be heavy snowfall this year.
lagtā hai is sāl bahut barf paṛegī.
लगता है इस साल बहुत बर्फ़ पड़ेगी।

...freezing cold...

...kaṛake kī ṭhaṇḍ... ...कड़ाके की ठण्ड ...

The river is flooded.

nadī meṁ bāṛh āī hai. नदी में बाढ़ आई है।

There is drought in our State.
hamāre prades meṁ sūkhā paṛā hai.
हमारे प्रदेश में सूखा पड़ा है।

The entire crop has been ruined.
sab fasal kharāb ho gaī hai.
सब फ़सल खराब हो गई है।

SEASONS

India has six seasons.
bhārat meṁ chah ṛtueṁ hotī haiṁ.
भारत में छः ऋतुएँ होती हैं।

spring	**basant ṛtu**	बसन्त ऋतु
summer	**grīṣma ṛtu**	ग्रीष्म ऋतु
rainy season	**varṣā ṛtu**	वर्षा ऋतु
fall	**patjhaṛ**	पतझड़
early winter	**śiśir ṛtu**	शिशिर ऋतु
late winter	**hemant ṛtu**	हेमन्त ऋतु

TELLING TIME

What time is it?
kitne baje haiṁ? कितने बजे हैं?

It is one o'clock. **ek bajā hai.** एक बजा है।

It is two o'clock. **do baje haiṁ.** दो बजे हैं।

It is three o'clock. **tīn baje haiṁ.** तीन बजे हैं।

It is a quarter past one.
savā ek bajā hai. सवा एक बजा है।

It is a quarter past two.
savā do baje haiṁ. सवा दो बजे हैं।

...a quarter past three..
....savā tīn baje haiṁ... ...सवा तीन बजे हैं...

It is a quarter to one.
paun bajā hai. पौन बजा है।

It is a quarter to two.
paune do baje haiṁ. पौने दो बजे हैं।

It is a quarter to three.
paune tīn baje haiṁ. पौने तीन बजे हैं।

It is half past one.
deṛh bajā hai. डेढ़ बजा है।

It is two thirty.
ḍhāī baje haiṁ. ढाई बजे हैं।

It is three thirty.

sāṛhe tīn baje haiṁ. साढ़े तीने बजे हैं।

...four thirty...

sāṛhe cār baje haiṁ. साढ़े चार बजे हैं।

It is ten to two.

do bajne meṁ das 'minaṭ' haiṁ.

दो बजने में दस मिनट हैं।

It is ten past two.

do bajkar das 'minaṭ' hue haiṁ.

दो बजकर दस मिनट हुए हैं।

How long does it take?

kitnā samay lagtā hai? कितना समय लगता है?

MONTHS

Indians use the international calendar for most private or official business. They pronounce the months differently though.

January	**janvarī**	जनवरी
February	**farvarī**	फरवरी
March	**mārc**	मार्च
April	**aprail**	अप्रैल
May	**maī**	मई
June	**jūn**	जून
July	**julāī**	जुलाई
August	**agast**	अगस्त

September	**sitambar**	सितम्बर
October	**aktūbar**	अक्तूबर
November	**navambar**	नवम्बर
December	**disambar**	दिसम्बर

For religious ceremonies, lunar calendar is used.

names of the months		**corresponding English months**
cait	चैत	mid March- mid April
baisākh	बैशाख	mid April-mid May
jyeṣṭh	ज्येष्ठ	mid May- mid June
āsāṛh	आषाढ़	mid June- mid July
sāvan	सावन	mid July- mid August
bhādoṁ	भादों	mid August- mid September
kwār	कुआर	mid September- mid October
kātik	कातिक	mid October- mid November
ag'han	अगहन	mid November- mid December
pūs	पूष	mid December- mid January
māgh	माघ	mid January- mid February
phāgun	फागुन	mid February - mid March

DAYS OF THE WEEK

Monday	**somvār**	सोमवार
Tuesday	**maṅgalvār**	मंगलवार
Wednesday	**budhvār**	बुधवार

Thursday	**bṛhaspativār**	बृहस्पतिवार
	guruvār	गुरुवार
Friday	**śukravār**	शुक्रवार
Saturday	**śanivār**	शनिवार
Sunday	**ravivār**	रविवार
	itvār	इतवार

Use ko with days of the week e.g.

on Monday	**sombvar ko**	सोमवार को
on Tuesday	**mangalvar ko**	मंगलवार को

TIME DIVISIONS

day	**din**	दिन
night	**rāt**	रात
dawn	**prabhāt**	प्रभात
morning	**subah**	सुबह
noon	**dopahar**	दोपहर
afternoon	**aprāhn**	अपराह्न
evening	**śām/sandhyā**	शाम/सन्ध्या
night	**rāt/rātri**	रात/रात्रि
midnight	**ardh rātri**	अर्ध रात्रि
	ādhī rāt	आधी रात
week	**haftā / saptāh**	हफ़्ता/सप्ताह
month	**mahīnā**	महीना

year	**sāl/varṣ**	साल/वर्ष
sunrise	**sūryodayă**	सूर्योदय
sunset	**sūryāst**	सूर्यास्त
today	**āj**	आज
tomorrow	**kal**	कल
these days	**ājkal**	आजकल
yesterday	**kal**	कल
day after tomorrow	**parsoṁ**	परसों
day before yesterday	**parsoṁ**	परसों
two days after tomorrow	**narsoṁ**	नरसों
two days before yesterday	**narsoṁ**	नरसों

USEFUL TIPS

Indian Time Perceptions

Indian concept of time is cyclic, not linear. That explains the same words being used for 'time gone by' and 'time to come'. e.g. kal (yesterday/tomorrow), parsom (day before yesterday/day after tomorrow), narsom (two days before yesterday/two days after tomorrow) etc. To avoid confusion the present, past and future forms of the verb 'to be' are used.

Direction (diśa)

north	**uttar**	उत्तर
south	**dakṣiṇ**	दक्षिण
east	**pūrv**	पूर्व
west	**paścim**	पश्चिम
north-west	**uttar-dakṣiṇ**	उत्तर–दक्षिण
north- east	**uttar-pūrv**	उत्तर–पूर्व
east-west	**pūrv-paścim**	पूर्व–पश्चिम
south-west	**dakṣiṇ-paścim**	दक्षिण–पश्चिम
above	**ūpar**	ऊपर
below	**nīce**	नीचे
ahead	**āge**	आगे
behind	**pīche**	पीछे
over here	**idhar**	इधर
over there	**udhar**	उधर
right	**dāyeṁ**	दायें
left	**bāyeṁ**	बायें
towards right	**dāyīṁ or**	दायीं ओर
towards left	**bāyīṁ or**	बायीं ओर
all round	**cāroṁ or**	चारों ओर
all over	**sarvatra**	सर्वत्र
straight ahead	**sīdhe**	सीधे

Walk on the right side!	**dāyīṁ or calie.**	दायीं ओर चलिए
Stop!	**rukie!**	रुकिए!
Follow me!	**mere pīche āie.**	मेरे पीछे आइए।
Look ahead!	**āge dekhie!**	आगे देखिए!

Go straight and at the first crossing, turn to right
sīdhe jākar pahle caurāhe par bāyīṁ or muṛie.
सीधे जाकर पहले चौराहे पर बायीं ओर मुड़िए।

He lives on the floor above.
vah ūparwālī manjil par rahtā hai.
वह ऊपरवाली मंज़िल पर रहता है।

I don't know the one who lives above.
maiṁ ūparwāle ko nahīṁ jāntā.
मैं ऊपरवाले को नहीं जानता।

HOBBIES

What hobbies do you have?
āpke śauk kyā haiṁ?
आपके शौक क्या हैं?

What do you do in your free time?
āp apne khālī samay meṁ kyā karte haiṁ?
आप अपने खाली समय में क्या करते हैं?

I am fond of playing chess.
mujhe śatrañj khelne kā śauk hai.
मुझे शतरंज खेलने का शौक है।

... of doing photography...

... foto khīṁcne kā... ...फोटो खींचने का...

... of long walks...

... lambī sair karne kā... ...लम्बी सैर करने का...

... of making dolls...

... guṛiā banāne kā... ...गुड़िया बनाने का...

... of reading novels...

... upanyās paṛhne kā... ...उपन्यास पढ़ने का...

... of swimming...

... tairne kā... ...तैरने का...

... of playing cricket...

... kriket khelne kā... ...क्रिकेट खेलने का...

... of watching a game of cricket/ football/ hockey...

... kriket/fuṭbaul/hāki kā khel dekhne kā...

... क्रिकेट/फुटबॉल/हाकी का खेल देखने का...

Flower arrangement is my hobby.

phūl sajānā ... merā pasandīdā śauk hai.

फूल सजाना मेरा पसन्दीदा शौक है।

cooking special dishes..

khās vyañjan pakānā.. खास व्यन्जन पकाना...

shopping..

kharīdārī karnā.. ख़रीदारी करना...

The truth is that only the rich people can afford to have hobbies.

sac to yah hai ki sirf amīr log śauk pāl sakte haiṁ.

सच तो यह है कि सिर्फ़ अमीर लोग शौक पाल सकते हैं।

A common man in India has neither free time, nor any hobby.
hindustān meṁ ām ādmī ke pās nā khālī samay hotā hai, nā koī śauk .
हिन्दुस्तान में आम आदमी के पास ना खाली समय होता है, ना कोई शौक।

Daily life is quite stressful.
din bhar kī dauṛ-bhāg rahtī hai.
दिन भर की दौड़–भाग रहती है।

Normally, I eat dinner and go to sleep early.
sāmānyatā, maiṁ to śām kā khānā khā kar jaldī so jātā hūṁ.
सामान्यता, मैं तो शाम का खाना खा कर जल्दी सो जाता हूँ।

Sometimes, on holidays I visit friends and relatives.
chuṭṭī ke din kabhī-kabhī dostoṁ aur riśtedāroṁ se mil letā hūṁ.
छुट्टी के दिन कभी–कभी दोस्तों और रिश्तेदारों से मिल लेता हूँ।

This is what you people think.
aisā āp log bhārat meṁ socte haiṁ.
ऐसा आप लोग भारत में सोचते हैं।

In western countries people believe that a hobby is the key to good mental and physical health

pascimī deśoṁ meṁ logoṁ kā mānanā hai ki 'hāubī' acchī mānsik aur śārīrik sehat kī kunjī hai.
पश्चिमी देशों में लोगों का मानना है कि हॉबी अच्छी मानसिक और शारीरिक सेहत की कुञ्जी है।

POLITICS

In India, the elections take place once every five years.
bharat meṁ har pañc sāl par cunāv hote haiṁ.
भारत में हर पाँच साल में चुनाव होते हैं।

Both women and men have equal voting rights in this country.
is deś meṁ auratem aur ādmī dono voṭ dene ke samān adhikārī haiṁ.
इस देश में औरतें और आदमी दोनों वोट देने के समान अधिकारी हैं।

Voting age is 18 years.
voṭ dene kī umra aṭṭhārah sāl hai.
वोट देने की उम्र अट्ठारह साल है।
rājnīti meṁ bhrṣṭācār bahut hai.
राजनीति में भ्रष्टाचार बहुत है।

Voting is not honest.
matdān īmāndārī se nahīṁ hotā.
मतदान ईमानदारी से नहीं होता।
Big scams take place.
baṛe-baṛe ghotale hote haiṁ.
बड़े–बड़े घोटाले होते हैं।

For petty personal gains, the leaders keep changing parties.
thoṛe se niji fāyade ke lie, netā log dal badalte rahte haiṁ.
निजि फ़ायदे के लिए, नेता लोग दल बदलते रहते हैं।

These days, every now and then, the governments keep falling and elections keep taking place.
ājkal āe din sarkāreṁ girtī rahtī haiṁ aur cunāv hote rahte haiṁ
आजकल, आए दिन, सरकारें गिरती रहती हैं और आए दिन चुनाव होते रहते हैं।

candidate	**ummīdwar**	उम्मीदवार
constitution	**saṃvidhān**	संविधान
minorities	**alpsaṅkhyak**	अल्पसंख्यक
majority	**bahusaṅkhyak**	बहुसंख्यक
nomination	**nāmāṅkan**	नामांकन
parliament	**saṁsad**	संसद
President	**rāṣṭrapati**	राष्ट्रपति
Prime minister	**pradhān mantrī**	प्रधानमन्त्री
voting	**janmat**	जनमत
voter	**matdātā**	मतदाता
scam	**ghotālā**	घोटाला
central government **kendrīyă sarkār**		केन्द्रीय सरकार
politics	**rājnīti**	राजनीति

member of parliament
sāṁsad सांसद

member of legislative assembly
vidhāyak विधायक

legislative assembly
vidhānsabhā विधानसभा

DOWRY PROBLEM

In the West we hear that in India, for dowry, brides are burnt to death.
paścim meṁ ham sunte haiṁ ki bhārat meṁ dahej ke lie nav vadhū ko jalā diyā jātā hai.
पश्चिम में हम सुनते हैं कि भारत में दहेज के लिए नव वधू को जला दिया जाता है।

Yes, this happens, but it is not very common.
hāṁ, aisā hotā hai, lekin yah bahut ām bāt nahīṁ hai.
हाँ, ऐसा होता है, लेकिन यह बहुत आम बात नहीं है।

This is true that in several homes the groom and his parents together torture the bride.
yah sac hai ki bahut gharoṁ meṁ var aur uske mātā-pitā milkar vadhū kā utpīṛan karte haiṁ.
यह सच है कि बहुत घरों में वर और उसके माता–पिता मिलकर वधू का उत्पीड़न करते हैं।

NUMBERS

CARDINALS

zero	**śūnyă**	शून्य
one	**ek**	एक
two	**do**	दो
three	**tīn**	तीन
four	**cār**	चार
five	**pāṁc**	पाँच
six	**chah**	छः
seven	**sāt**	सात
eight	**āṭh**	आठ
nine	**nau**	नौ
ten	**das**	दस
eleven	**gayārah**	ग्यारह
twelve	**bārah**	बारह
thirteen	**terah**	तेरह
fourteen	**caudah**	चौदह
fifteen	**pandrah**	पन्द्रह
sixteen	**solah**	सोलह
seventeen	**satrah**	सत्रह
eighteen	**aṭhārah**	अट्ठारह
nineteen	**unnīs**	उन्नीस
twenty	**bīs**	बीस

twenty-one	**ikkīs**	इक्कीस
twenty-two	**bāīs**	बाईस
twenty-three	**teīs**	तेईस
twenty-four	**caubīs**	चौबीस
twenty-five	**paccīs**	पच्चीस
twenty-six	**chabbīs**	छब्बीस
twenty-seven	**satāīs**	सताईस
twenty-eight	**aṭhāīs**	अठाईस
twenty-nine	**untīs**	उनतीस
thirty	**tīs**	तीस
thirty-one	**iktīs**	इकतीस
thirty-two	**battīs**	बत्तीस
thirty-three	**taiṁtīs**	तैंतीस
thirty-four	**cauṁtīs**	चौंतीस
thirty-five	**paiṁtīs**	पैंतीस
thirty-six	**chattīs**	छत्तीस
thirty-seven	**saiṁtīs**	सैंतीस
thirty-eight	**aṛtīs**	अड़तीस
thirty-nine	**untālīs**	उन्तालीस
forty	**cālīs**	चालीस
forty-one	**iktālīs**	इकतालीस
forty-two	**bayālīs**	बयालीस
forty-three	**taiṁtālīs**	तैंतालीस
forty -four	**cauvālīs**	चौवालीस

forty-five	**paiṁtālīs**	पैंतालीस
forty-six	**chiyālīs**	छियालीस
forty-seven	**saiṁtālīs**	सैंतालीस
forty-eight	**aṛtālīs**	अडतालीस
forty-nine	**uncās**	उन्चास
fifty	**pacās**	पचास
fifty-one	**ikyāvan**	इक्यावन
fifty-two	**bāvan**	बावन
fifty-three	**trepan**	तिरपन
fifty-four	**cauvan**	चौवन
fifty-five	**pacpan**	पचपन
fifty-six	**chappan**	छप्पन
fifty-seven	**sattāvan**	सत्तावन
fifty-eight	**aṭṭhāvan**	अट्ठावन
fift-nine	**unsaṭh**	उनसठ
sixty	**sāṭh**	साठ
sixty-one	**iksaṭh**	इकसठ
sixty-two	**bāsaṭh**	बासठ
sixty-three	**tirsaṭh**	तिरसठ
sixty-four	**causaṭh**	चौसठ
sixty-five	**paiṁsaṭh**	पैसठ
sixty-six	**chiyāsaṭh**	छियासठ
sixty-seven	**saṛsaṭh**	सड़सठ
sixty-eight	**aṛsaṭh**	अड़सठ

sixty-nine	**unhattar**	उनहत्तर
seventy	**sattar**	सत्तर
seventy-one	**ik'hattar**	इकहत्तर
seventy-two	**bahattar**	बहत्तर
seventy-three	**tihattar**	तिहत्तर
seventy-four	**cauhattar**	चौहत्तर
seventy-five	**pac'hattar**	पचहत्तर
seventy-six	**chi'hattar**	छिहत्तर
seventy-seven	**satattar**	सतत्तर
seventy-eight	**aṭh'hattar**	अठहत्तर
seventy-nine	**unnāsī**	उन्नासी
eighty	**assī**	अस्सी
eighty-one	**ikyāsī**	इक्यासी
eighty-two	**bayāsī**	बयासी
eighty-three	**tirāsī**	तिरासी
eighty-four	**caurāsī**	चौरासी
eighty-five	**pacāsī**	पचासी
eighty-six	**chiyāsī**	छियासी
eighty-seven	**sattāsī**	सत्तासी
eighty-eight	**aṭṭhāsī**	अट्ठासी
eighty-nine	**navāsī**	नवासी
ninety	**nabbe/navve**	नब्बे
ninety-one	**ikānve**	इकानवे

ninety-two	**bānve**	बानबे
ninety-three	**tirānve**	तिरानवे
ninety-four	**caurānve**	चौरानवे
ninety-five	**pacānve**	पचानवे
ninety-six	**chiyānve**	छियानवे
ninety-seven	**sattānve**	सत्तानवे
ninety-eight	**aṭṭhānve**	अट्ठानवे
ninety-nine	**ninyānve**	निन्यानवे
hundred	**sau**	सौ
thousand	**hazār**	हज़ार
a hundred thousand	**lākh**	लाख
a thousand thousand	**croṛe**	करोड़

ORDINALS

first	**pahlā**	पहला
second	**dūsrā**	दूसरा
third	**tīsrā**	तीसरा
fourth	**cauthā**	चौथा
fifth	**pāṁçvāṁ**	पाँचवाँ
sixth	**chaṭhā**	छठा
seventh	**sātvāṁ**	सातवाँ
eighth	**āṭhvāṁ**	आठवाँ
ninth	**nauvāṁ**	नौवाँ

tenth	**dasvāṁ**	दसवाँ
eleventh	**gyārahvāṁ**	ग्यारहवाँ
twelfth	**bārahvāṁ**	बारहवाँ

MULTIPLICATIVES

twice as much	**dugunā**	दुगुना
three times as much	**tigunā**	तिगुना
four times as much	**caugunā**	चौगुना
five times as much	**pāṁcgunā**	पाँचगुना
six times as much	**chahgunā**	छःगुना
seven times as much	**sātgunā**	सातगुना
eight times as much	**āṭhgunā**	आठगुना
nine times as much	**naugunā**	नौगुना
ten times as much	**dasgunā**	दसगुना
hundred times as much	**saugunā**	सौगुना

AGGREGATIVES

both	**donoṁ**	दोनों
all three	**tīnoṁ**	तीनों
all four	**cāroṁ**	चारों
all five	**pāṁcoṁ**	पाँचों
all six	**chahoṁ**	छहों
all seven	**sātoṁ**	सातों
all eight	**āṭhoṁ**	आठों

scores of	**bīsoṁ**	बीसों
hundreds of	**saiṅkṛoṁ**	सैकड़ों
thousands of	**hazāroṁ**	हजारों
millions of	**lākhoṁ**	लाखों

HOW MANY TIMES

once	**ek bār**	एक बार
twice	**do bār**	दो बार
thrice	**tīn bār**	तीन बार
four times	**car bār**	चार बार
five times	**pāṁc bār**	पाँच बार

HOW MANY FOLD

single layer	**Ikahrā**	इकहरा
double fold	**dohrā**	दोहरा
threefold	**tihrā/tehrā**	तिहरा/तेहरा
fourfold	**cauhrā**	चौहरा

FRACTIONS

one half	**ādhā**	आधा
one fourth	**ek cauthāī**	चौथाई
one third	**ek tihāī**	एक तिहाई
two thirds	**do tihāī**	दो तिहाई

FESTIVALS AND NATIONAL HOLIDAYS

Republic Day	**gaṇtantra divas**	January 26
Independence Day	**swatantratā divas**	August 15

Rām Navamī (राम नवमी) : Rām Navamī is celebration of birth of Rām.on the 9th day of the month Cait, the 1st month of the Hindu calendar.The Lord is believed to have incarnated as Rām, the son of the kṣatrya King Daśratha of Ayodhyā, to restore order in society in the Dwāpar yuga.

Tīj (तीज) : A festival of the rainy season held on the third day of the bright lunar fortnight in the month of Sāvan, the 5th month of the Hindu calendar.

Janamāṣṭmī (जन्माष्टमी) : The birthday of Lord Kṛṣṇa, on the 8th day of the dark half of the month Bhadoṁ. Most people do a day long fast, participate in group singing and narration of the glories of Lord Kṛṣṇa.

Rākhī (राखी) : A unique festival, held on the full moon of the month Savan, bonding brothers and sisters. The sisters tie a band round the wrist of brothers. They pray for their long lives and in turn, the brothers take the responsibility of protecting them all through their lives.

Durgā pūjā (दुर्गा पूजा) : First 10 days of the bright half of Aśvin, the 7th month of Hindu calendar are packed with festivities celeberating worship of the Goddess Durga in her various manifestations. People believe that the Goddess actually visits their homes , and that all their desires are fulfilled and prosperity comes to them through pleasing the Goddess.

Daśahrā (दशहरा) : Also known as Vijay Daśamī, this festival is celebrated on the 10th day of the bright half of the month of Aśvin, the 7th month of Hindu calendar to commemorate the victory of Rām over Rāvaṇ, symbolic of the victory of good over evil

Dīwālī (दीवाली) : This is the festival of lights, celebrated on new moon of Kārtik, 8th month of Hindu calendar, to commemorate the return of Rām to Ayodhyā after 14 years of exile. The homes, shops and every nook and corner of the country are illuminated with lamps. Lakṣmī, the Goddess of wealth is worshipped.

Bhaiyā Dūj (भैया दूज) : This festival is celebrated two days after Diwali, on the second day of the bright half of the month Kārtik. It strengthens bonding between sisters and brothers. Sisters put a dot of rice and saffron on the forehead of their brothers, offer them various delicacies and sweets and pray for their long life.

Guru Pūrṇimā (गुरु पूर्णिमा) : Birthday of Guru Nanak, the founder of Sikh religion, is observed as a day of obeisance and reverence for the spiritual preceptor, on the 15th of Kārtik, the eighth month of the Hindu calendar.

Makar Saṅkrānti (मकर सन्क्रान्ति) : This comees every year on the 14th of January. This marks the sun's entry in the Zodiac sign Capricorn and its progress northward. Death during the six months following this time is considered very auspicious

Basant Pañcamī (बसन्त पंचमी) : This spring festival falls on the fifth day of the bright half of Magh, 9th month of the Hindu calendar. Saraswatī, the Goddess of learning, is worshipped on this day.

Śivarātri (**शिवरात्रि**) **:** This is held on the 14th of the dark half of Phālgun, the 12th month of the Hindu calendar. Wedding of Lord Śivā and Goddess Pārvatī is celebrated.

Id-al-Fiṭr (**ईद-अल-फित्र**) **:** This is celebration of Ramzān believed to be the month of inception as well as completion of the Kurān, and is observed by Muslims as the month of self-purification through fasting and intense prayers.

Id-al-Aḍḥā (**ईद-अल-अधा**) **:** This is commemoration of Abrāham's sacrifice to God of his only son who, at the last moment, was substituted by a ram.

Muharram (**मुहर्रम**) **:** This commemorates the martyrdom of Imāmhusain.

Budh Pūrnimā (**बुद्ध पूर्णिमा**) **:** This is celebration of birth, enlightenment and nirvāṇa (liberation from earthly body) of Lord Budha. They all fall on the same day.

Mahāvīr Jayantī (**महावीर जयन्ती**) **:** Birthday of Mahāvīr, the founder of Jainism.

RELIGIONS

India is a secular country. All religions are equally respected here.

Buddhism	**bauddh-mat**	बुद्ध–मत
Christianity	**īsāī-mat**	ईसाई–मत
	islām	इस्लाम
Jainism	**jain-mat**	जैन–मत
Śaivism	**śiva bhakti**	शिव भक्ति
Sikhism	**sikh-mat**	सिख–मत
Bahaīsm	**bahāī-mat**	बहाई–मत

SAINT CELEBRITIES

Dādu	दादु;	**Guru Nānak**	गुरुनानक;
Kabīr	कबीर;	**Mīrā Bāī**	मीरा बाई;
Paramhansa	परमहंस;	**Raidās**	रैदास;
Śri Aurobindo	श्री अरबिन्दो;	**Vivekānanda**	विवेकानन्द

HINDUISM

SCHOOLS OF PHILOSOPHY

Hindu philosophy is divided into six systems of thought.

Sānkhya of Kapilā
Yoga of Patañjali
Vaiśeṣika of Kanada
Nayaya of Gautama
Purva - mimansa of Jaimini
Uttar - mimansa or Vedanta of Vyasa

SCRIPTUAL TEXTS

Sṛutis -Vedas

Smṛtis-- 108 Upaniṣads

18 Puraṇas, Mahabharata, Ramayana

Mahābhārata is the longest poem in the world. It was written by sage Ved Vyas. The book is divided into 18 chapters and has 110,000 couplets

Rāmāyaṇa is the story of Lord Rām, incarnation of Lord

Viśnu, to destroy evil and establish righteous order in society. Its sanskrit version was written by sage Vālmiki. Its popular version is by Tulsīdās, written about 600 years ago. This immortal and cherished epic has 24000 couplets. The story of Rāmāyaṇa projects through its characters, perfect family, high social and political ideals.

The Bhāgvad Gītā, which is actually a part of the Mahābhārata, is the sacred book of Hindus. It has 18 chapters and 700 verses. It is in the form of a dialogue between the divine teacher lord Kṛṣṇa and his earthly disciple Arjuna. It is not a collection of commandments. It only explains pros and cons of various dilemmas and crises that the earthly beings tend to confront, and leaves it to the judgement of the individual to choose the right path.

The entire setting of the situation is novel—the divine teacher talking to the earthly pupil in the battle field.

It does not teach renunciation of action. In fact it prompts one to act—the action being selflessly performed as an oblation to all life-sacrifice dedicated to the Lord.

PATHS OF SALVATION

Bhaktl Yoga (भक्ति योग) : This is the path of devotion to personal God. It is a spiritual quest through love and complete self surrender to the Lord.

Jñana Yoga (ज्ञान योग) : The path of knowledge.Here knowledge does not mean theoretical knowledge gotten through scriptures. It is spiritual knowledge attained through constant meditation on the Supreme reality culminating in the experience of oneness of the atman(individual soul) and the brahman(supreme soul). All dualities and doubts disappear. The Truth dawns: Aham brahm asmi'= I am brahm.

Karma Yoga (कर्म योग) : This is the path of salvation through action. Lord Kṛṣṇa in the Bagvad Gīta tells Arjuna, not to renounce the karma, but to renounce the fruit of karma. One should rise above dualities, to remain equipoised in sorrow and joy, success or failure, gain or loss. All actions must be done in the spirit of offering to the Lord. To be engaged in yoga while doing all works. Even though engaged in work one should not crave for the fruit of one's actions. One's engagement in action should be one's duty, not passion for work or its result. All his works are oblations to brahmyajna.Through Arjuna all of us are advised to do karma in a spirit of enlightened consciousness.

Raja Yoga (राज योग) : This is the path of salvation given by Patañjali in his Yoga Sūtra, It professes the practice of praṇayam and mind control.

CLASSIFICATION OF SOCIETY (Varaṇāśrama)

Bhrāhmaṇa (ब्राह्मण) is the class of thinkers and scholars. Their duty is to perpetuate knowledge in the society.

Kṣatriya (क्षत्रिय) is the warrior class. Their primary duty is to rule and defend the country and its people.

Vaiśya (वैश्य) are the trading class. Their occupations are commerce and agriculture.

Śūdra (शूद्र) is the service class. Their duty is to obey the command and execute orders from the higher classes.

The above caste system is now fast disappearing.

STAGES OF LIFE (āśramas)

Hindu scriptures believe the incarnation of the embodied soul in human body to be the result of meritorius deeds in several previous lives. Human beings alone through judicious use of discriminatory intelligence can strive to become liberated from the cycle of rebirth and death. They put the life span of a human being at a hundred years. As prescription for its righteous use, this span has been divided into four stages (āśramas) and their duties in respective phase clearly defined.

Brahmacarya (ब्रह्मचर्य) denotes the period of religious studentship at the feet of a qualified teacher and absolute abstinence during the first 25 years of one's life.

Gārhasthyă (गार्हस्थ्य) is the householder's stage from 25-50 years. During this period one is expected to marry, have children and do his best to provide for them.

Vānaprasth (वानप्रस्थ) is the period of semi-retirement from 50-75. One leaves home and retires to some secluded place. He is not supposed to return home , but his family can approach him for occasional consultation and advice. This allows transitional detachment from kith and kin as well as worldly belongings that he may have accumulated during his active years as householder.

Saṃnyās (संन्यास) is the final stage of complete withdrawal, without any belongings, from worldly life and retirement to the forest or the mountains. There should be no possibility of being approached by relatives. One spends one's time practising meditation and aspiring for salvation or freedom from the cycle of birth and death.

FOUR GOALS (cār puruṣārth)

Dharmā (धर्म) : righteous conduct

Arth (अर्थ) : acquisition and utilization of wealth in the light of dharma, by ethical and honest had work

Kām (काम) : sensual enjoyment

Mokṣ (मोक्ष) : liberation from the wheel of death and rebirth.

They are all mutually linked. Arth and kām within the purview of dharma pave the path for mokṣ.

MYSTICAL TOPICS

Most tourists are interested in talking with mendicants, sadhus, swamis and temple priests. They have innumerable questions. This interest is sometimes just curiosity, sometimes academic, genuinely exploring alternative philosophy and thought to find answers to the universal as well as

their personal conflicts. Given below are some useful words that come in handy to discuss and understand topics related to Hindu religion, philosophy and mythology.

ārtī (आरती): Arti is a singing of the Lord's glory with incense and lit lamps performed at the end of puja rituals.

Avtār (अवतार): manifestation of the Lord appearing from time to time to protect the universe from oppression by demonic powers

Bhagvān (भगवान): Bhagvān is He who is aware of creation and dissolution of the universe, of the appearances and disappearances of the beings.

Bhagvān is entire glory, entire virtue, entire renown, entire prosperity, entire wisdom, entire dispassion, all in one.

bhakta (भक्त): devotee

bhakti (भक्ति): devotion

darśan (दर्शन): vision of the Lord

guru (गुरु): Guru is a spiritual teacher who can transmit spiritual knowledge, who through initiation helps people to break the bindings of the soul in this world and cross the ocean of existence. Institution of guru by birth is not the essence of Hinduism.

karma (कर्म): actions

kīrtan (कीर्तन): singing the glories of the Lord.

mālā (**माला**) : rosary of 108 beads used by devotees to recite the name of the Lord. Different explanations are offered for the auspiciousness of the number 108. Twelve signs of the Zodiac multiplied by nine planets is one hundred and eight. Again twenty-seven constellations of stars, each further divided into four parts is one hundred and eight. Completing one round of the rosary while reciting the name of the Lord, or any mantra suggested by one's guru is believed to maintain mystical contact between the individual soul and the Absolute Supreme Truth.

mantra (**मन्त्र**): mantra is based on sound vibrations. Letters of the devanāgrī script put together in different combinations and permutations and learnt and chanted as per instructions of the guru are believed to produce varied energy to attain desired goals. In Hinduism various deities have their own mantra, by chanting which the respective deity can be invoked.

nām (**नाम**) : name of the Lord. The Lord is worshipped in various forms and by various names in India.

pāp (**पाप**) : sin

prāṇ (**प्राण**) : vital air/life force

prārabdh (**प्रारब्ध**) : destiny predetermined by the creator of the universe. One's actions from several previous lives that are ripe enough to bear fruit in the current life span of the individual.

pūjā (**पूजा**) : worshipping the Lord.

punarjanam (**पुर्नजन्म**) : rebirth

puṇyă (**पुण्य**) : meritorious deeds

sādhnā (**साधना**) : spiritual practice leading to realization of God

sādhū (साधु) : holy men

saṃskār (संस्कार) :

- an inborn power or faculty:
- any of the various sanctifying rites in Hinduism, such as naming the baby, wearing the sacred thread, marriage, funeral rites etc.

satsaṅg (सत्संग) : company of good spiritual people. They sing, chant, narrate and listen to the glories of the Lord.

simran (सिमरन) : remembering the name of the Lord.

tilak (तिलक) : a dot on the forehead. The substances commonly used for this purpose are red lead, vermillion, sandalwood powder or even ash.

Om (ओम) : Om is the sound symbol for the Supreme Reality. It stands for the Hindu trinity, Brahma, Viṣṇu, and Maheś, the creative, sustaining and destructive cosmic energies.

PROVERBS

Birds of the same feather

cor-cor mausere bhāī चोर–चोर मौसेरे भाई

Birds of the same feather flock together

ek hī thālī ke caṭṭe-baṭṭe

एक ही थाली के चट्टे–बट्टे

To have one's bread buttered on both sides

pāṁcoṁ uṅgliyāṁ ghī meṁ honā

पाँचो उंगलियाँ घी में होना

Drink as you have brewed

jaisī karnī, vaisī bharnī जैसी करनी, वैसी भरनी

A new broom sweeps clean

nayā naukar tīrandāz नया नौकर तीरन्दाज़

All tarred with the same brush

Sab dhān bāīs paserī सब धान बाईस पसेरी

Cut root and branch

nā rahe gā bāṁs, nā bajegī bāṁsurī

ना रहेगा बाँस, ना बजेगी बाँसुरी

When the cat is away the mice will play

gharwāle ghar nahīṁ, hameṁ kisī kā ḍar nahīṁ

घरवाले घर नहीं, हमें किसी का डर नहीं

To count one's chickens before they are hatched

sūt nā kapās, kolī se lāṭhī-laṭh

सूत ना कपास, कोली से लाठी–लठ

A burnt child dreads fire
dūdh kā jalā chāch phūṁk-phūṁk kar pītā hai
दूध का जला छाछ फूंक–फूंक कर पीता है।

Thundering clouds seldom rain
bādal jo garajte haiṁ ve baraste nahīṁ
बादल जो गरजते हैं वे बरसते नहीं

A guilty conscience needs no accuser
Cor kī dāṛhī meṁ tinkā
चोर की दाढ़ी में तिनका

Too many cooks spoil the broth
adhik jogī maṭh ujāṛ अधिक जोगी मठ उजार
Do mulloṁ meṁ ek murgī harām
दो मुल्लों में एक मुर्गी हराम

Cut according to cloth
teto pāṁv pasārie jeto cādar hoy
तेतो पाँव पसारिए जेतो चादर होए

Danger passed, God forgotten
dukh meṁ simran sab kare, sukh meṁ kare nā koy
दुख में सिमरन सब करे, सुख में करे ना कोए

Death day is Doom's Day
āp ḍūbe to saṁsār ḍūbā आप डूबे तो संसार डूबा

Death defies the doctor
maut kī davā nahīṁ मौत की दवा नहीं

Death cannot be had for asking
māṁge muṁh maut nahīṁ miltī

माँगे मुँह मौत नहीं मिलती

Pull devil, pull baker
donoṁ maśāloṁ meṁ tel denā
दोनों मशालों में तेल देना

An empty mind is a devil's workshop
khālī dimāg, śaitān kā ghar   खाली दिमाग़, शैतान का घर

Do in Rome as the Romans do
jaisā deś, vaisā bheṣ   जैसा देश, वैसा भेष
Jaisī dekhe gāṁv kī rīt, vaisī uṭhāe apnī bhīt
जैसी देखे गाँव की रीत, वैसी उठाए अपनी भीत

Do good and forget
nekī kar kueṁ meṁ ḍāl   नेकी कर कुएँ में डाल

Act in haste and repent in leisure
binā vicāre jo kare so pīche pachtāe
बिना विचारे जो करे सो पीछे पछताए

To carry coals to Newcastle
ulte bāṁs barelī ko   उल्टे बाँस बरेली को

Barking dogs seldom bite
jo garajte haiṁ ve baraste nahīṁ
जो गरजते हैं वे बरसते नहीं

Every dog has his day
har kutte ke din badalte haiṁ
हर कुत्ते के दिन बदलते हैं

Give a dog a bad name and hang him
bad se badnām burā   बद से बदनाम बुरा

śahar meṁ ūṁṭ badnām शहर में ऊँट बदनाम

Let sleeping dogs lie

gaṛhe murde mat ukhāṛo गढे मुर्दे मत उखाड़ो

Faith moves mountains

man caṅgā to kaṭhautī meṁ gaṅgā

मन चंगा तो कठौती में गंगा

To fish in troubled waters

kisī kā ghar jale, aur koī āg tāpe

किसी का घर जले और कोई आग तापे

Forbidden fruit is sweetest

sahaj pake so mīṭhā hoy सहज पके सो मीठा होय

A friend in need is a friend indeed

mitra vahī jo samay par kām āe

मित्र वही जो समय पर काम आए

No gains without pains

binā sevā ke mevā nahīṁ बिना सेवा के मेवा नहीं

A little knowledge is a dangerous thing

nīm hakīm khatrā e jān, nīm mullā khatrā īmān

नीम हकीम ख़तरा ए जान, नीम मुल्ला ख़तरा ईमान

Good mind, good find

āp bhalā to jag bhalā आप भला तो जग भला

To make mountain out of a molehill

rāī kā pahāṛ banānā राई का पहाड़ बनाना

A bad man is better than a bad name

bad se badnām burā बद से बदनाम बुरा

One who excuses himself, accuses himself

cor kī dāṛhī meṁ tinkā — चोर की दाढ़ी में तिनका

Many hands make work light

ek ek, do gayārah — एक एक, दो ग्यारह

You can't run with the hare and hunt with the hounds

ek miyān meṁ do talwāreṁ nahīṁ rah saktīṁ

एक म्यान में दो तलवारें नहीं रह सकतीं

To strike while the iron is hot

tatte tave kām karnā — तत्ते तवे काम करना

To advance by leaps and bounds

din dūnī rāt caunī tarakkī karnā

दिन दूनी रात चौनी तरक्की करना

Half a loaf is better than none

jāte cor kī laṅgoṭī hī sahī

जाते चोर की लंगोटी ही सही

It is no use crying over spilt milk

āb pachtāy kyā hot, jab ciṛiya cug gaī khet

अब पछताए क्या होत, जब चिड़िया चुग गई खेत

Half a mouthful for a starving man

ūṁṭ ke muṁh meṁ jīrā — ऊँट के मुँह में जीरा

Necessity is the mother of invention

āvaśyaktā āviṣkār kī jananī hai

आवश्यकता आविष्कार की जननी है

Reap as you sowed

jaisā bonā, vaisā kāṭnā — जैसा बोना, वैसा काटना

Over shoes, over boots
okhlī meṁ sir diyā, to mūsloṁ se kyā ḍar
ओखली में सिर दिया, तो मूसलों से क्या डर

A rolling stone gathers no moss
dhobī kā kuttā, nā ghaṛ kā nā ghāt kā
धोबी का कुत्ता, ना घर का ना घाट का

Time and tide wait for none
samay kisī ke lie ruktā nahīṁ
समय किसी के लिए रुकता नहीं

A word spoken is past recalling
kamān se niklā tīr vāpas nahīṁ ātā
कमान से निकला तीर वापस नहीं आता

Bad workman always blames his tools
nāc nā jāne āṅgan ṭeṛhā नाच ना जाने आंगन टेढ़ा

USEFUL TIPS

Expressing Anger!

Often you hear a native shouting at somebody.

calānā nahīm ātā to saṛak par nikalte kyoṁ ho?
चलाना नहीं आता तो सड़क पर निकलते क्यों हो?
Why do you come out on the road, when you don't know how to drive?
khud bhī maroge, dūsaroṁ ko bhī māroge.
खुद भी मरोगे, दूसरों को भी मारोगे।
He almost died because of somebady's rash, careless driving.

IDIOMS

get things off one's chest
kah dālnā　　कह डालना

to make someone dance to one's tune
uṅgalī par nacānā　　उंगली पर नचाना

a negligible difference
unnīs-bīs kā farak　　उन्नीस–बीस का फ़रक

very close friends
ek jān do kālib　　एक जान दो कालिब

to add insult to injury　　jale par namak chiṛaknā
जले पर नमक छिड़कना

to be in the jaws of death
jān ke lāle paṛnā　　जान के लाले पड़ना

to be green with envy
chātī par sāṁp loṭnā　　छाती पर साँप लोटना

to exaggerate
namak mirc lagānā　　नमक मिर्च लगाना

enemy in the garb of a friend
āstīn kā sāṁp　　आस्तीन का साँप

for there to be something fishy
dāl meṁ kālā honā　　दाल में काला होना

to be a source of constant vexation
chātī par mūṅg dalnā　　छाती पर मूंग दलना

be in a sad plight

nānī yād ānā नानी याद आना

to call a spade a spade

kharī-kharī sunānā खरी–खरी सुनाना

tit for tat

īṁṭ ka jawāb patthar se denā ईंट का जवाब पत्थर से देना

to die of shame

cullū bhar pānī meṁ ḍūb marnā

चुल्लू भर पानी में डूब मरना

to lose one's wits

hoś uṛ jānā होश उड़ जाना

to be in the seventh heaven

phūlā na samānā फूला न समाना

to raise false hopes

sabz bāg dikhānā सब्ज़ बाग दिखाना

to be a traditionalist

lakīr kā fakīr honā लकीर का फ़कीर होना

to be terror struck

muṁh par havāiyāṁ uṛnā मुँह पर हवाइयाँ उड़ना

to be meek and quiet

bhīgī billī bananā भीगी बिल्ली बनना

a child's play

bāeṁ hāth kā khel बाएँ हाथ का खेल

for a happy occasion to be marred

raṅg meṁ bhaṅg ḍālnā रंग में भंग डालना

VOCABULARY

A

able	yogyă (adj.)	योग्य
abortion	garbhpāt (m.)	गर्भपात
above	ūpar (adv.)	ऊपर
abroad	videś (m.)	विदेश
absolutely	bilkul (adv.)	बिल्कुल
accept	mānanā (v.t.)	मानना
	swīkār karnā (v.t.)	स्वीकार करना
accident	durghaṭnā (f.)	दुर्घटना
accommo-dation	āvās (m.)	आवास
	rahne kī jagah (f.)	रहने की जगह
accompany	sāth honā (v.i.)	साथ होना
across	pār (adv.)	पार
accuse	doṣ lagānā (v.t.)	दोष लगाना
acidity	khaṭṭī ḍakār(f.)	खट्टी डकार
	amlīyat(f.)	अमलीयत
aquarius	kumbh	कुम्भ
addiction	lat (f.)	लत
address	patā (m.)	पता
admire	sarāhnā (v.t.)	सराहना
	praśaṃsā karnā (v.t.)	प्रशंसा करना
admission	dākhilā (m.)	दाखिला

A

adult	vayask (adj.)	वयस्क
	bālig (adj.)	बालिग
advantage	lābh (m.)	लाभ
advice	salāh (f.)	सलाह
	parāmarś (m.)	परामर्श
advise	salāh denā (v.t.)	सलाह देना
	parāmarś denā (v.t.)	परामर्श देना
ad verbum	śabdśaḥ (adv.)	शब्दशः
advertise	vijñāpan denā (v.t.)	विज्ञापन देना
advertisement	vijñāpan (m.)	विज्ञापन
aeroplane	havāī jahāz (m.)	हवाई जहाज
after	ke bād (pp.)	के बाद
afternoon	aprāhn (m..)	अपराह्न
against	ke khilāf (pp.)	के ख़िलाफ
age	umra (f.)	उम्र
	āyu (f.)	आयु
ago	pahale (adv.)	पहले
aggressive	ugra (f.)	उग्र
agriculture	kheti-bāṛī (f.)	खेती–बाड़ी
	kṛṣi (f.)	कृषि
ahead	āge (adv.)	आगे
air	vāyu (f.)	वायु
	havā (f.)	हवा
airconditioned	vātānukūlit (adj.)	वातानुकूलित

A

airport	havāī aḍḍā (m.)	हवाई अड्डा
alert	sajag (adj.)	सजग
allow	anumati denā (v.t.)	अनुमति देना
almond	bādām (m.)	बादाम
almost	lagbhag (adv.), takrīban (adv.)	लगभग, तकरीबन
alone	akele (adv.)	अकेले
already	pahle se hī (adv.)	पहले से ही
also	bhī (particle.)	भी
altitude	ūṁcāī (f.)	ऊँचाई
always	hameśā (adv.)	हमेशा
amateur	śaukiyā (adj.)	शौकिया
ambiguous	golmol (adj.)	गोलमोल
	dohre matlabwālā (adj.)	दोहरे मतलबवाला
among	meṁ (pp.)	में
	ke bīc(pp.)	के बीच
amusement	manorañjan (m)	मनोरंजन
analyses	viśleṣaṇ (m.)	विश्लेषण
anarchy	arājaktā (f.)	अराजकता
and	aur (conj.)	और
anger	krodh (m.)	क्रोध
angry	kupit (adj.)	कुपित
	krodhit(adj.)	क्रोधित

A

animal	jānvar(m.)	जानवर
aniseed,fennel	saumph (f.)	सौंफ
ankle	ṭakhnā (m.)	टखना
announce	ghoṣṇā karnā (v.t.)	घोषणा करना
announcement	ghoṣṇā (f.)	घोषणा
annoy	khijhānā (v.i.)	खिझाना
annoyed	nārāz (adj.)	नाराज़
annual	salānā (adj.)	सलाना
	iksālā (adj.)	इकसाला
ant	cīṁtī (f.)	चींटी
antique	purātan(adj.)	पुरातन
	purāne samay kā	पुराने समय का
anticipate	pratyāśā karnā (v.t.),	प्रत्याशा करना
	aṭkal lagānā (v.t.)	अटकल लगाना
any	koī	कोई
apology	kṣamā (f.)	क्षमा
apologise	kṣamā māṁgnā (v.t.)	क्षमा मांगना
appendix	uṇḍuk	उण्डुक
applaud	praśaṃsā karnā (v.t.)	प्रशंसा करना
	vāh-vāh karnā (v.t.)	वाह–वाह करना
apple	seb (m.)	सेब
application	āvedan patra (m.)	आवेदन पत्र
appointment	milne kā samay (m.)	मिलने का समय
apricot	khumānī (f.)	खुमानी

A

approximately	lagbagh (adv.)	लगभग
archaeological	purātattvīyă (adj.)	पुरातत्तवीय
architect	vāstukār (m.)	वास्तुकार
argue	bahas karnā (v.t.)	बहस करना
aries	meṣa	मेष
arm	bāṁh (f.)	बाँह
arrange	prabandh karnā (v.t.)	प्रबन्ध करना
arrive	pahuṁcnā (v.i)	पहुँचना
arrival	āgman (m.)	आगमन
arrogance	ghamaṇḍ (m.)	घमण्ड
arrogant	ghamaṇḍī (adj.)	घमण्डी
art	kalā (f.)	कला
arteries	dhamniyāṁ (f.)	धमनियाँ
artificial	kṛtrim (adj.)	कृत्रिम
artist	kalākār (m.)	कलाकार
ascend	caṛhnā (v.i.)	चढ़ना
ascending node of the moon	rāhū	राहू
ascent	caṛhāī (f.)	चढ़ाई
ask	pūchnā (v.t.)	पूछना
ashtray	rākhdānī (m.)	राखदानी
asthma	damā	दमा
at least	kam-az-kam	कम–अज़–कम

B

babysitter	āyā	आया
back	pīṭh	पीठ
backpack	pīṭh par sāmān ḍhone kā jholā	पीठ पर सामान ढोने का झोला
backstitch	bakhiā	बखिया
bacteria	jīvāṇū	जीवाणु
baggage	sāmān	सामान
baggage claim	sāmān milne kī jagah	सामान मिलने की जगह
baker	ḍabal rotī banānewālā	डबल रोटी बनानेवाला
balance	bākī, śeṣ	बाकी, शेष
balcony	chajjā	छज्जा
ball	geṁd	गेंद
banana	kelā	केला
bandage	paṭṭī	पट्टी
bank	baiṅk	बैंक
bank account	khātā	खाता
barber	nāī	नाई
bargain	molbhāv	मोलभाव
barley	jau	जौ
basket	ṭokrī	टोकरी
basting (of a garment)	kacca taṁka	कच्चा टांका

bat	ballā	बल्ला
bathe	nahānā	नहाना
bathroom	gusalkhānā	गुसलख़ाना
batting	ballebājī	बल्लेबाजी
bayleaf	tejpattā	तेजपत्ता
beach	samudrataṭ	समुद्रतट
bear	bhālū	भालू
beautiful	sundar(adj.)	सुन्दर
bed	palaṅg(m.)	पलंग
bedbug	khaṭmal(m.)	खटमल
bedroom	śayan kakṣ(m.)	शयन कक्ष
	sone kā kamrā (m.)	सोने का कमरा
bee	madhumakkhī(f.)	मधुमक्खी
beet root	cukandar(m.)	चुकन्दर
before	pahle(adv.)	पहले
beggar	bhikhārī(m.)	भिखारी
begin	śurū karnā (v.t.)	शुरू करना
	śurū honā (v.i.)	शुरू होना
beginning	śurū(m.)	शुरू
behind	ke pīche (pp.)	के पीछे
belch	ḍakār lenā(v.t)	डकार लेना
bell	ghaṇṭī(f.)	घण्टी
below	nīce(adv.)	नीचे
beside	ke pās (pp)	के पास

B

besides	ke alāvā (pp)	के अलावा
	ke atirikt(pp)	के अतिरिक्त
best	sab se acchā	सब से अच्छा
	(adj. superlative)	
bet	śart (f.),	शर्त
	bāzī (f.)	बाज़ी
better	behtar	बेहतर
	(adj. comparative)	
	x se acchā	x से अच्छा
	(adj. comparative)	
between	ke bīc(pp)	के बीच
bicycle	sāikil(m.)	साइकिल
biennials	do-sālā (m.)	दो–साला
big	baṛā(adj.)	बड़ा
binoculars	dūrbīn(m.)	दूरबीन
biography	jīvnī (f.)	जीवनी
bird	ciṛiā (f.)	चिड़िया
birth certificate	janmpramāṇak(m.)	जन्मप्रमाणक
birth control	janm-niyantraṇ(m.)	जन्म–नियन्त्रण
birthday	janm-din(m.)	जन्म–दिन
birth rate	janm-dar(m.)	जन्म–दर
bite	kāṭnā (v.t.)	काटना
bitter	kaṛvā (adj.)	कड़वा
black	kālā (adj.)	काला

black cumin	śah jīrā (m.)	शह जीरा
black gram	kālā canā	काला चना
bladder	mūtrāśyă (m.)	मूत्राशय
blanket	kambal (m.)	कम्बल
bleat	mimiyānā (v.i.)	मिमियाना
bleed	khūn bahnā (v.i.)	खून बहना
bless	aśīrvād denā (v.t.)	आशीर्वाद देना
blessing	aśīrvād (m.)	आशीर्वाद
blink	āṁkh jhapaknā (v.i.)	आँख झपकना
blister	chālā (m.)	छाला
blood	khūn (m.)	खून
blood group	khūn kī kism (f.)	खून की किस्म
blood pressure	rakt cāp (m.)	रक्त चाप
blood pressure high	ucc rakt cāp (m.)	उच्च रक्त चाप
blood pressure low	nimn rakt cāp (m.)	निम्न रक्त चाप
blood test	khūn kī jāṁc (f.)	खून की जाँच
blue	nīlā (adj.)	नीला
blue sapphire	nīlam (m.)	नीलम
blush	lajjā se cehrā lāl honā (v.i.)	लज्जा से चेहरा लाल होना
body	śarīr (m.)	शरीर
boil	phoṛā (m.)	फोड़ा

B

bone	haḍḍī (f.)	हड्डी
book	pustak (f.)	पुस्तक
	kitāb (f.)	किताब
book fair	pustak mela (m.)	पुस्तक मेला
bookshop	kitāb kī dukān (f.)	किताब की दुकान
	pustak bhaṇḍār (m.)	पुस्तक भण्डार
boring	ubāū (adj.)	उबाऊ
borrow	udhār lenā (v.i.)	उधार लेना
both	donoṁ	दोनों
bottle	botal (f.)	बोतल
	śīśī (f.)	शीशी
bottle opener	botal kholnewālā (m.)	बोतल खोलनेवाला
bottle gourd	laukī (f.)	लौकी
bottom	niclā bhāg (adj. + m.)	निचला भाग
box	sandūk (m.)	सन्दूक
boxing	mukkebāzī (f.)	मुक्केबाज़ी
boy	laṛkā (m.)	लड़का
boyfriend		
brackish	khārā (adj.)	खारा
brain	dimāg (m.)	दिमाग
branch	ṭahnī (f.)	टहनी
	śākhā (f.)	शाखा
brass	pītal (m.)	पीतल

brave	bahādur (adj.)	बहादुर
bray	reṁknā (v.i.)	रेंकना
bread	ḍabal roṭī (f.)	डबल रोटी
break	ṭūṭnā (v.i.)	टूटना
breakfast	nāśtā (m.)	नाश्ता
breathe	śvās lenā (v.)	श्वास लेना
	sāṃs lenā (v.)	सांस लेना
bribe	riśvat (f.)	रिश्वत
bribe (give..)	riśvat denā (v.t.)	रिश्वत देना
(take..)	riśvat lenā (v.t.)	रिश्वत लेना
bridge	pul (m)	पुल
bright	camkīlā (adj.)	चमकीला
brilliant	pratibhāśālī (adj.)	प्रतिभाशाली
bring	lānā (v.t.)	लाना
brinjal	baiṅgan (m.)	बैंगन
broad	cauṛā (adj.)	चौड़ा
brother	bhāī (m.)	भाई
brown	bhūrā (adj.)	भूरा
bruise	kharoc (f.)	खरोच
bucket	bālṭī (f.)	बाल्टी
bud	kalī	कली
building	bhavan(m.)	भवन
buffalo	bhaiṁs (f.)	भैंस
burp	ḍakār dilānā (v.)	डकार दिलाना

bus	bas (f.)	बस
bus stop	bas aḍḍā (m.)	बस अड्डा
bush	jhaṛī (f.)	झड़ी
business	vyāpār (m.)	व्यापार
businessman	vyāpārī (m.)	व्यापारी
busy	vyast (adj.)	व्यस्त
but	lekin (coj.)	लेकिन
butcher	kasāī (m.)	कसाई
butter	makkhan (m.)	मक्खन
buy	kharīdnā (v.t.)	खरीदना
buyer	kharīdār (m.)	खरीदार
cabbage	pattā-gobhī (f.)	पत्ता–गोभी
calendar	kalaṇḍar (m.)	कलण्डर
	pañcāṅg (m.)	पंचांग
camel	ūṁṭ (m.)	ऊँट
camera	kaimrā (m.)	कैमरा
can	saknā (v)	सकना
can	ḍibbā (m.)	डिब्बा
cancer	kark	कर्क
can opener	ḍibbā kholnewālā (m.)	डिब्बा खोलनेवाला
candidate	ummīdvār (m.)	उम्मीदवार
candle	mombattī (f.)	मोमबत्ती
car	kār (f.)	कार
	gāṛī (f.)	गाड़ी

C

care(n.)	cintā (f.)	चिन्ता
cap	topī (f.)	टोपी
capricorn	makar	मकर
capsicum	pahāṛī mirc (f.)	पहाड़ी मिर्च
carpenter	baṛhaī(m.)	बढ़ई
carrom seed	ajwāyan (f.)	अजवायन
carrot	gājar (f.)	गाजर
carry	le jānā (v.i.)	ले जाना
cartilage	upasthi (f.)	उपस्थि
carton	ḍabbā (m.)	डब्बा
cash	nakad (f.), rokaṛ(f.)	नकद, रोकड़
cashew	kājū	काजू
cashier	khajāncī (m.)	खजान्ची
cathedral	baṛa girjā (m.)	बड़ा गिरजा
cat	billī (f.)	बिल्ली
cat's eye	lahsuniyā (m.)	लहसुनिया
cauliflower	phūl-gobhī (f.)	फूल–गोभी
caution	sāvdhānī (f.)	सावधानी
cave	gufā (f.)	गुफ़ा
ceiling	chat (f.)	छत
cemetery	kabristān (m.)	कब्रिस्तान
	śavbhūmī(f.)	शवभूमी
central-government	kendrīyă sarkār (f.)	केन्द्रीय सरकार

C

certificate	pramāṇ patra (m.)	प्रमाण पत्र
chair	kursī (f.)	कुर्सी
chalk	căk	चॉक
cheap	sastā (adj.)	सस्ता
check	jāṁcnā (v.t.)	जाँचना
check out	choṛnā (v.t.) (होटल)	छोड़ना
cheek	gāl (m.)	गाल
cheese	panīr (m.)	पनीर
chef	mahārāj (m.)	महाराज
	<u>kh</u>ānsāmā (m.)	खानसामा
chest	sīnā (m.)/chātī (f.)	सीना/छाती
chew	cabānā (v.t.)	चबाना
chicken	murgā (m.)	मुर्गा
chick peas(m.)	kābulī cane	काबुली चने
chief minister	mukhyă mantrī (m.)	मुख्य मन्त्री
child	baccā (m.)	बच्चा
childhood	bacpan (m.)	बचपन
childish	backānā (adj.)	बचकाना
chin	ṭhoṛī (f.)	थोड़ी
chirp	cahaknā (v.i.)	चहकना
church	girjāghar (m.)	गिरजाघर
cinnamon	dārcīnī (f.)	दारचीनी
citizen	nāgrik (m.)	नागरिक

C

city	śahar (m.)	शहर
clap	tālī bajānā (v.t.)	ताली बजाना
class	kakṣā (f.)	कक्षा
	varg (m.)	वर्ग
class system	varṇvyavasthā (f.)	वर्णव्यवस्था
clean	sāf (adj.)	साफ़
clever	catur (f.)	चतुर
cleverness	caturāī (adj.)	चतुराई
client	grāhak (m.)	ग्राहक
climb	caṛhnā (v.i.)	चढ़ना
clinic	upcārālay (m.)	उपचारालय
clock	ghaṛī (f.)	घड़ी
clogged	band ho jānā (v.i.)	बन्द हो जाना
	ruk jānā (v.i.)	रुक जाना
close	band karnā (v.t.)	बन्द करना
closed	band (adj.)	बन्द
clothes	kapṛe (m.pl.)	कपड़े
cloud(s)	bādal (m.)	बादल
cloves	lauṅg (m.)	लौंग
cobbler	mocī (m.)	मोची
cocoanut oil	nāriyal kā tel (m.)	नारियल का तेल
cockroach	tilcaṭṭā (m.)	तिलचट्टा
cold	jukhām (m.)	जुख़ाम
cold(have a..)	jukhām honā (v.i.)	जुख़ाम होना

C

cold	ṭhaṇḍā (adj.)	ठण्डा
color	raṅg (m.)	रंग
colorful	raṅg-biraṅgā (adj.)	रंग–बिरंगा
comb	kaṅghī (f.)	कंघी
comb	kaṅghī karnā (v.t.)	कंघी करना
	bāl banānā (v.t.)	बाल बनाना
comedy	sukhant nāṭak (m.)	सुखन्त नाटक
comfortable	sukhkar (adj.)	सुखकर
	ārāmdeh (adj.)	आरामदेह
comic	vinod patrikā (f.)	विनोद पत्रिका
command	ādeś (m.)	आदेश
communism	sāmyăvād (m.)	साम्यवाद
communist	sāmyăvādī (m.)	साम्यवादी
companion	sāthī (m.)	साथी
compare	tulnā karnā (v.t.)	तुलना करना
comparison	tulnā (f.)	तुलना
compass	kampas (m.)	परकार
compensate	kṣatipūrti karnā (v.t.)	क्षतिपूर्ति करना
	muāvzā denā (v.t.)	मुआवज़ा देना
complaint	śikāyat (f.)	शिकायत
compliment	praśaṃsā karnā (v.t.)	प्रशंसा करना
concert	goṣṭhī (f.)	गोष्ठी
condolences	mātampursī (f.)	मातमपुसी

confused	vikṣipt (adj..)	विक्षिप्त
confused (..state)	vikṣipt avasthā (f.)	विक्षिप्त अवस्था
constable	sipāhī (m.)	सिपाही
constipation	kabz (f.)	कब्ज़
contraceptive	garbhnirodhak (m.)	गर्भनिरोधक
convenience	suvidhā (f.)	सुविधा
convenient	suvidhā janak (adj.)	सुविधाजनक
conversation	bāt-cīt (f.)	बात–चीत
cook	khānā pakānā (v.t.)	खाना पकाना
copper	tāṁbā (m.)	ताँबा
coriander	dhaniyā (m.)	धनिया
corn(maize)	makkā (m.)	मक्का
corner	konā (m.)	कोना
corrupt	bhraṣṭ (adj.)	भ्रष्ट
corruption	bhraṣṭācār(m.)	भ्रष्टाचार
cough	khāṁsī (f.)	खाँसी
	khāṁsnā (v.i.)	खाँसना
count	ginanā (v.t.)	गिनना
country	deś(m.)	देश
countryside	dehāt (m.)	देहात
courage	himmat(f.)	हिम्मत
	sāhas(m.)	साहस

C

C

court	kacharī	
courtesy	saujanyă(m.)	सौजन्य
courtship	śādī se pahle	शादी से पहले
	mel-jol(m.)	मेल–जोल
cow	gāy (f.)	गाय
cowardly	asāhasī (adj.)	असाहसी
cramps	maroṛ (m.)	मरोड़
cream	malāī (f.)	मलाई
creeper	bel (f.) latā (f.)	बेल; लता
crematorium	śmaśān (m.)	शमशान
crime	aprādh (m.)	अपराध
criminal	aprādhī (m.)	अपराधी
criminal law	daṇḍvidhān (m.)	दण्डविधान
croak	ṭarrānā (v.i.)	टर्राना
crochet	kirośiyā	किरोशिया
crocodile	magarmacch (m.)	मगरमच्छ
crop	fasal (f.)	फ़सल
crossing	caurāhā (m.)	चौराहा
crow	kauvā (m.)	कौवा
crowded	khacā-khac bhārā	खचा–खच भरा
	huā (adj.)	हुआ
	saṅkul(adj.)	संकुल
cruel	krūr(adj.)	क्रूर

cube	ghan (m.)	घन
	trighāt(m.)	त्रिघात
cucumber	khīrā(m.)	खीरा
cumin seed	safed jīrā (m.)	सफ़ेद जीरा
cunning	cālāk (adj.)	चालाक
cup	pyālā (m.)	प्याला
cupboard	ālmārī (f.)	आलमारी
curator	saṅgrahpāl (m.)	संग्रहपाल
curiosity	utsuktā (f.)	उत्सुकता
currency	mudrā (f.)	मुद्रा
current-account	cālū khātā (m.)	चालू खाता
curtain	pardā (m.)	पर्दा
custard apple	śarīfā (m.)	शरीफ़ा
custom	prathā (f.)	प्रथा
customs duty	sīmā-śulk (m.)	सीमा–
cut	kāṭnā(v.t.)	काटना
cylinder	belan ke ākār kā rambh (m.)	बेलन के आकार का रम्भ
daily	roz (adv.)	रोज़
dairy products	dugdh padārth (m.)	दुग्ध पदार्थ
damaged	kṣatigrast (adj.)	क्षतिग्रस्त
danger	khatrā (m.)	ख़तरा
dangerous	khatarnāk (adj.)	ख़तरनाक

D

daring	sāhsī (adj.)	साहसी
dark	andherā (m.)	अन्धेरा
dark color	gahrā raṅg (adj. + m.)	गहरा रंग
dark - complexion	sāṁvlā raṅg (adj.+m.)	साँवला रंग
darn	rafū karnā	रफू करना
data	āṅkṛe(m.)	आंकड़े
date	tārīkh (f.)	तारीख़
dates	khajūr	खजूर
dates (dried)	chuhārā	छुहारा
date of birth	janm tithi (f.)	जन्म तिथि
daughter	laṛkī (f.)	लड़की
dawn	prabhāt (m.)	प्रभात
day	din (m.)	दिन
day after tomorrow	parsoṁ (adv)	परसों
day before yesterday	parsoṁ (adv.)	परसों
deaf	bahrā (adj./n.)	बहरा
death	mṛtyu (f.)	मृत्यु
debility	kamzorī	कमज़ोरी
decide	faislā karnā (v.t.)	फ़ैसला करना
deep	gahrā (adj.)	गहरा
defence	pratirakṣā (f.)	प्रतिरक्षा

delay (n.)	vilamb (m.)	विलम्ब
	der (f.)	देर
delay	vilamb /der karnā (v.t.)	विलम्ब/देर करना
	vilamb/der honā (v.i.)	विलम्ब/देर होना
delicious	swādiṣṭ (adj.)	स्वादिष्ट
democracy	loktantra (m.)	लोकतन्त्र
demonstration	pradarśan(m.)	प्रदर्शन
dentist	dāṁt kā dāukṭar(m.)	दाँत का डॉक्टर
deny	nā mānanā (v.t.)	ना मानना
deodorant	durgandhhar (adj.)	दुर्गन्धहर
depart	calā jānā (v.i.)	चला जाना
	ravānā honā (v.i.)	रवाना होना
department	vibhāg (m.)	विभाग
departure	chūtnā (m.)	छूटना
	ravānăgī (f.)	रवानगी
descend	utarnā (v.i.)	उतरना
desert	registān (m.)	रेगिस्तान
detour	cakkarwālā rāstā	चक्करवाला रास्ता
diabetes	madhumeh (m.)	मधुमेह
diamond	hīrā (m.)	हीरा
diet	āhār (m.)	आहार
diet-control	āhār niyantraṇ (m.)	आहार नियन्त्रण
different	bhinn (adj.)	भिन्न

D

difficult	kaṭhin (adj.)	कठिन
difficulty	kaṭhināī (f.)	कठिनाई
dilemma	duvidhā (f.)	दुविधा
	a'samañjas (m.)	असमन्जस
diligent	mehntī (adj.)	मेहनती
dinner	rāt kā khānā (m.)	रात का खाना
direction	diśā (f.)	दिशा
disappointed	nirāś (adj.)	निराश
disappointment	nirāśā (f.)	निराशा
discount	chūṭ (f.)	छूट
discover	khojnā (v.t.)	खोजना
disease	bīmārī (f.)	बीमारी
	rog (m.)	रोग
dispensary	davākhānā (m.)	दवाखाना
	ḍispainsarī (f.)	डिसपेन्सरी
distress	hairānī (f.)	हैरानी
distributor	vitrak (m.)	वितरक
disturb	aśānt karnā (v.t.)	अशान्त करना
dive	gotā lagānā (v.t.)	गोता लगाना
	ḍubkī lagānā (v.t.)	डुबकी लगाना
dizziness	cakkar ānā (v.i.)	चक्कर आना
do	karnā (v.t.)	करना
dog	kuttā (m.)	कुत्ता
dog-bite	kutte kā kāṭnā (m.)	कुत्ते का काटना

E

door	darvāzā (m.)	दरवाज़ा
downhill	ḍhāl (f.)	ढाल
drain	nālī (f.)	नाली
dream	svapn (m.)	स्वप्न
dress	pośāk (f.)	पोशाक
drought	sūkhā (m.)	सूखा
drowse	ūṁghnā (v.i.)	ऊँघना
drug	davāī (f.)	दवाई
drug store	davāī kī dukān(f.)	दवाई की दुकान
dry	sūkhā (adj.)	सूखा
	sukhānā (v.t.)	सुखाना
	sūkhnā (v.i.)	सूखना
dumb	gūṅgā (adj./n)	गूंगा
each	pratyek (adv.)	प्रत्येक
ear	kān (m.)	कान
early	jaldī (adv)	जल्दी
early morning	subah-subah	सुबह–सुबह
earn	kamānā (v.t.)	कमाना
earning	kamāī (f.)	कमाई
earth	dharatī (f.)	धरती
earthquake	bhūkamp (m.)	भूकम्प
east	pūrv	पूर्व
Easter	īsā ke punarjanm kā din (m.)	ईसा के पुनर्जन्म का दिन

E

easy	āsān (adj.)	आसान
eat	khānā (v.t./n)	खाना
economics	arthśāstra (m.)	अर्थशास्त्र
economy	arthvyavasthā (f.)	अर्थव्यवस्था
editor	sampādak (m.)	सम्पादक
education	śikṣā (f.)	शिक्षा
elections	cunāv (m.)	चुनाव
electorate	cunāv-kṣetra (m.)	चुनाव–क्षेत्र
electricity	bijlī (f.)	बिजली
elephant	hāthī (m.)	हाथी
elegance	prāñjaltā (f.)	प्राञ्जलता
	cārutā (f.)	चारुता
elegant	prāñjal (adj.)	प्राञ्जल
	suśiṣṭ (adj.)	सुशिष्ट
egg plant	baiṅgan (m.)	बैंगन
egoism	ahaṃbhāv (m.)	अहंभाव
egoist	ahaṃvādī (m.)	अहंवादी
embassy	dūtāvās (m.)	दूतावास
embroidery	kaṛhāī	कढ़ाई
emerald	pannā (m.)	पन्ना
emergency	āpāt (m.)	आपात
emeritus	sevāmukt (adj.)	सेवामुक्त
employee	karmcārī (m.)	कर्मचारी
employer	mālik (m.)	मालिक

emotion	bhāv (m.)	भाव
empty	khālī (adj.)	खाली
empty	khālī karnā (v.t.)	खाली करना
encourage	protsāhit karnā (v.t.)	प्रोत्साहित करना
end	ant (m.)	अन्त
endanger	khatre meṁ ḍālnā (v.t.)	ख़तरे में डालना
enemy	śatru (m.)	शत्रु
engagement	sagāī (f.)	सगाई
engineer	abhiyantā (m.)	अभियन्ता
engineering	abhiyāntrikī (f.)	अभियांत्रिकी
enjoy	ānand lenā (v.t.)	आनन्द लेना
enough	bas! (interj.)	बस!
	kāfī (adv./adj.)	काफ़ी
enter	praveś karnā (v.t.)	प्रवेश करना
entrance	praveś (m.)	प्रवेश
	bhītar jāne kā mārg	भीतर जाने का मार्ग
envelope	lifāfā (m.)	लिफ़ाफ़ा
envious	spardhī (adj.)	स्पर्धी
	īrśyālu (adj.)	ईर्ष्यालु
environment	paryāvaraṇ (m.)	पर्यावरण
envy	spardhā (f.)	स्पर्धा
	īrśyā (f.)	ईर्ष्या
epidemic	mahāmārī (f.)	महामारी

E

epilepsy	mirgī (f.)	मिर्गी
equal-opportunity	samān avsar (m.)	समान अवसर
equal rights	samān adhikār(m.)	समान अधिकार
equality	samāntā (f.)	समानता
	barābarī (f.)	बराबरी
equipment	upkaraṇ(m.)	उपकरण
errata	śuddhi-patra (m.)	शुद्धि–पत्र
etcetera	ādi (adv.)	आदि
eternal	nityă (adj.)	नित्य
euthanasia	sukh mṛtyu (f.)	सुख मृत्यु
evaluate	mūlyāṅkan karnā	मूल्यांकन करना
evening	śām (f.)	शाम
	sandhyā (f.)	सन्ध्या
everdry	sadāśuṣk	सदा शुष्क
evergreen	sadābahār	सदा बहार
every day	har roz (adv.)	हर रोज़
everything	sab kuch	सब कुछ
example	udāharaṇ (m.)	उदाहरण
excellent	bahut baṛhiyā	बहुत बढ़िया
	utkṛṣṭ (adj.)	उत्कृष्ट
exchange	badalnā (v.t.)	बदलना
excitement	utsāh (m.)	उत्साह
Excuse me!	māf kījie	माफ़ कीजिए

E

exhale	śvās bāhar nikālnā	श्वास बाहर निकालना
exhibition	pradarśanī (f.)	प्रदर्शनी
exit	nikās (m.)	निकास
exotic	vijātīyă (adj.)	विजातीय
	haṭ ke	हट के
expensive	mahaṁgā (adj.)	महँगा
experience	anubhav(m.)	अनुभव
experiment	prayog (m.)	प्रयोग
experimental	prāyogic (adj.)	प्रायोगिक
explain	samjhānā (v.t.)	समझाना
exploitation	śoṣaṇ (m.)	शोषण
export	niryāt karnā (v.t.)	निर्यात करना
export	niryāt (m.)	निर्यात
express	abhivyakt karnā (v.t.)	अभिव्यक्त करना
express train	drutgāmī rel (f.)	द्रुतगामी रेल
expression	abhivyakti (f.)	अभिव्यक्ति
extra	atirikt	अतिरिक्त
	fāltū	फ़ालतू
extraordinary	asādhāraṇ (adj.)	असाधारण
extravagant	kharcīlā (adj.)	खर्चीला
extreme	ati (adv.)	अति
	bahut zyādā	बहुत ज़्यादा
eye	āṁkh (f)	आँख

F

faith	śraddhā (f.)	श्रद्धा
face	muṁh (m.)	मुँह
faded	badraṅg	बदरंग
fall	girnā (v.i)	गिरना
	patjhaṛ (m.)	पतझड़
false	asatyă (adj./m.)	असत्य
family	parivār (m.)	परिवार
famine	akāl (m.)	अकाल
famous	maśhūr (adj.)	मशहूर
fan	paṅkhā (m.)	पंखा
fan(turn on..)	paṅkhā kholnā (v.t.)	पंखा खोलना
fan(turn off..)	pankhā band karnā (v.t.)	पंखा बन्द करना
fantastic	anokhā (adj.)	अनोखा
	adbhut (adj.)	अद्‌भुत
far	dūr (adv.)	दूर
farewell	vidāī (f.)	विदाई
farm	khet (m.)	खेत
farmer	kisān (m.)	किसान
fast	tej (adj.)	तेज
	drutgāmī (adj.)	द्रुतगामी
	upvās (m.)	उपवास
	vrat (m.)	व्रत
	upvās karnā (v.t.)	उपवास करना

F

	vrat karnā (v.t.)	व्रत करना
fat	moṭā (adj.)	मोटा
	ciknāī (f.)	चिकनाई
	carbī (f.)	चर्बी
fatal	prāṇghātak (adj.)	प्राणघातक
fatalism	bhāgyavād (m.)	भाग्यवाद
fatigue	thakān (f.)	थकान
fault	doṣ (m.)	दोष
fee	śulk (m.)	शुल्क
feel	mahsūs karnā (v.t.)	महसूस करना
feelings	anubhūti(f.)	अनुभूति
feet	pair (m.)	पैर
fence	jaṅglā (m.)	जंगला
fenugreek seed	methī dānā (m.)	मेथी दाना
festival	tyohār (m.)	त्योहार
fever	bukhār (m.)	बुखार
few	kuch (adj.)	कुछ
	katipay (adj.)	कतिपय
fiance/fiancee	maṅgetar (m./f.)	मंगेतर
field	maidān (m.)	मैदान
fight	laṛāī (f.)	लड़ाई
fill	bharnā (v.t.)	भरना
find	milnā (v.i.)	मिलना
find out	patā lagānā (v.t.)	पता लगाना

F

fine	daṇḍ (m.)	दण्ड
	jurmānā (m.)	जुर्माना
fine	bahut baṛhiyā (adj.)	बहुत बढ़िया
finger	uṅglī (f.)	उंगली
fire	agni (f.)	अग्नि
fire engine	damkal gāṛī (f.)	दमकल गाड़ी
fire station	damkal ghar	दमकल घर
	agniśaman kendra	अग्निशमन केन्द्र
fire-works	paṭākhe (m.)	पटाखे
first	pahlā (adj.)	पहला
first aid kit	farsṭ ed kiṭ;	फर्स्ट एड किट;
	prāthmik upcār ke	प्रारम्भिक उपचार
	sāmān kī peṭī (m.)	के सामान की
		पट्टी
F.I.R.	aif. āī. ār	एफ आई आर
	prāthmik sūcnā	प्रारम्भिक सूचना
	rapaṭ (f.)	रपट
fish	machlī (f.)	मछली
flea	pissū (m.)	पिस्सू
flight	uṛān (f.)	उड़ान
flood	bāṛh (f.)	बाढ़
floor	farś (m.)	फर्श
flour (black gram)	besan (m.)	बेसन

F

flour (wheat)	ātā (m.)	आटा
flower	phūl (m.)	फूल
fly	uṛnā (v.i.)	उड़ना
fly(house..)	makkhī (f.)	मक्खी
food	khānā (m.)	खाना
footpath	pagḍaṇḍī (f.)	पगदण्डी
forbidden	varjit (adj.)	वर्जित
	niṣiddh (adj.)	निषिद्ध
forebearance	sahanśīltā (f.)	सहनशीलता
forehead	māthā (m.)	माथा
foreign	videśī (adj.)	विदेशी
foreigner	videśī (n.)	विदेशी
forenoon	pūrvāhn (m.)	पूर्वाह्न
forest	jaṅgal (m.)	जंगल
	van (m.)	वंन
forgive	kṣamā karnā (v.t.)	क्षमा करना
	māf karnā (v.t.)	माफ करना
fort	kilā (m.)	किला
fortune teller	jyotiṣī (m.)	ज्योतिषी
free	swatantra (adj.)	स्वतन्त्र
	āzād (adj.)	आज़ाद
free of cost	muft (adj.)	मुफ्त
freedom	swatantratā (f.)	स्वतन्त्रता
	āzādī (f.)	आज़ादी

G

freeze	ṭhiṭhurnā (v.i.)	ठिठुरना
frequently	bār-bār (adv.)	बार–बार
fresh	tāzā (adj.)	ताज़ा
Friday	śukravār (m.)	शुक्रवार
friend	dost (m./f.)	दोस्त
	mitra (m./f.)	मित्र
frog	meṁḍhak (m.)	मेंढक
frown	tayorī caṛhnā (v.i.)	त्योरी चढ़ना
fried	talā hua	तला हुआ
fry	talnā (v.t.)	तलना
frozen	jamā hua (adj.)	जमा हुआ
fruit	phal (m.)	फल
full	bharā huā (adj.)	भरा हुआ
fun	mauj-mastī (f.)	मौज–मस्ती
	dillagī (f.)	दिल्लगी
funeral	dāh saṃskār (m.)	दाह संस्कार
future	bhaviṣyă (m.)	भविष्य
games	khel (m.)	खेल
garbage	kūṛā (m.)	कूड़ा
gain	lābh (m.)	लाभ
garden	bāgīcā (m.)	बागीचा
gardner	mālī (m.)	माली
gardening	bāgwānī (f.)	बागवानी
garlic	lahsun (m.)	लहसुन

gate	phāṭak (m.)	फाटक
gemini	mithun	मिथुन
generous	dānī (adj.)	दानी
	udār (adj.)	उदार
ghee	ghī (m.)	घी
giddiness	cakkar ānā (v.i.)	चक्कर आना
ginger	adrak (m.)	अदरक
girl	laṛkī (f.)	लड़की
give	denā (v.t.)	देना
gloves	dastāne (m.)	दस्ताने
glue	goṁd (f.)	गोंद
go	jānā (v.i.)	जाना
goal	lakṣyă (m.)	लक्ष्य
goat	bakrī (f.)	बकरी
god	devtā (m.)	देवता
God	bhagvān (m.)	भगवान
gold	sonā (m.)	सोना
golden	sunahrā (adj.)	सुनहरा
gossip	gap mārnā (v.t.)	गप मारना
gossip	gap (f.)	गप
government	sarkār (f.)	सरकार
gout	gaṭhiyā (m.)	गठिया
grain	dānā (m.)	दाना

G

grains	anāj (m.)	अनाज
grandson	potā (son' son)	पोता
	nātī (daughter's son)	नाती
granddaughter	potī (son's daughter)	पोती
	nātin (daughter's daughter)	नातिन
grandfather	dādā (father's father)	दादा
	nānā (mother's father)	नाना
grandmother	dādī (father's mother)	दादी
	nānī (mother's mother)	नानी
grapes	aṅgūr (m.)	अंगूर
grass	dūb (f.)	दूब
grate	retnā (v.t.)	रेतना
grave	kabra (f.)	कब्र
graveyard	kabristān (m.)	कब्रिस्तान
greasy	ciknā (adj.)	चिकना
green	harā (adj.)	हरा
greenery	hariyālī (f.)	हरियाली
greengrocer	śāk vikretā (m.)	शाक विक्रेता
	sabzīwālā (m.)	सब्ज़ीवाला
greet	abhivādan karnā (v.t.)	अभिवादन करना
grief	śok (m.)	शोक
grocer	kiranewālā (m.)	किरानेवाला

H

groundnuts	mūṁgphalī	मूंगफली
guide	gāīḍ (m.)	गाईड
grunt	ghurghurānā (v.i.)	घुरघुराना
guava	amrūd (m.)	अमरूद
gulf	khāṛī (f.)	खाड़ी
guidebook	gāīḍbuk (f.)	गाईडबुक
guilt sense	aprādhbodh(m.)	अपराधबोध
hair	bāl (m.)	बाल
half	ādhā	आधा
hammer	hathauṛā (m.)	हथौड़ा
hand	hāth (m.)	हाथ
handicrafts	dastkārī (f.)	दस्तकारी
handkerchief	rūmāl	रूमाल
happiness	khuśī (f.)	खुशी
happy	*kh*uś (adj.)	खुश
harbour	bandargāh(m.)	बन्दरगाह
harvest	fasal kāṭnā (v.t.)	फ़सल काटना
haughtiness	abhimān (m.)	अभिमान
haughty	abhimānī (adj.)	अभिमानी
have(to...)	ke pas honā	के पास होना
hazelnuts	piṅgal phal	पिंगल फल
head	sir (m.)	सिर
health	swāsthyă (m.)	स्वास्थ्य
healthy	swāsthyăprad (adj)	स्वास्थ्यप्रद

H

heart	dil (m.)	दिल
heart attack	dil kā daurā	दिल का दौरा
hell	narak (m.)	नरक
help	madad (f.)	मदद
hemming	turpan	तुरपन
herb	jaṛī būṭī	जड़ी बूटी
hexagon	ṣaṭkoṇ (m.)	षटकोण
to hiccough	hickī lenā (v.t.)	हिचकी लेना
high	ūṁcā (adj.)	ऊँचा
highway	rājpath	राजपथ
hill	ṭīlā (m.)	टीला
hire	kirāye par lenā (v.t.)	किराये पर लेना
hiss	phuphkārnā (v.i.)	फुफकारना
historical	aitihāsik (adj.)	ऐतिहासिक
holiday	chuṭṭī kā din (m.)	छुट्‌टी का दिन
horrible	ḍrāvanā (adj.)	डरावना
	arucikar (adj.)	अरुचिकर
horse	ghoṛā (m.)	घोड़ा
horse-riding	ghuṛswārī(f.)	घुड़सवारी
hospitable	satkārśīl (adj.)	सत्कारशील
hospital	aspatāl (m.)	अस्पताल
hospitality	ātithyă (m.)	आतिथ्य
	āvbhagat (f.)	आवभगत

house	ghar (m.)	घर
housework	ghar ka kām (m.)	घर का काम
hug	āliṅgan (m.)	आलिंगन
	āliṅgan karnā (v.t.)	आलिंगन करना
human	mānavīyă (adj.)	मानवीय
humanist	mānavvādī (m./adj.)	मानववादी
resources	jan-saṁsādhan (m.)	जन–संसाधन
human rights	mānav-adhikār (m.)	मानव–अधिकार
hundred	sau	सौ
hungry	bhūkhā (adj.)	भूखा
hunt	śikār karnā (v.t.)	शिकार करना
husband	pati (m.)	पति
hurricane	pracaṇḍ āndhī (f.)	प्रचण्ड आँधी
hypertension	atiśay mānsik	अतिशय मानसिक
	tanāv (m.)	तनाव
hypocrisy	dambh (m.)	दम्भ
hypocrite	dambhī vyakti (m.)	दम्भी व्यक्ति
I	maiṁ (pron.)	मैं
Idea	vicār (m.)	विचार
Identity card	paricayă patra (m.)	परिचय पत्र
Idiot	mūṛh (adj.)	मूर्ख
	jāṛmati (adj.)	जाड़मति
irrigation	siṁcāī (f.)	सिंचाई
irrigate	sīṁcnā (v.t.)	सींचना

I

	khet meṁ pānī denā (v.t.)	खेत में पानी देना
immigration	āvasan (m.)	आवसन
	videś nivās (m.)	विदेश निवास
immortal	amar (adj.)	अमर
import	āyāt (m.)	आयात
	āyāt karnā (v.t.)	आयात करना
important	zarūrī (adj.)	ज़रूरी
impossible	asambhav (adj.)	असम्भव
	duṣkar (adj.)	दुष्कर
impress	prabhāvit karnā (v.t.)	प्रभावित करना
improper	anucit (adj.)	अनुचित
in a hurry	jaldī meṁ	जल्दी में
including	ke sahit(pp)	के सहित
income	āya (f.)	आय
	āmdanī (f.)	आमदनी
income tax	āya-kar (m.)	आय-कर
	inkam taiks (m.)	इनकम टैक्स
incomprehen-sible	abodhyă (adj.)	अबोध्य
in front of	ke sāmne (pp)	के सामने
indigestion	badhazmī (f.)	बदहज़मी
industry	udyog (m.)	उद्योग
industrialist	udyogpati	उद्योगपति

inequality	asamāntā (f.)	असमानता
inferiority complex	hīn bhāvnā (f.)	हीन भावना
inform	sūcnā denā (v.t.)	सूचना देना
information	sūcnā (f.)	सूचना
inhale	śvās andar lenā (v.t.)	श्वास अन्दर लेना
inject	suī lagānā (v.t.)	सुई लगाना
injury	coṭ (f.)	चोट
injustice	anyāy (m.)	अन्याय
inside	andar (adv.)	अन्दर
insipid	phīkā (adj.)	फीका
inspect	nirīkṣaṇ karnā (v.t.)	निरीक्षण करना
instructor	praśikṣak (m.)	प्रशिक्षक
insurance	bīmā (m.)	बीमा
intelligent	buddhimān (adj.)	बुद्धिमान
interesting	rocak (adj.)	रोचक
international	antarrāśtrīyă (adj.)	अन्तर्राष्ट्रीय
intermission	antrāl (m.)	अन्तराल
intestines	aṁtaṛiyāṁ (f.)	अँतडियाँ
intolerable	asahnīyă (adj.)	असहनीय
invite	āmantrit karnā (v.t.)	आमन्त्रित करना
island	dwīp (m.)	द्वीप
itch	khujlī (f.)	खुजली
itinerary	yātrā vivraṇ (m.)	यात्रा विवरण

J

jackfruit	kaṭ'hal(m.)	कटहल
jail	jel (m.)	जेल
	bandīgṛh(m.)	बन्दीगृह
jar	kalaś (m.)	कलश
jealous	īrṣyālu (adj.)	ईर्ष्यालु
jealousy	īrṣyā (f.)	ईर्ष्या
jewellery	ābhūṣaṇ(m.)	आभूषण
	gahnā(m.)	गहना
job	dhandhā (m.)	धन्धा
	naukrī (f.)	नौकरी
joke	mazāk karnā (v.t.)	मज़ाक करना
journalist	patrakār (m.)	पत्रकार
journey	yātrā (f.)	यात्रा
judge	nyāyādhīś (m.)	न्यायाधीश
juice	ras (m.)	रस
jump	kūdnā (v.i.)	कूदना
jupiter	bṛhaspati	बृहस्पति
just now	abhī-abhī (adv.)	अभी–अभी
justice	nyāy (m.)	न्याय
key	cābhī (f.)	चाभी
kidney beans	rājmāṁ (m.)	राजमां
kidney	gurdā (m.)	गुर्दा
kill	marnā (v.i.)	मरना
kill	mārnā (v.t.)	मारना

kilogram	kilogrām (m.)	किलोग्राम
kilometer	kilomīṭar (m.)	किलोमीटर
kind	dayālu (adj.)	दयालु
kindness	dayā (f.)	दया
king	rājā (m.)	राजा
kiss	cūmnā (v.t.)	चूमना
kith and kin	sage sambandhī (m.)	सगे सम्बन्धी
kitchen	rasoīghar (m.)	रसोईघर
knapsack	jholā (m.)	झोला
knead	gūṁdhnā (v.t.)	गूँधना
knee	ghuṭnā (m.)	घुटना
knife	cākū (m.)	चाकू
knit	bunaănā (v.t.)	बुनना
knitting	bunāī (f.)	बुनाई
knock	khaṭkhaṭānā (v.t.)	खटखटाना
knol kohl	gāṁṭh-gobhī (f.)	गाँठ–गोभी
know	jānănā (v.t.)	जानना
knowledge	jñān(m.)	ज्ञान
lady's finger	bhiṇḍī (f.)	भिण्डी
lake	jhīl (f.)	झील
lame	laṅgṛā (m./adj.)	लंगड़ा
land	zamīn (f.)	ज़मीन
landscape	bhū-driṣyă(m.)	भू–दृश्य
language	bhāṣā (f.)	भाषा

L

large	baṛā (adj.)	बड़ा
last	pichlā (adj.)	पिछला
last month	pichle mahīne	पिछले महीने
last night	kal rāt	कल रात
last time	pichlī bār	पिछली बार
last week	pichle hafte	पिछले हफ़्ते
last year	pichle sāl	पिछले साल
laugh	haṁsnā (v.i.)	हँसना
law	kānūn (m.)	कानून
law-practice	vakālat (f.)	वकालत
lawyer	vakīl (m.)	वकील
lazy	ālsī (adj.)	आलसी
lead	sikkā (m.)	सिक्का
lead	āge jānā (v.i.)	आगे जाना
	netṛtva karnā (v.t.)	नेतृत्व करना
leader	netā (m.)	नेता
leaf	pattā (m.)	पत्ता
learn	sīkhnā (v.t.)	सीखना
leech	joṁk (f.)	जोंक
left	bāyāṁ (adj.)	बायाँ
leftover	bacā huā (adj.)	बचा हुआ
leg	ṭāṅg (f.)	टांग
legislation	vidhān (m.)	विधान
lemon	nīmbū (m.)	नींबू

L

lentil	dāl (f.)	दाल
leo	siṁh	सिंह
leprosy	koṛh (m.)	कोढ़
less	kam (adj.)	कम
letter	patra (m.)	पत्र
libra	tulā	तुला
lice	jūṁ (f.)	जूं
lick	cāṭna (v.t).)	चाटना
life	jīvan (m.)	जीवन
light	prakāś (m.)	प्रकाश
light (turn on..)	battī jalānā	बत्ती जलाना
light (turn off..)	battī bujhānā	बत्ती बुझाना
like	pasand karnā (v.t.)	पसन्द करना
lion	śer (m.)	शेर
lips	hoṁṭh (m.)	होंठ
lipstick	surkhī	सुर्खी
listen	sunănā (v.t.)	सुनना
live(in a place)	rahnā (v.i.)	रहना
live(life)	jīnā (v.t.)	जीना
local	sthānīyă (adj.)	स्थानीय
locality	ilākā (m.)	इलाका
	kṣetra (m.)	क्षेत्र
lock	tālā (m.)	ताला
	tālā lagānā (v.t.)	ताला लगाना

L

long	lambā (adj.)	लम्बा
look	dekhnā (v.t.)	देखना
look for	ḍhuṁḍhnā (v.t.)	ढूँढना
loose change	chuṭṭā paisā (m.)	छुट्टा पैसा
loose motions	patlī ṭaṭṭī (f.)	पतली टट्टी
lose	khonā (v.t.)	खोना
	hārnā (v.i.)	हारना
loss	hāni (f.)	हानि
lotus root	kamal-kakṛī (f.)	कमल–ककड़ी
loyal	vafādār (adj.)	वफ़ादार
luggage	sāmān (m.)	सामान
lump	gāṁṭh (f.)	गाँठ
lunch	din kā khānā (m.)	दिन का खाना
luxury	aiśvaryă (m.)	ऐश्वर्य
lungs	phephṛe (m.)	फेफड़े
mace	jāvitrī (f.)	जावित्री
maize	makkā (f.)	मक्का
mad	pāgal (adj./n)	पागल
magazine	patrikā (f.)	पत्रिका
make	banānā (v.t.)	बनाना
mailbox	dāk-peṭī (f.)	डाक–पेटी
manager	prabandhak	प्रबन्धक
main square	cauk (m.)	चौक

magic	jādu	जादु
magic spell	tilasm	तिलस्म
majority	bahusaṅkhyǎ	बहुसंख्य
majority vote	kāmcalāū (adj.)	कामचलाऊ
man	puruṣ (m.)	पुरुष
	ādmī (m.)	आदमी
manager	prabandhak (m.)	प्रबन्धक
mango	ām (m.)	आम
mango powder	āmcūr (m.)	आमचूर
manual worker	mazdūr (m.)	मज़दूर
map	nakśā (m.)	नक्शा
market	bāzār (m)	बाज़ार
marriage	śādī (f.)	शादी
	vivāh(m.)	विवाह
married	śādīśudā (adj,)	शादीशुदा
	vivāhit (adj.)	विवाहित
marry (to...)	śādī karnā (v.t.)	शादी करना
mars	maṅgal	मंगल
marvellous	asādhāraṇ (adj.)	असाधारण
	alaukik (adj.)	अलौकिक
massage	māliś (f.)	मालिश
massage (to ...)	māliś karnā (v.t.)	मालिश करना
massage (to get..)	māliś karvānā (v.t.)	मालिश करवाना

M

matter	māmlā (m.)	मामला
may be	śāyad	शायद
measuring tape	nāpne kā phītā	नापने का फीता
medal	padak (m.)	पदक
meditation	dhyān (m.)	ध्यान
meet	milnā (v.)	मिलना
meeting	baiṭhak (f.)	बैठक
	sabhā (f.)	सभा
melon seeds	magaz	मगज़
member	sadasyă (m.)	सदस्य
membership	sadasyatā (f.)	सदस्यता
memorize	yād karnā (v.t.)	याद करना
memory	yād (f.)	याद
merciless	nirday (adj.)	निर्दय
mercy	dayā (f.)	दया
message	sandeś (m.)	सन्देश
messenger	dūt (m.)	दूत
mew	miyāūṁ - miyāūṁ karnā (v.t.)	मियाऊँ–मियाऊँ करना
midnight	ardh rātri (f.)	अर्ध रात्रि
military	senā (f.)	सेना
milk	dūdh (m.)	दूध
millets	bājrā (m.)	बाजरा

M

million	das lākh (m̐.)	दस लाख
minister	mantrī (m.)	मन्त्री
minority	alpsaṅkhyă (f.)	अल्पसंख्य
	alpsaṅkhyak varg (m.)	अल्पसंख्यक वर्ग
minority vote	alpmat (m.)	अल्पमत
mint	pudīnā (m.)	पुदीना
minute	minaṭ (m.)	मिनट
mirror	darpaṇ (m.)	दर्पण
	śīśā (m.)	शीशा
mischievous	śaitān(m.)	शैतान
mock at	mazāk uṛānā (v.t.)	मज़ाक उड़ाना
monastery	maṭh (m.)	मठ
money	paisā (m.)	पैसा
money deposit	paisā jamā karnā (v.t.)	पैसा जमा करना
money withdrawal	paisā nikālnā (v.t.)	पैसा निकालना
monk	saṃnyāsī (m.)	सन्यासी
	maṭhvāsī (m.)	मठवासी
monkey	bandar(m.)	बन्दर
month	mahīnā (m.)	महीना
monument	imārat (f.)	इमारत
moo	rambhānā (v.i.)	रंभाना
moon	cāṁd; candra (m.)	चाँद, चन्द्र

M

moonlight	cāṁdnī (f.)	चाँदनी
more	zyādā	ज़्यादा
morning	subah (f.)	सुबह
mosque	masjid (f.)	मस्जिद
mosquito	macchar (m)	मच्छर
mother	mātā (f.)	माता
mother-in-law	sās (f.)	सास
mountain	pahāṛ (m.)	पहाड़
	parvat (m.)	पर्वत
mountaineous-path	pahāṛī rāstā (m)	पहाड़ी रास्ता
mountain-ranges	parvat sṛṅkhlā (f.)	पर्वत श्रृंखला
mouse	cūhā (m.)	चूहा
mouth	muṁh (m.)	मुँह
movie	film (f.)	फ़िल्म
muscle	mānspeśī (f.)	मांसपेशी
museum	saṅgrahālay (m.)	संग्रहालय
music	saṅgīt (m.)	संगीत
musician	saṅgītkār(m.)	संगीतकार
musk melon	kharbūzā (m.)	खरबूज़ा
muslim	musalmān(m.)	मुसलमान
mustard	rāī (f.)	राई
mustard oil	sarsoṁ kā tel (m.)	सरसों का तेल

N

mute	gūṅgā (m./adj.)	गूंगा
nail	kīl (m.)	कील
nails	nākhūn (m.)	नाखून
narrow	saṁkṛā (adj.)	संकरा
near	pās	पास
needle	suī	सुई
neighbour	paṛosī (m.)	पड़ोसी
nerve	nas (f.)	नस
never	kabhī nahīṁ	कभी नहीं
newspaper	akhbār (m.)	अखबार
	samācārpatra (m.)	समाचारपत्र
next week	agle hafte	अगले हफ़्ते
night	rāt/rātri (f.)	रात/रात्रि
nondairy	binā dugdh padārth kā	बिना दुग्ध पदार्थ का
non-violence	ahiṁsā (f.)	अहिंसा
noon	dopahar (m.)	दोपहर
north	uttar	उत्तर
north-west	uttar-dakṣiṇ	उत्तर–दक्षिण
novel	upanyās(m.)	उपन्यास
numb	sunn	सुन्न
numbness	sunnat (f.)	सुन्नत
nutmeg	jāyafal (m.)	जायफल

O

nuts	meve (m.)	मेवे
oats	jaī	जई
obese	moṭā (adj.)	मोटा
	sthūl (adj.)	स्थूल
occasionally	samay-samay par	समय–समय पर
ochre	bhagvā (adj.)	भगवा
octagon	aṣṭkoṇ (m.)	अष्टकोण
oesophagus	bhojan kī nalī (f.)	भोजन की नली
offer	peś karnā (v.t.)	पेश करना
often	aksar (adv.)	अक्सर
oil	tel (m.)	तेल
ointment	marham	मरहम
olive oil	jaitūn kā tel	जैतून का तेल
okra	bhiṇḍī (f.)	भिण्डी
once a week	hafte meṁ ek bār	हफ्ते में एक बार
onion seed	kalauñjī (f.)	कलौंजी
onion	pyāz (m.)	प्याज़
open	kholnā (v.t.)	खोलना
opposition	vipakṣ (m.)	विपक्ष
	pratipakṣ	प्रतिपक्ष
optimist	āśāvādī(adj.)	आशावादी
orange	santrā (m.)	सन्तरा
oval	aṇḍal (adj.)	अण्डल
over here	idhar	इधर

over there	udhar	उधर
overdone	zyādā pakā huā (adj.)	ज़्यादा पका हुआ
owl	ullū (m.)	उल्लू
pace	barābar kadmoṁ se calnā	बराबर कदमों से चलना
papaya	papītā (m.)	पपीता
paper	kāgaz (m.)	काग़ज़
paralysis	lakvā (m.)	लकवा
parents	mātā -pitā (m.)	माता–पिता
parliament	samsad (m.)	संसद
parrot	totā (m.)	तोता
party	dāvat (f.)	दावत
	pārṭī (f.)	पार्टी
party(to..)	mauj-mastī karnā (v.t.)	मौज–मस्ती करना
pass	darrā (m.)	दर्रा
passbook	lekha pustikā (f.)	लेख पुस्तिका
pastime	śagal	शगल
patience	dhairyă (m)	धैर्य
patient (n)	rogī (m.)	रोगी
	bīmār (m.)	बीमार
patient	dhairyăvān (adj.)	धैर्यवान
	sahanśīl (adj.)	सहनशील
pattern	namūnā	नमूना

P

payment	bhugtān (m.)	भुगतान
payment (make..)	bhugtān karnā (v.t.)	भुगतान करना
peach	āṛū (m.)	आड़ू
peak	coṭī (f.)	चोटी
pear	nāśpātī (f.)	नाशपाती
pearl	motī (m.)	मोती
peas	maṭar (m.)	मटर
peasant	kisān (m.)	किसान
peel	chīlnā (v.t.)	छीलना
penance	prāyaścitt (m.)	प्रायश्चित
pentagon	pañckoṇ (m.)	पंचकोण
perennials	sadābahār	सदाबहार
	bārāhmāsī	बाराहमासी
perhaps	śāyad	शायद
pessimist	nirāśāwādī (adj.)	निराशावादी
philanthropist	paropkārī (adj.)	परोपकारी
	janhitaiṣī (adj.)	जनहितैषी
pig	sūar (m.)	सूअर
piles	bavāsīr (m.)	बवासीर
pill	golī(f.)	गोली
pillow	takiyā (m.)	तकिया
	sirhānā (m.)	सिरहाना
pillow cover	takiye ka gilāf (m.)	तकिये का गिलाफ़

P

pimples	muhāse(m.)	मुहासे
pineapple	anānās(m.)	अनानास
pinenuts	cilgozā	चिलगोज़ा
pink	gulābī (adj.)	गुलाबी
pisces	mīn	मीन
pistachio	pistā	पिस्ता
plague	tāūn (m.)	ताऊन
planet	graha	ग्रह
plant	paudhā (m.)	पौधा
	bonā (v.t.)	बोना
pleasant	manohar (adj.)	मनोहर
	suhāvnā (adj.)	सुहावना
pleased	khuś (adj.)	खुश
	prasann (adj.)	प्रसन्न
plum	ālūbūkhārā (m.)	आलूबुख़ारा
plumber	nal ṭhīk karnewālā (m.)	नल ठीक करनेवाला
	nalkar (m.)	नलकर
poet	kavi (m.)	कवि
police	pulis (f.)	पुलिस
police station	thānā (m.)	थाना
policy	nīti (f.)	नीति
politics	rājnīti (f.)	राजनीति
politician	rājnetā (m.)	राजनेता

P

pollen	parāg	पराग
pomegranate	anār (m.)	अनार
pond	tālāb (m.)	तालाब
poor	garīb (adj.)	गरीब
poppy seed	khaskhas (f.)	खसखस
post	ḍāk (f.)	डाक
postal stamp	ḍāk ṭikaṭ (m./f.)	डाक टिकट
postman	ḍākiyā (m.)	डाकिया
post-mortem	śav-parīkṣā (f.)	शव–परीक्षा
potato	ālū (m.)	आलू
power	sattā (f.)	सत्ता
probably	sambhavtā	सम्भवता
pray	prārthnā karnā (v.t.)	प्रार्थना करना
president	rāṣṭrapati (m.)	राष्ट्रपति
pride	garv(m.)	गर्व
prime minister	pradhān mantrī (m.)	प्रधानमन्त्री
prison	kārāvās (m.)	कारावास
producer	utpādak	उत्पादक
profane	sāṃsārik (adj.)	सांसारिक
	apavitra (adj)	अपवित्र
profit	lābh (m.)	लाभ
profitable	lābhdāyak (adj.)	लाभदायक
pronounce	uccāraṇ karnā (v.t.)	उच्चारण करना
	ghoṣit karnā (v.t.)	घोषित करना

P

proper	ucit (adj.)	उचित
proposal	prastāv (m.)	प्रस्ताव
protect	rakṣā karnā (v.t.)	रक्षा करना
provisions	rasad (f.)	रसद
	khāne pīne kā	खाने पीने का
	sāmān (m.)	सामान
pulse	nāṛī (f.)	नाड़ी
	dāl (f.)	दाल
pumpkin	laukī (f.)	लौकी
pungent	tīkhā (adj.)	तीखा
	tītā (adj.)	तीता
purple	jāmunī (adj.)	जामुनी
pyramid	konstūpākār (m.)	कोन्सतुपाकार
quack	nīm hakīm (m.)	नीम हकीम
(an unqualified doctor)		
qualified	yogyă (adj.)	योग्य
quality	guṇvattā (f.)	गुणवत्ता
queue	katār (f.)	कतार
	lāin (f.)	लाइन
quickly	jaldī se	जल्दी से
quiet (be..)	cup honā (v.i.)	चुप होना
	śānt (adj.)	शान्त
quilt	razāī (f.)	रज़ाई
quit	choṛnā (v.t.)	छोड़ना
radish	mūlī (f.)	मूली

Q

R

raisins	kiśmiś	किशमिश
ramble	vihār karnā (v.t.)	विहार करना
	sair karnā (v.t.)	सैर करना
raw mango	kaccā ām (m.)	कच्चा आम
reasonable	vājib (adj.)	वाजिब
recently	hāl meṁ (adv.)	हाल में
rectangle	āyatākār (m.)	आयताकार
red	lāl (adj.)	लाल
red pepper	lāl mirc (f.)	लाल मिर्च
refreshing	sphūrtidāyak (adj.)	स्फूर्तिदायक
refuge	āśray(m.)	आश्रय
	śaraṇ(f.)	शरण
refuse	inkār karnā (v.t.)	इन्कार करना
	manā karnā (v.t.)	मना करना
refuse	kacrā (m.)	कचरा
regret	khed (m.)	खेद
reject	choṛ denā (v.t.)	छोड़ देना
remaining	bākī (adj./f.)	बाकी
repair	marammat karnā (v.t.)	मरम्मत करना
repentance	pachtāvā (m.)	पछतावा
representative	pratinidhi (m.)	प्रतिनिधि
republic	gaṇtantra (m.)	गणतन्त्र
reserved	ārakṣit (adj.)	आरक्षित

rheumatism	bāy (f.)	बाय
ribs	pasliyāṁ (f.)	पसलियाँ
rice	cāval (m.)	चावल
	dhān (m.)	धान
rice field	dhān kā khet (m.)	धान का खेत
rich	amīr (adj.)	अमीर
right	dāyāṁ (adj.)	दायाँ
ringworm	dād (m.)	दाद
riots	daṅge (m.)	दंगे
river	nadī (f.)	नदी
roar	dahāṛnā (v.i.)	दहाड़ना
roll	belnā (v.t.)	बेलना
root	jaṛ	जड़
rope	rassī (f.)	रस्सी
rouge	lālī	लाली
rough	khurdurā (adj.)	खुरदुरा
round	gol (adj.)	गोल
ruby	māṇik (m.)	माणिक
rumour	afvāh (f.)	अफ़वाह
sad	udās (adj.)	उदास
safe	surakṣit (adj.)	सुरक्षित
saffron	kesar (m.)	केसर
sage	ṛṣi (m.)	ऋषि
sagittarius	dhanu	धनु

S

salary	vetan (m.)	वेतन
salt	namak (m.)	नमक
salt-free	namak ke binā (adj.)	नमक के बिना
salty	namkīn (adj.)	नमकीन
sand	ret (f.)	रेत
sapodilla	cīkū (m.)	चीकू
satisfaction	santoṣ (m.)	सन्तोष
satisfactory	santoṣprad (adj.)	सन्तोषप्रद
saturn	śani	शनि
savings account	bacat khātā (m.)	बचत खाता
savoury	caṭpaṭā (adj.)	चटपटा
scandal	ghoṭālā (m.)	घोटाला
scene	dṛśya (m.)	दृश्य
science	vijñān	विज्ञान
scientist	vaijñānik	वैज्ञानिक
scissors	kaiṁcī	कैंची
scoff	avajña karnā (v.t.)	अवज्ञा करना
scorn	upekṣāpūrṇ uphās karnā (v.t.)	उपेक्षापूर्ण उपहास करना
scorpio	vṛścik	वृश्चिक
scorpion	bicchū	बिच्छू
scream	cīkhnā (v.i.)	चीखना
script	lipi (f.)	लिपि

S

sea	samudra (m.)	समुद्र
seacoast	samudrataṭ (m.)	समुद्रतट
seafood	samudrajāt bhojan (m.)	समुद्रजात भोजन
seamstress	darzin	दर्ज़िन
season	mausam (m.)	मौसम
seasonal	mausmī (adj.)	मौसमी
secular	dharmnirpekṣ(adj.)	धर्मनिरपेक्ष
secular state	dharmnirpekṣ deś (adj.+m.)	धर्मनिरपेक्ष देश
security	surakṣā	सुरक्षा
seed	bīj (m.)	बीज
self-confidence	ātmviśvās (m.)	आत्मविश्वास
self-evident	svatahsiddh (adj.)	स्वतःसिद्ध
self-help	ātmnirbhartā (f.)	आत्मनिर्भरता
self-interest	swārth (m.)	स्वार्थ
semolina	sūjī (f.)	सूजी
sentiment	manobhāv (m.)	मनोभाव
sentimentalism	atibhāvuktā (f.)	अतिभावुकता
sermon	pravacan (m.)	प्रवचन
	updeś (m.)	उपदेश
sesame oil	til kā tel (m.)	तिल का तेल
sesame seed	til (m.)	तिल
several times	kaī bār	कई बार

S

shake	hilnā (v.i)	हिलना
shake	hilānā (v.t.)	हिलाना
shapes	ākār (m.)	आकार
sheep	bheṛ (f.)	भेड़
sheet	cādar (f.)	चादर
shimmer	jhalmalānā (v.i.)	झलमलाना
	timtimānā (v.i.)	टिमटिमाना
shine	camaknā (v.i.)	चमकना
shirker	kāmcor (m.)	कामचोर
shirt	kamīz	कमीज़
shivering	kaṁpkaṁpī (f.)	कँपकँपी
shoemaker	mocī (m.)	मोची
shoot	aṅkur	अंकुर
shopkeeper	dukāndār	दुकानदार
short	choṭā (adj.)	छोटा
	nāṭā (adj.)	नाटा
shoulder	kandhā	कंधा
shout	cillānā (v.i.)	चिल्लाना
shrub	jhāṛī	झाड़ी
sick	bīmār (adj./m)	बीमार
sigh	āh bharnā (v.t.)	आह भरना
signal	saṅketak (m.)	संकेतक
	signal (m.)	सिगनल
signpost	nām-stambh (m.)	नाम–स्तम्भ

signature	dastkhat (m.)	दस्तख़त
silly	bevkūf (m./adj.)	बेवकूफ़
silver	cāṁdī (f.)	चाँदी
sip	ghūṁt bharnā (v.t.)	घूँट भरना
sister	bahan (f.)	बहन
skin disease	carm rog (m.)	चर्मरोग
skirt	ghāghrā	घाघरा
sky	ākāś (m.)	आकाश
sleep	nīṁd (f.)	नींद
slip	phisalnā (v.i.)	फिसलना
slipperiness	phislan (f.)	फिसलन
small	choṭā (adj.)	छोटा
smile	muskarānā (v.i.)	मुस्कराना
smuggle	taskarī karnā (v.t.)	तस्करी करना
smuggling	taskarī	तस्करी
snake	sāṁp (m.)	साँप
sneer	mazāk uṛānā (v.t.)	मज़ाक उड़ाना
sneeze	chīṁknā (v.i.)	छींकना
sniff	sūṁ-sūṁ karnā (v.t.)	सूँ–सूँ करना
snooze	uṁghnā (v.i.)	उँघना
snore	kharraṭe bharnā (v.t.)	खर्राटे भरना
soak	bhigonā (v.t.)	भिगोना

soap	sābun (m.)	साबुन
socialism	samājvād (m.)	समाजवाद
socks	jurābeṁ	जुराबें
soft	mulāyam (adj.)	मुलायम
sometimes	kabhī-kabhī (adv.)	कभी–कभी
sore throat	galā khrāb	गला ख़राब
sorrow	dukh (m.)	दुख
sound	āvāz (f.)	आवाज़
sour	khaṭṭā (adj.)	खट्टा
south	dakṣiṇ (m./adj.)	दक्षिण
souvenir	smṛti cihn (m.)	स्मृति चिन्ह
sowing	buāī (f.)	बुआई
speak	bolnā (v.t.)	बोलना
speech	bhāṣaṇ (m.)	भाषण
spend (v.)	kharchnā (v.t.)	ख़र्चना
spendthrift	kharcīlā (adj.)	ख़र्चीला
sphere	golā (m.)	गोला
	ākāśvṛt (m.)	आकाशवृत्त
spices	masāle (m.)	मसाले
spicy	masāledar (adj.)	मसालेदार
	tītā (adj.)	तीता
spider	makṛī (f.)	मकड़ी
spinach	pālak (m.)	पालक
spiral	sarpil (adj.)	सर्पिल

	kuṇḍlit (adj.)	कुण्डलित
spleen	tillī (f.)	तिल्ली
splendid	śāndār (adj.)	शानदार
	bhavyă (adj.)	भव्य
spread	bichānā (v.t.)	बिछाना
sprout	aṅkur	अंकुर
square	samāyatākār (m.)	समायताकार
	caṭuṣkoṇ (m.)	चतुष्कोण
squeak	karkaś śabd karnā (v.t.)	कर्कश शब्द करना
	ciciyānā (v.i.)	चिचियाना
stairs	sīṛhiyāṁ	सीढ़ियाँ
stale	bāsī (adj.)	बासी
stamp	ṭikaṭ (m./f.)	टिकट
	muhar (f.)	मुहर
stamp (to...)	ṭikaṭ lagānā (v.t.)	टिकट लगाना
	muhar lagānā (v.t.)	मुहर लगाना
stationery	lekhan sāmagrī (f.)	लेखन सामग्री
statue	mūrti (f.)	मूर्ति
sternness	niṣṭhurtā (f.)	निष्ठुरता
sticky	cipcipā (adj.)	चिपचिपा
stitching	silāī	सिलाई
stir	hilānā (v.t.)	हिलाना
stomach	peṭ (m.)	पेट

S

stool test	ṭaṭṭī kī jāṁc (f.)	टट्टी की जाँच
straight ahead	sīdhe (adv.)	सीधे
strain	chānănā (v.t.)	छानना
strainer	channī (f.)	छन्नी
	jhārā (m.)	झारा
strange	vicitra (adj.)	विचित्र
steep	kharā ḍhāl (m.)	खड़ा ढाल
street	saṛak (f.)	सड़क
street car	trām (f.)	ट्राम
still	abhī (adv.)	अभी
stroll	ṭahlnā (v.i.)	टहलना
strong	balvān (adj.)	बलवान
	mazbūt (adj.)	मजबूत
student	vidyārthī (m.)	विद्यार्थी
stupid	mūrkh ādmī (m.)	मूर्ख आदमी
stye	bilnī (f.)	बिलनी
sublimity	mahāntā (f)	महानता
substitute	pratisthāpan (m.)	प्रतिस्थापन
	pratisthāpan karnā (v.t.)	प्रतिस्थापन करना
suburb	nagarañcal (m.)	नगरांचल
subway	antarbhūmārg (m.)	अन्तरभूमार्ग
success	saphaltā (f.)	सफलता

successful	saphal (adj.)	सफल
suck	cūsnā (v.t.)	चूसना
sudden death	akāl mṛityu (adj.+f.)	अकाल मृत्यु
sugar	cīnī (f.)	चीनी
sugar cane	gannā (m.)	गन्ना
suggest	sujhāv denā (v.t.)	सुझाव देना
suitcase	sandūk (m.)	सन्दूक
sun	sūryă	सूर्य
sunglasses	dhūp kā caśmā (m.)	धूप का चश्मा
sunrise	sūryoday (m.)	सूर्योदय
sunset	sūryāst (m.)	सूर्यास्त
superiority complex	ahaṃ mānyatā	अहम् मान्यता
swallow	nigalnā (v.t.)	निगलना
sweat	pasīnā (m.)	पसीना
sweat (to...)	pasīnā ānā (v.i)	पसीना आना
sweet & sour	khaṭṭā -mīṭhā (adj.)	खट्टा–मीठा
sweet potato	śakarkandī (f.)	शकरकन्दी
sweet	mīṭhā (adj.)	मीठा
sweet	miṭhāī (f)	मिठाई
sweetheart	premī (m.)	प्रेमी
	premikā (f.)	प्रेमिका
swelling	sūjan (f.)	सूजन
swim	tairnā (v.i.)	तैरना

T

swimming pool	taraṇ tāl (m.)	तरण ताल
symbol	pratīk (m.)	प्रतीक
sympathy	sahānubhūti (f.)	सहानुभूति
table	mez (f.)	मेज़
tablet	golī(f.)	गोली
tailor	darzī (m.)	दर्ज़ी
take	lenā (v.t.)	लेना
take care	dhyān rakhnā (v.t.)	ध्यान रखना
take off	uṛān bharnā	उड़ान भरना
talkative	bātūnī (adj.)	बातूनी
tall	lambā (adj.)	लम्बा
tamarind	imlī (f.)	इमली
tap(water..)	nal (m.)	नल
tap(turn on..)	nal kholnā	नल खोलना
tap(turn off..)	nal band karnā	नल बन्द करना
taro	arbī (f.)	अरबी
	kacālū (m.)	कचालू
tasty	svādiṣṭ (adj.)	स्वादिष्ट
taurus	vṛṣabh	वृषभ
tax	kar (m.)	कर
tea	cāy	चाय
tea (black..)	binā dūdh kī cāy	बिना दूध की चाय
tea (strong..)	kaṛak cāy	कडक चाय
tea with spices	masālewālī cāy	मसालेवाली चाय

T

teacher	adhyāpak(m.)	अध्यापक
	śikṣak (m.)	शिक्षक
team	dal (m.)	दल
telegram	tār (m.)	तार
telephone	dūrbhāṣ (m.)	दूरभाष
	ṭailifon (m.)	टैलिफ़ोन
telescope	dūrbīn (m.)	दूरबीन
television	dūrdarśan (m.)	दूरदर्शन
	ṭī.vī. (m.)	टी.वी.
television (to turn on..)	ṭī.vī. calānā.	टी.वी. चलाना
television (to turn off..)	ṭī.vī. band karnā	टी.वी. बन्द करना
temperature	tāp (m.)	ताप
temple	mandir (m.)	मन्दिर
	kanpaṭī (f.)	कनपटी
temptation	pralobhan (m.)	प्रलोभन
tempting	pralobhī (adj.)	प्रलोभी
	lubhāvnā (adj.)	लुभावना
tension	tanāv (m.)	तनाव
that	vah	वह
these	ye	ये
these days	ājkal (adv.)	आजकल
thick	moṭā (adj.)	मोटा

T

thief	cor (m.)	चोर
tiger	cītā (m.)	चीता
thin	patlā (adj.)	पतला
this	yah	यह
those	ve	ये
thought	vicār (m.)	विचार
throat	galā (m.)	गला
thread	dhāgā (m.)	धागा
thumb	aṅgūṭhā (m.)	अंगूठा
tobacco	tambākū(m.)	तम्बाकू
today	āj	आज
toe	pair kā aṅgūthā	पैर का अंगूठा
toilet	śaucālay	शौचालय
toilet-accessories	śṛṇgār kā sāmān (m.)	श्रंगार का सामान
tomato	ṭamāṭar (m.)	टमाटर
tomorrow	kal	कल
tongue	jībh (f.)	जीभ
tonight	āj rāt ko	आज रात को
too much	bahut zyādā	बहुत ज़्यादा
too expensive	bahut mahaṁgā	बहुत महँगा
tooth	dāṁt (m)	दाँत
toothache	dāṁt dard (m.)	दाँत दर्द
tooth brush	dāṁt kā buruś (m.)	दाँद का बुरुश

T

tooth paste	mañjan (m.)	मञ्जन
tornadoes	bavaṇḍar (m.)	बवण्डर
	tūfān (m.)	तूफ़ान
touch	chūnā (v.)	छूना
touchy person	atibhāvuk vyakti (adj.+m.)	अतिभावुक व्यक्ति
touchy topic	samvedanśīl viṣay (adj.+m)	संवेदनशील विषय
tourist	paryaṭak (m.)	पर्यटक
tourist bureau	ṭūrisṭ byoro (m.)	टूरिस्ट बयोरो
	paryaṭak sevak maṇḍal (m.)	पर्यटक सेवक मण्डल
tourist office	paryaṭan daftar (m.)	पर्यटन दफ़्तर
tout	dalāl (m.)	दलाल
towards	kī or	की ओर
towards left	bāyīṁ or	बायीं ओर
towards right	dāyīṁ or	दायीं ओर
towel	tauliā (m.)	तौलिया
trachea	śvās kī nalī (f.)	श्वास की नली
traffic	yātāyāt (m.)	यातायात
tragedy	trāsadī (f.)	त्रासदी
tragical/	trāsad (adj.)	त्रासद
tragic	dukhad(adj.)	दुखद
triangle	trikoṇ (m.)	त्रिकोण

T

trainer	praśikṣak (m.)	प्रशिक्षक
training	praśikṣaṇ (m.)	प्रशिक्षण
transcendent	anubhvātīt (adj.)	अनुभवातीत
transient	kṣaṇik (adj.)	क्षणिक
	alpkālik (adj.)	अल्पकालिक
translation	anuvād (m.)	अनुवाद
translate	anuvād karnā (v.t.)	अनुवाद करना
travel	yātrā (f.)	यात्रा
	safar (m.)	सफ़र
traveller	yātrī (m.)	यात्री
treatment	ilāj (m.)	इलाज
trekking	lambī pad yātrā (f.)	लम्बी पद यात्रा
tree	peṛ (m.)	पेड़
trench	khāī (f.)	खाई
trend	ghaṭnā-pravāh (m.)	घटना–प्रवाह
trouble	pareśānī (f.)	परेशानी
	pareśān karnā (v.t.)	परेशान करना
troublesome	kaṣṭdāyak (adj.)	कष्टदायक
trousers	paiṇṭ	पैण्ट
true	sac (adj.)	सच
truly	sacmuc (adv.)	सचमुच
trunk	tanā	तना
trust	viśvās (m.)	विश्वास

T

trustworthy	viśvās ke yogyă	विश्वास के योग्य
truth	satya(m.)	सत्य
try	kośiś karnā(v.t.)	कोशिश करना
turmeric	haldī (m.)	हल्दी
turning	moṛ (m.)	मोड़
twice	do bār	दो बार
twin	juṛvāṁ (adj.)	जुड़वाँ
twitch	akasmāt pharaknā	अकस्मात फड़कना
ugly	badsūrat (adj.)	बदसूरत
	bhaddā (adj.)	भद्दा
umbrella	chātā (m.)	छाता
unconscious-ness	behośī (f.)	बेहोशी
undercooked	kam pakā huā (adj.)	कम पका हुआ
understand	samajhnā	समझना
underwear	jāṁghiyā (m.)	जांघिया
	kacchā (m.)	कच्छा
unemployment	berozgārī (f.)	बेरोज़गारी
unlimited	asīmit (adj.)	असीमित
unforgettable	avismarṇīyă (adj.)	अविस्मणीय
unique	anokhā (adj.)	अनोखा
universe	saṁsār (m.)	संसार
university	viśvavidyālay (m.)	विश्वविद्यालय
unparallelled	atulyă (adj.)	अतुल्य

U

unsafe	asurakṣit (adj.)	असुरक्षित
until	jab tak	जब तक
until now	ab tak	अब तक
untimely	asāmayik (adj.)	असामयिक
unusual	asādhāran (adj.)	असाधारण
uphill	caṛhāī (f.)	चढ़ाई
upon	ke ūpar (pp)	के ऊपर
urgent	atyāvaśyak (adj.)	अत्यावश्यक
	śīghra (adv.)	शीघ्र
urine test	peśāb kī jāṁc (f.)	पेशाब की जाँच
useful	upyogī (adj.)	उपयोगी
	fāydemand (adj.)	फ़ायदेमन्द
useless	bekār (adj.)	बेकार
vacant	khālī (adj.)	खाली
	rikt (adj.)	रिक्त
vacancy	khālī jagah (adj.+f.)	खाली जगह
	rikt sthān (adj.+m.)	रिक्त स्थान
vacation	chuṭṭī (f.)	छुट्टी
	dīrgh avkāś (m.)	दीर्घ अवकाश
vaccination	ṭīkā (m.)	टीका
valley	ghāṭī (f.)	घाटी
valuable	kīmtī (adj.)	कीमती
value	kīmat (f.)	कीमत

vegetable	sabzī (f.)	सब्ज़ी
vegetarian	śākāhārī (adj.)	शाकाहारी
vegetation	vanaspati	वनस्पति
ventilator	rośandān (m.)	रोशनदान
venus	śukra	शुक्र
verify	jāṁcnā (v.t.)	जाँचना
vest	baniyān	बनियान
village	gāṁv	गाँव
village council	pañcāyat (f.)	पंचायत
vine	aṅgūr kī bel (f.)	अंगूर की बेल
vinegar	sirkā (m.)	सिरका
virgo	kanyā	कन्या
visit	milne jānā (v.i.)	मिलने जाना
vision	darśan (m.)	दर्शन
vital air	prāṇ (m.)	प्राण
vocabulary	śabdāvalī (f.)	शब्दावली
volunteer	svayaṁsevak (m.)	स्वयंसेवक
volcano	jwālāmukhī (m.)	ज्वालामुखी
vomit	kai karnā (v.t.)	कै करना
vote	voṭ ḍālnā (v.t.)	वोट डालना
	matdān karnā (v.t.)	मतदान करना
wage	mazdūrī (f.)	मज़दूरी
waist	kamar (f.)	कमर
wait	intzār karnā (v.t.)	इन्तज़ार करना

V

	pratīkṣā karnā (v.t.)	प्रतीक्षा करना
waiting list	pratīkṣā sūcī (f.)	प्रतीक्षा सूची
waiting room	pratıkṣalay (m.)	प्रतीक्षालय
wake up	jagānā (v.t.)	जगाना
	jāgnā (v.i.)	जागना
walk	calnā (v.i.)	चलना
wall	dīvār (f.)	दीवार
want	cāhnā	चाहना
war	laṛāī (f.)	लड़ाई
	yuddh (m.)	युद्ध
warm	garam (adj.)	गरम
warm (to...)	garam karnā (v.t.)	गरम करना
warn	cetāvanī denā (v.i.)	चेतावनी देना
wash	dhonā (v.t.)	धोना
washerman	dhobī	धोबी
waste	barbād karnā (v.t.)	बर्बाद करना
watch	ghaṛī (f.)	घड़ी
watch	dekhnā (v.t.)	देखना
watchman	caukīdār (m.)	चौकीदार
water	jal (m.)	जल
waterfall	jharnā (m.)	झरना
watermelon	tarbūz (m.)	तरबूज़
wave	lahar (f.)	लहर
way	rāstā (m.)	रास्ता

W

weakness	kamzorī (f.)	कमज़ोरी
wealth	dhan (m.)	धन
wealthy	amīr (adj.)	अमीर
	dhanī (adj.)	धनी
weather	mausam (m.)	मौसम
wedding	śādī (f.)	शादी
	vivāh (m.)	विवाह
week	haftā (m.)	हफ़्ता
	saptāh (m.)	सप्ताह
weigh	tolnā (v.i.)	तोलना
	vazan karnā (v.t.)	वज़न करना
weight	vazan (m.)	वज़न
welcome	swāgat (m.)	स्वागत
	swāgat karnā (v.t.)	स्वागत करना
welfare	kalyāṇ (m.)	कल्याण
west	paścim (adj./m.)	पश्चिम
wet	gīlā (adj.)	गीला
what for	kis lie	किस लिए
wheat	gehūṁ (m.)	गेहूँ
weeds	khar patvār	खर पतवार
	niraunā	निरौना
wheel	pahiyā (m.)	पहिया
when	kab	कब
where	kahāṁ	कहाँ

W

white flour	maidā (m.)	मैदा
white	safed (adj.)	सफ़ेद
who	kaun	कौन
why not	kyoṁ nahiṁ	क्यों नहीं
why so	aisā kyoṁ	ऐसा क्यों
why	kyoṁ	क्यों
wide	cauṛā (adj.)	चौड़ा
wife	patnī (f.)	पत्नी
win	jītnā (v.t.)	जीतना
window	khirkī (f.)	खिड़की
wings	paṅkh (m.)	पंख
wink	āṁkh mārnā (v.t.)	आँख मारना
winter	ṭhaṇḍ (f.)	ठण्ड
	jāṛā (m.)	जाड़ा
wisdom	buddhi (f.)	बुद्धि
wise	buddhimān (adj.)	बुद्धिमान
wish	icchā (f.)	इच्छा
wishful thinking	khyālī pulāo	खयाली पुलाव
within	ke andar	के अन्दर
woman	aurat (f.)	औरत
	nārī (f.)	नारी
	mahilā (f.)	महिला
wonderful	āścaryăjanak (adj.)	आश्चर्यजनक

W

	apūrv (adj.)	अपूर्व
wood	lakṛī (f.)	लकड़ी
word	śabd (m.)	शब्द
world	duniā (f.)	दुनिया
work	kām (m.)	काम
worker	karmcārī (m.)	कर्मचारी
worried	cintit (adj.)	चिन्तित
worry	cintā (f.)	चिन्ता
worship	pūjā (f.)	पूजा
worth	ke yogyă	के योग्य
wound	jakhm (m.)	जख्म
wrist watch	hāth ki ghaṛī(f.)	हाथ की घड़ी
write	likhnā (v.t.)	लिखना
writer	lekhak (m.)	लेखक
wrong	galat (adj.)	ग़लत
wry face (make a..)	muṁh sikoṛnā	मुंह सिकोड़ना
yawn	jamhāī lenā (v.t.)	जम्हाई लेना
year	sāl (m.)	साल
yellow	pīlā (adj.)	पीला
yellow sapphire	pukhrāj (m.)	पुखराज
yet	abhī tak	अभी तक
yesterday	kal	कल
young	yuvā (adj.)	युवा

	javān (adj./m.)	जवान
zeal	jośa	जोश
zero	śunya	शून्य
zest	ānand	आनन्द
zoo	ciṛiyāghar	चिड़ियाघर

Y

USEFUL TIPS

Cultural Sensitivity

You might encounter strange looks if you appear in black at religious or wedding ceremonies. In this country, the auspicious colours are yellow, orange, pink and red, symbolizing energy and happiness.

Black is considered to be inauspicious and troublesome.

ENGLISH WORDS IN EVERYDAY USE

In India the English speaking people can get by with most of their work in English.

Indians themselves were first introduced to several new terms related to modern technology in English language. They have never seriously felt the need to replace this vast range of words by equivalent Hindi-terms. Quite a number of the natives speak English with sufficient ease, without excercising any mental conversion. A large number of people use English words without feeling any problem in using the alien language.

However there is usually some twist of the original word with difference in the pronunciation and accent. Also because of the difference in culture, the connotation is many times very different.

A list of some commonly used English words:

a.c.
admission
antiseptic
auntie
bank
bell
boarding pass
booking
break
cable backup disk

camera
car
cash
CD Rom disk
check
chip
cigarette
collect call
computer
concert
cricket
cursor
directory
double
driver's license
e-mail
embassy
emporium
engine
express
fax
firm
floppy
football
form
gear

guesthouse
handle
hardware
helmet
hotel

infection
injection
internet café
mineral water
mouse
museum

napkin
operator
parcel
passbook
passport
petrol
photo
pincode
postcard
postman
printer
pump
puncture
radiator
scanner
school
seat
serial
single
size
stadium
station
steering
taxi
team
telephone
ticket
tire
toilet paper
train
travel agency
travel agent
traveller check
tube
uncle
virus
visa

DEVANAGARI SCRIPT

VOWELS — SVARA (स्वर)

Devanāgarī	Transliteration	Vowel symbol	Position	Pronunciation
अ	a	Ø	(this is inherent in the consonant)	hut
आ	ā		(follows the consonant)	father
इ	i	ि	(precedes the consonant)	sit
ई	ī	ी	(follows the consonant)	meet
उ	u	ु	(subscript)	put
ऊ	ū	ू	(subscript)	rule
ऋ	r	ृ	(subscript)	ritu
ए	e	े	(superscript)	hate
ऐ	ai	ै	(superscript)	cat
ओ	o	ो	(follows the consonant)	hole
औ	au	ौ	(follows the consonant)	hot

Nasalized vowels

In Hindi vowels are nasalized by putting a crescent with a dot above it, known as 'anunāsik' or 'candrabindu'.

It is written above the headstroke of the vowel, e.g. माँ (māṁ), or above the headstroke of the consonants to which the vowel is affixed, e.g. हूँ (hūṁ).

However if the consonant already has a superscript vowel symbol, only a dot (ं) is put instead of a 'candrabindu' (ँ) to avoid crowding.

In practice, however, this rule is widely flouted. In printed matter, books or newspapers, and only a dot (ं) is commonly used to indicate nasal vowel sounds., e.g. चीं chīṁ; नहीं nahīṁ. Nasalized vowels are transliterated as 'ṁ'

PUNCTUATION

Use of punctuation in Hindi is the same as in English except that :

- A vertical stroke is used to mark the end of a sentence.
- Sometimes, more than one exclamation marks are used to indicate the degree of surprise or intensity of emotion.

CONSONANTS — VYAÑJAN - व्यञ्जन

non-aspirate	aspirate	non-aspirate	aspirate	nasal
क	ख	ग	घ	ङ
ka	kha	ga	gha	ṅa
च	छ	ज	झ (भ)	ञ
ca	cha	ja	jha	ña
ट	ठ	ड	ढ	ण/रा
ṭa	ṭha	ḍa	ḍha	ṇa
		ड़	ढ़	
		ṛ	ṛha	
त	थ	द	ध	न
ta	tha	da	dha	na
प	फ	ब	भ	म
pa	pha	ba	bha	ma
य	र	ल (ल)	व	
ya	ra	la	va	
श	ष	स	ह	
śa	ṣa	sa	ha	
क्ष	त्र	ज्ञ (ज्ञ)		
kṣa	tra	jña (gya)		

The first vowel अ is inherent in all the consonants for phonetic ease. The consonants without the vowel 'a' called hals have a subscript stroke written left to right down-wards e.g. क्, ख्, ग् etc.

MODIFIED LETTERS TO ACCOMMODATE SOUNDS FROM PERSIAN LANGUAGE.

क़	ख़	ग़	फ़	ज़
qa	<u>kh</u>a	ga	fa	za

NASAL CONSONANTS

☞ The Hindi alphabet provides a nasal consonant at the end of the first five groups of consonants i.e. the velars, the prepalatals, the retroflexes, the dentals and the labials. Of these the nasal consonants ङ and ञ are not used independently but as conjuncts preceded by some vowel and succeeded by some consonant.

Example : rañg (रङ्ग); rañj (रञ्ज).

☞ The remaining three nasal consonants ण, न, म can be used independently.

Examples : aṇū (अणु); dhan (धन); ām (आम)

☞ When these five nasal consonants precede the members of their own series, they can be and are usually written as a dot (̇) above the head stroke of the previous consonant but read before the following letter. This is known as 'anusvār'.

Examples:

रङ्ग	रंग	(raṅg)	चञ्चल	चंचल	(cañcal)
अण्डा	अंडा	(aṇḍā)	मन्दा	मंदा	(mandā)
चम्पा	चंपा	(campā)			

VISARGA : (:)

☞ **Visarga is written as two dots one below the other like colon (:), and is transliterated as 'ḥ', It is pronounced as ah (अह). It occurs mostly in words borrowed from Sanskrit such as प्राय: prāyaḥ (usually), छ: chaḥ (six) etc.**

LIGATURES: CONJUNCT CONSONANTS

s + ta =sta	namaste
स् + त = स्त	नमस्ते
k + ṣa = kṣa	kakṣā
क् + ष = क्ष	कक्षा
d + ya = dya	d + dha= ddha
द् + य = द्य	द् + ध = द्ध
dh + ya = dhya	c + cha = ccha
ध् + य = ध्य	च् + छ = च्छ
t + ta = tta uttar	ṣ + ṭa = ṣṭa
त् + त = त्त/त्त	ष् + ट = ष्ट

☞ **When r (र्) precedes any consonant, r (र्) is written as ि on top of the succeeding consonant but read between the two letters.**

r + la = rla　　　　　r + thī = rthī

र् + ल = र्ल;　　　　र् + थी = र्थी

k + r + ma = karma

क + र् + म = कर्म

vi + d + yā + r + thī = vidyārthī

वि + द् + या + र् + थी = विद्यार्थी

☞ **When ra (र) follows a consonant without inherent 'अ', it takes the form of a stroke under the preceding letter as shown below.**

k + ra = kra;　क् + र = क्र

p + re = pre　प् + रे = प्रे

k + ra + ma = kram क्रम

p + re + ma = prem प्रेम

☞ **ऋ following a consonant is written as ृ underneath.**

क् + ऋ = कृ kṛ;　प् + ऋ = पृ pṛ

क् + ऋ + ष् + ण = कृष्ण kṛṣṇa

CONSONANTS PLUS VOWELS

ka	kā	ki	kī	ku	kū	ke	kai	ko	kau	kaṁ	kah
क	का	कि	की	कु	कू	के	कै	को	कौ	कं	कः

but

r + u = ru   r + ū = rū

र + उ = रु   र + ऊ रू

USEFUL TIPS

How To Exprees

JOY

vāh — Splendid!, Wonderful!
vāh-vāh — Expression of applaud and praise
āhā — Vow! (to express pleasant surprise)

SURPRISE

kyā — what?
aiṁ — astonishment
bāp-re-bāp — astonishment
haiṁ — astonishment

ANGER, REGRET, WORRY

afsos — How sad! (to express sorrow)
rām rām — Oh God!

FEAR

trāhi — Help!
rām rām — God forbid!
duhāī — A cry for help

IRRITATION, COMTEMPT, SCORN, DISGUST

chī chī — Ugh! Shame!
hat — Out of the away!
cup — Be quiet!
thū thū — Shame
dur dur dur — Be off! Clear out!
dhikkār — Fie! Be cursed!

NOUNS

GENDER

Hindi has two genders, masculine and feminine. There is no neuter gender.

NUMBER

singular or plural

CASE

Direct case : When a noun or a pronoun is used as subject without a postposition it is said to be in the direct case, and controls the verb conjugation.

- Hindi uses postposition 'ne' after the subject in the past tense with transitive verb.

  Example :

  I read the book. maiṁne kitāb paṛhī.

- Also many constructions in Hindi have the subject in the dative case followed by the postposition 'ko'.

  Example :

  I am hungry. mujhko bhūkh lagī hai.

Oblique case : When a noun or pronoun is followed by a postposition, it is said to be in the oblique case such as accusative, dative, instrumental, ablative, possessive, locative.

Vocative case : Hindi has a special vocative form of noun which is used when addressing or invoking a person or thing. This is similar to the oblique form except that vocative plural is 'o' or 'yo' instead of 'oṁ' or 'yoṁ'.

Case Endings (see simple postpositions pg. 294):

ko	to, for	accusative, dative
se	with, from	instrumental, ablative
meṁ, par	in, on, at	locative
ka, ke, kī	of	genitive

DECLINATION OF MASCULINE NOUNS

ā-ending masculine nouns change to e-ending in direct plural as well as oblique singular cases; They change to oṁ-ending in the oblique plural. Nouns in the oblique case are followed by suitable postposition to meet the requirement of the case in which they are used.

Example :

		sg.	pl.
direct case	boy	larkā	larke
oblique case	boys	lark**e+pp**	lark**oṁ+pp**

All other masculine nouns remain the same in direct singular, direct plural and oblique singular case. oṁ or yoṁ is added to their oblique plural case.

- ☞ **yoṁ is added to the i- or ī- ending nouns in their oblique plural form. ī is shortened before adding yoṁ.**
- ☞ **ū is shortened before adding oṁ.**

Example :

		sg.	pl.
direct case	apple	seb	seb
oblique case	apple	seb	seb**oṁ**
direct case	poet	kavi	kavi
oblique case	poet	kavi	kavi**yoṁ**
direct case	man	ādmī	ādmī
oblique case	man	ādmī	ādm**iyoṁ**
direct case	child	śiśu	śiśu
oblique case	child	śiśu	śiśu**oṁ**
direct case	bear	bhālū	bhālū
oblique case	bear	bhālū	bhāl**uoṁ**

DECLINATION OF FEMININE NOUNS

- eṁ-ending is added in the direct case to pluralize feminine nouns ending in a consonant or the vowels ā, u, ū.
  ū is shortened before making the change.
- Oblique singular form is the same as direct singular form.
- Oblique plural has the ending oṁ or yoṁ.
- Symbol form of 'eṁ' is used with nouns ending in consonants.
  In all other cases, 'eṁ' or oṁ is physically added to the noun.

Examples :

		sg.	pl.
direct case	woman	aurat	aurat**eṁ**
oblique case		aurat	aurat**oṁ**

direct case	garland	mālā	mālā**eṁ**
oblique case		mālā	mālā**oṁ**
direct case	date	tithi	tithi**yāṁ**
oblique case		tithi	tithi**yoṁ**
direct case	girl	laṛkī	laṛk**iyāṁ**
oblique case		laṛkī	laṛk**iyoṁ**
direct case	thing	vastu	vastu**eṁ**
oblique case		vastu	vastu**oṁ**
direct case	daughter-in-law	bahū	bah**ueṁ**
oblique cause		bahū	bah**uoṁ**

PRONOUNS

PERSONAL PRONOUNS

	Nom. Case	**Obl. Case***
I	maiṁ	mujh
We	ham	ham
You	tū	tujh
You	tum	tum
You	āp	āp
He, she, it (near)	yah	is
He, she, it (far)	vah	us
They, these (near)	ye	in
They, those (far)	ve	un

* **Pronouns in the oblique case are followed by some postposition according to the case in which it is used.**

INTERROGATIVE PRONOUNS

what	kyā
who	kaun
whom	kisko
whose	kiskā, kiske, kiskī

INDEFINITE PRONOUNS

somebody (used as subject)	koī
somebody (sg.)	kisī*
somebody (pl.)	kinhī*

(* used in cases other than the subject)

POSSESSIVE PRONOUNS/ADJECTIVES

my, mine	merā	mere	merī
our, ours	hamārā	hamāre	hamārī
your, yours (sg.)	terā	tere	terī
your, yours (pl.)	tumhārā	tumhāre	tumhārī
your, yours (hon.)	āpkā	āpke	āpkī
his,her (far)	uskā	uske	uskī
his,her (near)	iskā	iske	iskı
their,theirs (far)	unkā	unke	unkī
their,theirs (near)	inkā	inke	inkī
whose(sg.)	kiskā	kiske	kiskī
whose(pl.)	kinkā	kinke	kinkī
somebody's(sg.)	kisīkā	kisīke	kisīkī
somebody's(pl.)	kinhīkā	kinhīke	kinhīkī

ADJECTIVES

DECLINATION

In Hindi, like the nouns, the adjectives are declined too.

All adjectives can be categorized as: (1) ā-ending adjectives and (2) all other adjectives with any other ending.

The ā-ending adjectives change to:

- e-ending when qualifying masculine nouns, in direct plural, oblique singular, or oblique plural.
- ī-ending when qualifying feminine nouns in singular or plural, in direct or oblique case.

tall	lambā	lambe	lambī
good	acchā	acche	acchī

☞ **All the other adjectives, while qualifying any noun in any number or case, remain the same.**

beautiful sundar; **kind** dayālu; **stale** bāsī

DEGREE OF THE ADJECTIVE

COMPARATIVES:

Let x be the object with which the comparison is made.

x+se+the base form of the adjective

older than me.	mujhse baṛā
younger than him.	usse choṭā
cleverer than Robert	raubart se hośiyār

SUPERLATIVE :

sab+se+ the base form of the adjective

the tallest	sab se lambā
the cleverest	sab se hośiyār
the most expensive	sab se mahṁgā
the best	sab se acchā

ADJECTIVAL SUFFIX 'vālā'

1. noun + vālā :

the sweets seller	miṭhāīvālā
the greengrocer	sabzīvālā
the houseowner	makānvālā

2. **Infinitive + vālā** :

the one who sings	gānevālā
the one who teaches	paṛhānevālā

3. **Adverb + vālā** :

the one that is above	ūparvālā
the one who is in front	sāmnevālā

4. **(v.r. + ने) + vālā/vāle/vālī (about to do something)**

I am about to sleep.	maiṁ sonevālā hūṁ.
We are about to go out.	ham bāhar jānevāle haiṁ.

REFLEXIVE ADJECTIVE—apnā

Tell your name.	apnā nām batāo.
Bring your book.	apnī kitāb lāo.
Wear your clothes.	apne kapṛe pahno.

COMMONLY USED ADJECTIVES

good	acchā	bad	kharāb
less	kam	more	zyādā
cheap	sastā	expensive	mahaṁgā
big	baṛā	small	chotā
old age	būṛhāpā	young	jawān
fresh	tāzā	stale	bāsī
new	nayā	old	purānā
sweet	mīthā	salty	namkīn
bitter	kaṛuvā	pungent	tītā
sour	khattā	insipid	phīka
rich	amīr	poor	garīb
light	halkā	heavy	bhārī
long	lambā	wide	cauṛā
dirty	gandā	clean	sāf

COMMONLY USED ADVERBS

now	ab	then	tab
quickly	jaldī	slow	dhīre
usually	prāyaḥ	often	aksar
always	hameśā	much	bahut
less	kam	more	adhik
approximately	lagbhag	a little	thoṛā
below	nīce	above	ūpar
as if	māno	hardly	yadā-kadā

VERBS

All verbs in their infinitive form have 'nā' ending.

Very few constructions in Hindi use the infinitive.

- **Infinitive minus the 'nā' ending is the verb root.**

VERB 'TO BE' (honā)

☞ **'honā' is used as the main verb when talking about being or state of things.**

☞ **'honā' is used as auxilliary verb along with present or past participle of the main action verbs when talking about activities in their indefinite or perfective forms in the required tense.**

PRESENT FORMS OF honā

hūṁ	ho	hai	haīṁ

I am.	maiṁ	hūṁ
you (inf.) are.	tum	ho
you (int.),he, she, it is.	tū, vah, yah	hai
we, they, you (formal) are.	ham, ve, ye, āp	haīṁ

PAST FORMS OF honā

thā (m.sg.)	the (m.pl.)
thī (f.sg.)	thīṁ (f.pl.)

	m.	f.
I, you, he, she, it, who, what		
maiṁ, tu, vah, yah, kaun, kyā	thā	thī
we, you (inf./form.) they, who		
ham, tum, āp, ve, ye, kaun-kaun	the	thīṁ

FUTURE FORM OF honā

I will be	maiṁ	hūṁgā	hūṁgī
		hoūṁgā	hoūṁgī
you (int.)	tū	hogā	hogī
he, she, it,	vah, yah	hogā	hogī
you (inf.)	tum	hoge	hogī
we, you (hon.)	ham, āp	hoṁge	hoṁgī
they	ve, ye	hoṁge	hoṁgī

☞ **Hindi is not very rich in one-word verbs for all activities.**

The verbs 'karnā'(to do) and 'honā' (to be) are most of the time added to a noun or an adjective to make new verbs.

band honā	(v.i.)	to be closed
band karnā	(v.t.)	to close

☞ **Another thing that baffles foreign students is the use of compound verbs i.e. of two or more verbs at one time.**

'baith jāie'.
The literal meaning is 'sit go'.

Sounds weird, isn't it? Yet a native speaker would not be satisfied using only one verb 'baithie'

It takes some time and practice for a novice learning Hindi as a foreign language to grasp an accurate sense of this usage.

Let us remember:

We use the root of the main verb plus the conjugated form of the helping verb. The helping verb is just an intensifier. It does not lend its inherent meaning.

Different intensifiers are used for different connotations such as change of state, completion, rashness or suddenness of action.

Compound verbs are used in affirmative and interrogative sentences. They are not used in the negative sentences.

☞ **Denā (give), lenā (take) and jānā (go) are three much used intensifiers.**

Denā is used when the beneficiary of the activity is someone other than the doer of the action.

Lenā is used when the beneficiary is the doer himself.

take	le lenā
give	de denā

jānā is used as intensifier to indicate completion of action or change of state.

to become ill.	bīmār ho jānā
milk to curdle	dūdh phaṭ jānā

☞ **Besides intransitive and transitive, hindi has two more categories of causative verbs.**

- **causative 1, where the person himself causes the other person to do the activity.**
- **causative 2, where a person has the work done by some third person.**

eat	khānā (v.t.)
feed	khilānā (causative 1)
to have some one fed	khilvānā (causative 2)

USEFUL TIPS

The Omnipresent Lord

People in India love to involve the Lord in everyday life!

★ **When they meet, they say the name of their deity.**

Devotees of Ram say : Rām Rām;
Devotees of Kṛṣṇa say : Jai Srī Kṛṣṇa
Devotees of the Goddess say : Jai Mātā dī
Devotees of Hanuman say : Jai Bajrang Bali
Devotees of Siva say : Har-Har Mahādev
Devotees of Jesus say : Jai Masīh

★ **When they are happy, they say:**
śukra hai bhagwān kā (Thank God!)

★ **When somebody dies, they say:**
Rām Nām Sat Hai (Name of the Lord is Truth.)

IMPERATIVE

PRESENT IMPERATIVE

tū + v.r.; tum + (v.r. + o); āp + (v.r.+ i + e/ye)

EXAMPLES: to go (jānā)

You go! tu jā; tum jāo; āp jāie

FUTURE IMPERATIVE

tū / tum + (v.r. + inf.); āp + (v.r. + i + e + gā)

tū / tum jānā; āp jāiegā

☞ **For negative commands use 'mat' with 'tū', 'tum' and 'na' with 'āp'.**

(You) don't go. tū mat jā; tum mat jāo

āp na jāie.

In practice, in cases where cultural requirement is to address somebody as 'tum', but the relations are very formal, 'na' is used instead of 'mat'. Similarly 'mat ' can be used with 'āp' where despite cultural requirement of formal address, the relationship is very close and gives one the right to stop the person concerned with force and authority.'

IRREGULAR IMPERATIVES :

		tū	tum	āp
to do	karnā	kar	karo	kījie
to drink	pīnā	pī	pio	pījie
to take	lenā	le	lo	lījie
to give	denā	de	do	dījie

SUBJUNCTIVE IMPERATIVE

v.r. + eṁ is used only with āp.

Please be seated.	āp baiṭheṁ.
Please eat.	āp khāeṁ.

■ **TWO VALUABLE TOOLS TO LEARN TENSE-CONSTRUCTIONS IN HINDI ARE:**

(1) the present participle i.e. v.r. + tā, te, tī

(2) the past participle i.e v.r. + ā / yā, e, ī

'y' is infixed for phonetic ease.

- the present participle + present form of the verb honā = present simple tense (pg. 290)
- the present participle + past form of hona = past habitual (pg. 291)
- past participle to agree with the subject in the nominative case = past simple tense with intransitive verbs. (pg. 295)
- past participle to agree with the object, and subject followed by ne = past simple tense with transitive verbs. (pg. 296)
- the past participle + present form of honā = present perfect tense (pg. 297)
- the past participle + past form of honā = past perfect tense (pg. 298)
- present participle + rahnā + honā = continuative compound. (pg. 309)
- present participle + jānā + honā = progressive compound. (pg. 309)
- present participle + future form of honā = present presumption. (pg. 309)
- past participle + future form of honā =perfective presumption. (pg. 310)

- present participle + jānā + honā =passive voice
- present participle of the main verb + past participle of honā = present participial construction used as adjective, adverb or noun. (pg. 311)
- past participle of the main verb + past participle of honā = past participial construction used as adjective, adverb or noun. (pg. 311)
- present participle (only ā/yā form) + karna + hona = frequentative compound. (pg. 311)

PRESENT SIMPLE TENSE

(This verb tense expresses habitual action in the present time)

LANGUAGE STRUCTURE

subj. + obj. + v.r. + $tā^{m.sg.}$, $te^{m.pl.}$, + hūṁ, ho, hai,
nom. case, if any; $tī^{f.sg./pl.}$ — written together; haiṁ — agree with the N and G of the subj.

I come.	maiṁ	ātā	huṁ	maiṁ	ātī	huṁ
We come.	ham	āte	haiṁ	ham	ātī	haiṁ
You (intimate) come.	tū	ātā	hai	tū	ātī	hai
You (informal) come.	tum	āte	ho	tum	ātī	ho
You (formal) come.	āp	āte	haiṁ	āp	ātī	haiṁ
He, she, it comes.	yah	ātā	hai	yah	ātī	hai
He, she, it comes.	vah	ātā	hai	vah	ātī	hai
They, these come.	ye	āte	haiṁ	ye	ātī	haiṁ
	ve	āte	haiṁ	ve	ātī	haiṁ

PAST HABITUAL TENSE

LANGUAGE STRUCTURE

subj. + obj. + v.r. + tā^m.sg., te^m.pl., + tha, the, thī,
nom. if any tī^f.sg./pl. thīṁ
case (v.r. + tā, te, tī: written together) (tha, the, thī, thīṁ: agree with the N and G of the subj.)

I used to come	maiṁ	ātā	thā	maiṁ	ātī	thī
We used to come	ham	āte	the	ham	ātī	thīṁ
You used to come	tū	ātā	thā	tū	ātī	thī
You used to come	tum	āte	the	tum	ātī	thīṁ
You used to come	āp	āte	the	āp	ātī	thīṁ
He, she, it used to come	yah	ātā	thā	yah	ātī	thī
He, she, it used to come	vah	ātā	thā	vah	ātī	thī
They, these used	ye	āte	the	ye	ātī	thīṁ
to come	ve	āte	the	ve	ātī	thīṁ

PRESENT PROGRESSIVE TENSE

LANGUAGE STRUCTURE

subj. + obj. + v.r. + rahā^m.sg. rahe^m.pl., + hūṁ, hai,
nom. if any rahī^f.sg./pl. ho, haiṁ
case (v.r. + rahā, rahe, rahī: written separately) (hūṁ, hai, ho, haiṁ: agree with the N and G of the subj.)

I am coming.	maiṁ	ā raha(m.)/rahī(f.)	huṁ
We are coming.	ham	ā rahe(m.)/rahī(f.)	haiṁ
You are coming.	tū	ā rahā(m.)/rahī(f.)	hai
You are coming.	tum	ā rahe(m.)/rahī(f.)	ho
You are coming.	āp	ā rahe(m.)/rahī(f.)	haiṁ
He, she, it (near) is coming.	yah	ā rahā(m.)/rahī(f.)	hai
He, she, it(far) is coming	vah	ā rahā(m.)/rahī(f.)	hai
They (near)are coming	ye	ā rahe(m.)/rahī(f.)	haiṁ
They(far) are coming.	ve	ā rahe(m.)/rahī(f.)	haiṁ

PAST PROGRESSIVE TENSE

LANGUAGE STRUCTURE

subj. + obj. + v.r. + rahā$^{m.sg.}$·rahe$^{m.pl.}$, + tha, the,
nom.   if any   rahī$^{f.sg./pl.}$ thī, thīṁ
case

              ‿‿‿‿‿
            written separately

                          ‿‿‿‿‿
                        agree with the N and
                        G of the subj.

I was coming.	maiṁ (m.)	ā	rahā	thā
	maiṁ (f.)	ā	rahī	thī
We were coming.	ham (m.)	ā	rahe	the
	ham (f.)	ā	rahī	thīṁ
You (int.) were coming.	tū (m.)	ā	rahā	thā
	tū (f.)	ā	rahī	thī
You (inf.) were coming.	tum (m.)	ā	rahe	the
	tum (f.)	ā	rahī	thīṁ
You (form.) were coming.	āp (m.)	ā	rahe	the
	āp (f.)	ā	rahī	thīṁ
He, she, it (near) was coming.	yah (m.)	ā	rahā	thā
	yah (f.)	ā	rahī	thī
He, she, it (far) was coming.	vah (m.)	ā	rahā	thā
	vah (f.)	ā	rahī	thī
They (near) were coming.	ye (m.)	ā	rahe	the
	ye (f.)	ā	rahī	thīṁ
These (far) were coming.	ve (m.)	ā	rahe	the
	ve (f.)	ā	rahī	thīṁ

PAST SIMPLE TENSE

Past simple tense language structures for verb transitive and verb intransitive are different.

In the case of intransitive verbs, the subject is in the nominative case and verb agrees with the number and gender of the subject.

In the case of transitive verbs, the subject is followed by ne′ and the verb agrees with the number and gender of the object.

PRONOUN / NOUN + ne

Singular	Plural
I	maiṁne
We	hamne
You (sg., intimate)	tūne
You (sg./pl., informal)	tumne
You (pl., informal)	tum logoṁ ne
You (sg., formal)	āpne
You (pl., formal)	āpne, āp logoṁ ne
He, she, it (near)	isne
They (near)	inhoṁne
He, she, it, (far)	usne
They (far)	unhoṁne
Who (sg.)	kisne
Who (pl.)	kinhoṁne

kisīne	kinhīṁne

'X'+ne — where 'X' stands for a proper noun.

e.g. Rām ne; auratoṁ ne

☞ **Pronouns + ne are written together. Noun + ne written separately.**

LANGUAGE STRUCTURE : VERB INTRANSITIVE

subject + (v.r. + ā/yā, e/ye, i/yi, īṁ/yīṁ)

agree with the N and G of the subject.

Intransitive Verb ānā (to come)

		m.	f.
I came.	maiṁ	āyā	āī
We came.	hum	āe	āīṁ
You (intimate) came.	tū	āyā	āī
You (informal) came.	tum	āe	āīṁ
You (formal) came.	ap	āe	āīṁ
He, She (far) came.	vah	āyā	āī
He, She (near) came.	yah	āyā	āī
They (far) came.	ve	āe	āīṁ
They (near) came.	ye	āe	āīṁ
who came	kaun	āyā	āi
who all came	kaun-kaun	āe	āīṁ

LANGUAGE STRUCTURE : VERB TRANSITIVE

(subj. + ne) + obj. + (v.r + ā/yā,e/ye,i/yi, īṁ/yīṁ)

agree with N and G of the object

Example : khānā (to eat)

subject	object	Verb
maine, hamne	santrā* (m.sg.)	khāyā
tūne, tumne	santre (m.pl.)	khāe
āpne, usne, isne	roṭī* (f.sg.)	khāī
unhoṁne, inhoṁne, kinhoṁne.	roṭiyāṁ (f. pl.)	khāīṁ

*santrā= orange; roṭī= Indian bread

☞ Everything else remaining the same, add present form of honā or past form of honā to above given constructions to derive the present perfect and past perfect tenses respectively, which in Hindi are just an extension of the past simple tense.

USEFUL TIPS

Praise, Acknowledgement, Inspirational Expressions

sābās — Bravo!
ṭhīk — Correct!
bas — thats all!
acchā — Okay

PRESENT PERFECT TENSE

This verb tense, expressing action completed at the present time, is formed by combining the past pariciple of the main verb with present tense of the auxiliary verb honā.

INTRANSITIVE VERB: ānā (to come)

		m.	f.	
I have come.	maiṁ	āyā	āī	hūṁ
We have come.	ham	āe	āī	haiṁ
You (intimate) have come.	tū	āyā	āī	hai
You (inf.) have come.	tum	āe	āī	ho
You (formal) have come.	āp	āe	āī	haiṁ
He, She (far) has come.	vah	āyā	āī	hai
He, She (near) has come.	yah	āyā	āī	hai
They (far) have come.	ve	āe	āī	haiṁ
They (near) have come.	ye	āe	āī	haiṁ

TRANSITIVE VERB : khānā (to eat)

maiṁne, hamne,			
tūne, tumne, āpne,	santra	khāyā	hai
usne, isne,	santre	khae	haiṁ.
inhoṁne unhoṁne	roti	khāī	hai.
kisne	roṭiyāṁ	khāī	haiṁ.
kinhoṁne			

PAST PERFECT TENSE

This verb tense, expressing action completed in the past, is formed in Hindi by combining the past participle of the main verb with the past tense of the auxiliary verb honā.

INTRANSITIVE VERB: ānā (to come)

I had come.	maiṁ	āyā thā	āī thī
We had come.	ham	āe the	āī thīṁ
You (intimate)	tū	āyā tha	āī thī
You (inf.)	tum	āe the	āī thīṁ
You (formal)	āp	āe the	āī thīṁ
He, She (far)	vah	āyā thā	āī thī
He, She (near)	yah	āyā thā	āī thī
They (far)	ve	āe the	āī thīṁ
They (near)	ye	āe the	āī thīṁ
Who(pl.)had come.	kaun-kaun	āe the	āī thīṁ

Transitive Verb: khānā (to eat)

maiṁne, hamne,			
tūne, tumne, āpne,	santrā	khāyā	thā
usne, isne,	santre	khāe	the
inhoṁne unhoṁne	roṭī	khāī	thī
kisne	roṭiyāṁ	khāī	thīṁ
kinhoṁne			

FUTURE

subj.	+	obj.	+	v.r.	+	ūṁ, e, o, eṁ	+	gā, ge, gī
nom. case		if any						

(v.r. + ūṁ, e, o, eṁ: written together)

(gā, ge, gī: agree with the N and G of the subject)

		m.	f.
I will come.	maiṁ	āūṁgā	āūṁgī
We will come.	ham	āeṁge	āeṁgī
You (int.) will come.	tū	āegā	āegī
You (inf.) will come.	tūm	āoge	āogī
You (formal) will come.	ap	āeṁge	āeṁgī
He/she (far) will come.	vah	āegā	āegī
He/she (near) will come.	yah	āegā	āegī
They (far) will come.	ve	āeṁge	āeṁgī
They (near) will come.	ye	āeṁge	āeṁgī
Who will come.	kaun	āegā	āegī
Who all will come.	kaun-kaun	āeṁge	āeṁgī

POSTPOSITIONS

Postpositions in Hindi function like prepositions in English. They follow the noun, hence they are called postpositions.Hindi uses simple as well as compound postpositions.

Simple postpositions are :

ko is used in accusative as well as dative case. i.e. with direct as well as indirect object.

If there is only one direct object, use of **ko** is obligatory with the living object, but not so with non-living object.

Call the child. bacce ko bulāo.

Read the book. kitāb paṛho.

☞ If there are both direct as well as indirect object in a sentence, use of ko is obligatory with the indirect object, but not so with the direct object.

Give the book to me. kitāb mujh ko do.

☞ However if both direct as well as indirect object happen to be living, then ko is used with both.

Give the child to me. bacce ko mujh ko do.

se is used in instrumental and ablative cases

with knife cākū se; from the tree peṛ se

on, in is used in the locative case

on the table mez par; in the room kamre meṁ

kā, ke , kī is used in possessive case

- **kā, ke, kī depends on the number and gender**

of the object possessed and not on the number and gender of the possesser, For example:

son of Kamlā	Kamlā kā betā (m.sg.)
sons of Kamlā	Kamlā ke bete (m.pl.)
daughter of Kamlā	Kamlā kī betī (f.sg.)
daughters of Kamlā	Kamlā kī betiyāṁ (f.pl.)

If the object possessed is a masculine noun in the oblique case i.e. followed by some postposition, the preceding 'kā' changes to 'ke'. e.g.

to son of Kamlā	Kamla ke bete ko
in Rām's room	Rām ke kamre meṁ

COMPOUND POSTPOSITIONS

on	ke ūpar	under	ke nīce
outside	ke bāhar	inside	ke andar
near	ke pās	ahead	ke āge
behind	ke pīche	in front of	ke sāmne
with	ke sāth	after	ke bād
before	ke pahle	without	ke binā
besides	ke alāvā	about	ke bāre meṁ
for	ke lie	because of	ke kāraṇ
towards	kī or	like	kī tarah
instead of		ke bajāe	
at the place of		ke yahāṁ	

CONJUNCTIONS

and	aur	but	lekin, parantu
therefore	islie	because	kyoṁki
so that	tāki	although	yadyapi
that	ki		
neither ... nor	na ... na		
either ... or	yā ... yā		

USE OF SOME VERBS

■ LIKE - pasand karnā

I like tea.	• maiṁ cāy pasand kartā hūṁ. • mujhko cāy pasand hai.
They like coffee.	• ve kaufī pasand karte haiṁ. • unko kaufī pasand hai.
What do you like?	• tumko kyā pasand hai? • tum kyā pasand karte ho?
I don't like coffee.	• mujhko kaufī pasand nahīṁ. • maiṁ kaufī pasand nahīṁ kartā.

■ WANT - cāhnā

I want to go out.
maiṁ bāhar jānā cāhtā hūṁ.

They don't want to come here.
ve yahāṁ ānā nahīṁ cāhte.

What do you want?   tum kyā cāhte ho?

I want to see a film.
maiṁ film dekhnā cāhtā hūṁ.

■ KNOW (how to do s.th.): ānā

I know how to cook.
mujko khānā pakānā ātā hai.

She knows how to swim.   usko tairnā ātā hai.

KNOW (somebody, something): jānanā

I know him.   maiṁ usko jāntā/jāntī hūṁ.

I don't know this matter.
maiṁ yah māmlā nahīṁ jāntā/jāntī.

KNOW (something) : patā honā, mālum honā

I don't know anything.
  • mujhko kuch nahīṁ patā.
  • mujhko kuch mālūm nahīṁ.

Do you Know?
  • kyā āpko patā hai?
  • kyā āpkko mālūm hai?

■ CAN—saknā

Language structure

subj. +	obj. +	v.r. +	saktā^m.sg.,	+	hūṁ,
nom.	if		sakte^m.pl.		hai,
case	any		saktī^f.sg./pl.		ho, haiṁ

written separately

agree with the N and G
of the subject

I(m.) can speak Hindi.
maiṁ hindī bol saktā hūṁ.

I(f.) cannot walk.
maiṁ paidal nahīṁ cal saktī.

Can you go on foot?
kyā āp paidal jā sakte haiṁ?

☞ **'pānā' is used instead of saknā, when one is unable to do something despite much effort, or one is able to accomplish something after much effort.**

I could not arrive on time.
maiṁ samay par nahīṁ pahuṁc pāyā.

I could come here with much difficulty.
maiṁ yahāṁ bahut muśkil se pahuṁc pāyā.

■ NEED—cāhie

(subj. + ko)	+	noun obj.	+	cāhie

I need water.	mujhko (mujhe) pānī cāhie.
They need a room.	unko kamrā cāhie.

■ SHOULD, OUGHT TO—cāhie

(subj. + ko)	+	verb infinitive	+	cāhie

I should go.	mujhko jānā cāhie.
You ought to sleep now.	ab āpko sonā cāhie.

■ COMPULSION — paṛnā, honā

• (subj. + ko) + v.inf. + honā (in the required tense)

I must go now. ab mujhko jānā hai

• (subj. + ko) + v.inf. + paṛna + honā (in the required tense)

I have to go everyday. mujhko roz jānā paṛtā hai.

■ PROBABILITY - śāyad, ho saktā hai:

Expressions like śāyad (perhaps), ho saktā hai (it is likely), sambhavtā (probably) are used at the beginning of the sentence in future tense without the endings gā, ge, gī.

They may not come today. śāyad ve āj na āeṁ.
It might rain today. ho saktā hai āj bāriś ho.

■ POSSESSION

☞ **ke pas honā : (non-living objects)**

He has many clothes. uske pās bahut kapṛe haiṁ.
I have many books. mere pās bahut kitābeṁ haiṁ

☞ **kā, ke, kī honā : (kith and kin; landed property)**

She has two houses. uske do makan haiṁ.

They have three daughters.

unkī tīn beṭiyāṁ haiṁ.

I have two brothers.

mere do bhāī haiṁ.

■ HABITUATED TO DO SOMETHING:

kā / ke / kī ādī honā

(kā, ke, kī depends upon the number and gender of the subject who is habituated to something).

I (m.) am used to drinking tea.
maiṁ cāy pine kā ādī hūṁ.

They (f.) are used to sleeping early.
ve jaldī sone kī ādī haiṁ.

ki ādat honā

I am used to drinking tea.
mujhko cāy pine kī ādat hai.

They are used to sleeping early.
unko jaldī sone kī ādat hai.

CONDITIONALS

If....., ... ; (yadi... to...)
If you call me, I will come.
yadi āp bulāeṁge, to maiṁ āūṁgā.

If they come, tell me.
yadi ve āeṁ, to mujhe batāeṁ.

■ BEGIN TO DO X — (v.r. + n

The child begins to cry.	baccā rone lagtā
The child began to cry.	baccā rone lagā.
The child will begin to cry.	baccā rone lagegā.

■ PERMISSION — (v.r. + ne) + denā

Please let me go.	mujhko jāne dījie.
He lets me go.	vah mujhko jāne detā hai.
He let me go.	usne mujhko jāne diyā.
He will let me go.	vah mujhko jāne degā.

■ KAR - conjunct :

- **When the same subject does several activities one following the other, Hindi speakers use the conjunct 'कर' to join the sentences.**
- **Only the verb of final activity is conjugated as per subject or object, depending upon (1) the tense and (2) the nature of activity, transitive or intransitive. In all the preceding sentences, only v.r. + कर or के is used.**
- **If the verb root happens to be कर then certainly के is used.**

v.r. + कर or के is written together.

...e) + lagnā

...hai.

...ginning of the

...ı. maiṁ paṛhtī hūṁ.
... paṛhtī hūṁ.

... maiṁ soī.
...kar soī.

... āūṁgī. maiṁ paṛhūṁgī.
...ṁ ākar paṛhūṁgī.

...e the verbs of two activities happ... in one and intransitive in the other s... subject of the final activity is placed at the b...ning of the sentence.

I came. I ate food.	maiṁ āī. maiṁne khānā khāyā.
I came and ate food.	maiṁne ākar khānā khāyā.
I ate food. I came.	maiṁne khānā khāyā. maiṁ āī.
I ate food and came.	maiṁ khānā khākar āī.

■ SIMULTANEOUS ACTIVITIES: (v.r. + te) + hī

Use : [ke + (v.r. + te) + hī]— when the subject of two sentences is different but living.

As soon as mother goes, the child cries.
mātā ke jāte hī baccā rotā hai. (pres. simple)

As soon as mother went, the child cried.
mātā ke jāte hī baccā royā. (past simple)

As soon as mother goes the child will cry.
mātā ke jāte hī baccā roegā. (future simple)

(v.r. + te) + hī—when the subject of the two sentences is different but at least the subject of one of the sentences is nonliving.

As soon as it is morning, we have bath.
subah hote hī ham snān karte haiṁ.

(v.r. + te) + hī—when the subject of the two sentences is the same.

As soon as the teacher comes, he teaches.
śikṣak āte hī paṛhātā hai.

■ CONTINUATIVE ACTIVITIES:

Present participle + rahnā + honā:

He keeps on reading. vah paṛhtā rahtā hai.
The children keep on playing.
bacce khelte rahte haiṁ.

■ GRADUAL CHANGES; DISAPPROVAL:

Present participle + jānā + honā:
He goes on talking.
vah boltā jātā hai. (disapproval)

Days gradually become shorter.
din choṭe hote jāte haiṁ. (gradual change)

■ PRESENT PRESUMPTION:

Present participle + future form of honā:
She must be eating meat. vah māṁs khātī hogī.

■ **PERFECTIVE PRESUMPTION:**

Past participle + future form of honā:

You must have driven fast.
tumne gāṛī tez calāī hogī.

■ **Repetitive use of present participle:** To talk about incomplete activities, to express ideas such as 'while doing' or 'constantly doing'.

I don't like talking while eating.

mujhe khāte-khāte bolna pasand nahīṁ.
She got tired from continuous walking.
vah callte-callte thak gaī.

■ **Repetitive use of past participle:To talk about completed activities.**

I am bored sitting.
maiṁ baithā-baithā ūb gaya hūṁ.

The woman was talking while sleeping.
aurat soyī-soyī bol rahī thī.

■ **Present participle of the main verb + past participle of honā is used as adjective, adverb or noun to express incomplete actions.**

The child came crying. (adv.)
baccā rotā huā āyā.

Console the crying child. (adjective)
rote hue bacce ko cup karāo.

Console the one (child) who is crying child. (noun)
rote (hue) ko cup karāo.

- **Similarly past participle of the main verb + past participle of the verb honā is used as adjective, adverb or noun to express complete activities.**

  ripened pakā huā
  washed dhulā huā

- **past participle of the main verb, only ā-form + karnā + honā in the required tense is used to express frequentative structures.**

In India I speak Hindi. (pres. freq.)
bhārat meṁ maiṁ hindi bolā kartā hūṁ.

In India I used to speak Hindi. (past freq.)
bhārat meṁ maiṁ hindi bolā kartā thā.

Please speak Hindi in India. (imperative freq.)
meṁ hindi āp bhārat bolā kījie.

In India I will speak Hindi. (future freq.)
bhārat meṁ maiṁ hindi bolā karūṁgā.

- **Past participle + jānā + honā is used to make sentences in the passive voice.**

The house is cleaned every day. (pres. passive)
ghar roz sāf kiyā jātā hai.

This road was construction last year. (past passive)
yah saṛak pichle sāl banāī gaī.

A cinema hall will be built here. (future passive)
yahāṁ ek sinemāghar banāyā jāegā.

COMMONLY USED VERBS

arrive	pahuṁcnā(v.i.)
ask	pūchnā(v.t.)
be	honā(v.i.)
begin	śurū karnā (v.t.)
	śurū honā(v.i.)
boil	ubālnā (v.t.)
	ubalnā (v.i.)
bring	lānā(v.t.)
buy	k̲h̲arīdnā(v.t.)
climb down	utarnā(v.i.)
climb up	caṛhnā(v.i.)
close	band karnā(v.t.)
	band honā(v.i.)
come	ānā (v.i.)
cook	pakānā(v.t.)
cool	ṭhaṇḍā karnā(v.t.)
cry	ronā(v.i.)
cut	kāṭnā(v.t.)
depart	ravānā honā(v.i.)
	chūṭnā (v.i.)
do	karnā(v.t.)
drink	pīnā (v.t.)
(to offer ..)drink	pilānā (v.t.)
dry	sukhānā (v.t.)
	sūkhnā (v.i.)
eat	khānā (v.t.)
explain	samjhānā(v.t.)

feed	khilānā (v.t.)
forget	bhūlnā (v.t.)
fry	talnā (v.t.)
get up	uṭhnā (v.i.)
give	denā (v.t.)
go	jānā (v.i.)
grow	baṛhnā (v.i.)
hear	sunănā (v.i)
hit	mārnā(v.t.)
jump	kūdnā (v.i.)
kill	mārnā (v.t.)
laugh	haṁsnā (v.i.)
(cause to..)laugh	haṁsānā (v.t.)
learn	sīkhnā (v.t.)
listen	sunanā (v.t.)
make	banānā (v.t.)
	bananā (v.i.)
meet	milnā (v.i.)
narrate	sunānā (v.t.)
open	kholnā (v.t.)
pick up	uṭhānā (v.t.)
play	khelnā (v.t.)
postpone	āge ṭālnā(v.t.)
praise	praśaṁsā karnā(v.t.)
pull	khīṁcnā(v.t.)
push	khiskānā(v.t.)
put down	nīce rakhnā (v.t.)
read	paṛhnā (v.t.)
recite	sunānā (v.t.)

remember	yād karnā (v.t.)
repair	marammat karnā (v.t.)
repeat	dohrānā (v.t.)
reserve	ārakṣaṇ karnā (v.t.)
return	lauṭnā (v.i.)
run	dauṛnā (v.i.)
say	kahnā (v.t.)
scold	dāṁṭnā(v.t.)
sell	becnā (v.t.)
send	bhejnā (v.t.)
sit down	baiṭhnā (v.i.)
sleep	sonā (v.i.)
speak	bolnā (v.t.)
stir	hilānā (v.t.)
soak	bhigonā (v.t.)
study	adhyayan karnā (v.t.)
	paṛhnā (v.t.)
take	lenā (v.t.)
taste	cakhnā (v.t.)
teach	paṛhānā (v.t.)
	sikhānā (v.t.)
understand	samajhnā (v.t.)
wake up(oneself)	jāgnā (v.i.)
wake some body up	jagānā (v.t.)
walk	paidal calnā (v.i.)
warn	cetāvni denā (v.t.)
wash	dhonā (v.t.)
wear	pahnanā (v.t.)
write	likhnā (v.t.)

CONJUNCT VERBS

to arrange for X	X kī vayasthā karnā
to attack X	X par hamlā karnā
to ask X for forgiveness	X se māfi maṁgnā
to ask X question	X se swāl pūchnā
to be angry at X	X par krodh karnā
to be attached to X	X se lagāv honā
to be of use to X	X ke kām ānā
to believe X	X par yakīn karnā
to benefit from X	X se fayādā uṭhānā
to beware of X	X se sāvdhān rahnā
to blame X	X ko doṣ denā
to confront X	X ka sāmnā karnā
to cut X into pieces	X ke ṭukṛe karnā
to deal with X	X se nipatnā
to depend on X	X par nirbhar honā
to explain to X	X ko samjhānā
to experience X	X kā anubhav karnā
to fall in love with X	X ko cāhne lagnā
to fight with X	X se laṛāī karnā
to get on X's nerves	X par hāvī honā
to hate X	X se ghṛṇā karnā
to insist on X	X kā āgrah karnā
to intend to do X	x karne kā irādā karnā
to kill X	X kā kām tamām karnā
to listen to X	X kī bāt mānanā
to love X	X se prem karnā
to make friendship with	X se dostī karnā

to make fun of X	X kā mazāk uṛānā
to meet X	X se mulākāt karnā
to marry X	X se śādī karnā
to offer to X	X ko peś karnā
t o permit X	X ko ijāzat denā
to praise X	X ke guṇ gānā
to promise X	X se vāyadā karnā
to quarrel with X	X se laṛāī karnā
to repair X	X kī marammat karnā
to request X	X se prārthnā karnā
to talk to X	X se bat karnā
to think of X	X par vicār karnā
to try X	X ka prayās karnā
to trust X	X par bhrosā karnā
to have faith in X	X par viśvās karnā
to use X	X kā prayog karnā

INDEX

About the Author

Kavita Kumar (nee Krishna Bhasin) holds a Masters degree in Economics from Delhi University, India, starting her career as lecturer in Economics at Janki Devi College, Delhi, she taught at a few other places, then dedicated herself to teaching English and Hindi as a second language. She runs her own school in Varanasi, India teaching Hindi, English and basic German to students from all over the world.

She has over twenty years of successful experience of teaching Hindi as a foreign language. Her long experience in this field has provided her with an unusual sensibility to the requirements of students learning a second language. Her book *Hindi for Non-Hindi Speaking People* has been widely acclaimed.